DEEP LEARNING
DISORIENTING W

Much has been written about the escalating intolerance of worldviews other than one's own. Reasoned arguments based on facts and data seem to have little impact in our increasingly post-truth culture dominated by social media, fake news, tribalism, and identity politics. Recent advances in the study of human cognition, however, offer insights on how to counter these troubling social trends. In this book, psychologist Jon F. Wergin calls upon recent research in learning theory, social psychology, politics, and the arts to show how a deep learning mindset can be developed in both oneself and others. Deep learning is an acceptance that our understanding of the world around us is only temporary and is subject to constant scrutiny. Someone who is committed to learning deeply does not simply react to experience, but engages fully with experience, knowing that the inevitable disquietude is what leads to efficacy in the world.

JON F. WERGIN is Professor of Education Studies at Antioch University's Graduate School of Leadership and Change, USA. He is also an educational psychologist with a professional background spanning nearly 50 years.

DEEP LEARNING IN A DISORIENTING WORLD

JON F. WERGIN

Antioch University

CAMBRIDGE
UNIVERSITY PRESS

University Printing House, Cambridge CB2 8BS, United Kingdom

One Liberty Plaza, 20th Floor, New York, NY 10006, USA

477 Williamstown Road, Port Melbourne, VIC 3207, Australia

314–321, 3rd Floor, Plot 3, Splendor Forum, Jasola District Centre, New Delhi – 110025, India

79 Anson Road, #06-04/06, Singapore 079906

Cambridge University Press is part of the University of Cambridge.

It furthers the University's mission by disseminating knowledge in the pursuit of education, learning, and research at the highest international levels of excellence.

www.cambridge.org
Information on this title: www.cambridge.org/9781108480222
DOI: 10.1017/9781108647786

© Cambridge University Press 2020

This publication is in copyright. Subject to statutory exception and to the provisions of relevant collective licensing agreements, no reproduction of any part may take place without the written permission of Cambridge University Press.

First published 2020

Printed in the United Kingdom by TJ International Ltd, Padstow Cornwall

A catalogue record for this publication is available from the British Library.

ISBN 978-1-108-48022-2 Hardback
ISBN 978-1-108-72715-0 Paperback

Cambridge University Press has no responsibility for the persistence or accuracy of URLs for external or third-party internet websites referred to in this publication and does not guarantee that any content on such websites is, or will remain, accurate or appropriate.

Contents

List of Figures		*page* vi
Preface		vii
Acknowledgments		xiii
1	Why Deep Learning Is So Important … and So Hard	1
2	How We Learn: A Short Primer	19
3	Mindful Learning	38
4	Constructive Disorientation	57
5	Critical Reflection	73
6	The Importance of Others	88
7	The Influence of Politics on Deep Learning	108
8	Constructive Disorientation Through the Arts	122
9	The Art of Maintaining Essential Tensions	140
10	Cultivating a Deep Learning Mindset	158
References		177
Index		193

Figures

1.1	Sources and outcome of confirmation (myside) bias	page 9
2.1	The human brain	20
2.2	The limbic system	21
2.3	Experiential learning cycle	27
3.1	Maslow's hierarchy of needs	39
5.1	The development of expertise	82
5.2	The deep learning mindset	85
6.1	The deep learning mindset, including the social learning field	106
8.1	World War II poster	136
8.2	The deep learning mindset with aesthetic experience added	138
9.1	The deep learning mindset, complete	151

Preface

I have approached this book with a sense of urgency, even alarm. I am normally an optimistic person, believing that yes, the world is always in crisis, somewhere; but I have also believed that "crises" are often overblown, sensationalized by media looking for ways to increase their viewership. In recent years, however, I have found my normal optimism shaken by the disharmony and polarization I witness in our social discourse, nearly every day. There is too much talking and not enough listening. There is too much dismissal of diverse points of view, and not enough effort to find common ground. There is too much moral judgment and not enough nuance. There is too much knee-jerk stereotyping and not enough appreciation of difference. And all of this, I fear, is getting worse, for reasons I explore in the coming chapters. What is needed, I submit, is a commitment to deep learning, a way of being that treats incoming information thoughtfully and critically. Those who learn deeply refuse to be seduced by messages that feed existing biases, and they embrace challenges to their worldviews. Deep learners assume that there is always more to learn.

The term "deep learning" has been used in other contexts, most recently artificial intelligence (cf. Goodfellow, Bengio, & Courville, 2016), *not* what this book is about, so let me define at the outset what deep learning is and what it is not:

(a) Deep learning is not stuff that is locked away in the brain and stays there. Deep learning is learning that lasts, but not vice versa. We all remember a lot of random things. I have no earthly idea why I remember a particular morning after a childhood sleepover, when my host told me at breakfast that his family used a spoon rather than a knife to get the jelly out of the jar.

(b) Deep learning is not the result of doing a lot of research on a topic. Knowing a lot about something does not necessarily mean that you have learned deeply to get there. Ask me which garage band recorded

"Wild Thing" and when, and I'll tell you.[1] The fact that I remember a lot of rock and roll trivia doesn't mean that I engaged in a lot of deep learning during my undergraduate days in the 1960s. (Far from it, sadly.)

(c) Deep learning is not what is taught in school. I don't mean to suggest that what we learned in school is not important. Children need to learn their multiplication tables; teenagers need to learn the foundations of their local and national governments; medical students need to learn the biochemistry of the Krebs cycle. Each of these is essential learning, needed to function in society or, in the case of medical school, the profession. None are useful, however, unless and until they are linked with lived experience, the challenges of life and work.

(d) And finally, deep learning is more than getting knocked off stride by an experience that encourages us to see things differently. Transformative learning, as this is known (Mezirow, 2000) is a necessary part of deep learning but not the whole of it.

So what, then, am I writing about in this book? Deep learning is learning that lasts, yes. And deep learning is the result of cognitive and emotional disorientation that makes us want to examine other ways of viewing the world, yes. But deep learning is also a way of being, a mindset, an orientation. It is a worldview that our understandings of the world around us are only temporary understandings, subject to constant inspection and scrutiny. Someone who is committed to learning deeply does not simply react to experience, but engages fully with experience, knowing that the inevitable disquietude is what leads to efficacy in the world.

Frankly, most of us don't do this very well. More than a quarter-century ago, in a widely reprinted article for the *Harvard Business Review* titled "Teaching Smart People How to Learn," psychologist Chris Argyris (1991) argued that "success in the marketplace increasingly depends on learning, yet most people don't know how to learn" (p. 99). This is a startling assertion from one of the eminent organizational theorists of his day. He argued that the reason for this dilemma stems from two misconceptions about the nature of learning itself: first that learning is all about "solving problems," and second that getting people to learn is all about creating external incentives, such as compensation programs and performance reviews. Argyris drew upon his research and professional experience as a consultant to argue that knowing how to learn requires the ability to reflect critically on one's own behavior, something people are rarely taught to do, whether in school or on the job.

An astonishing amount of research on human learning in the intervening years has largely supported and augmented Argyris' analysis from decades ago. And yet, his article remains provocative to this day. Why is this so? Why haven't schools, colleges, and professional development practices taken Argyris' and others' wisdom to heart? Or, when they have, why are the effects, if any, often so ephemeral? In this book I address this conundrum and offer some suggestions, based upon my own research and others', about how to deal with it.

Along the way I make several claims. First is the mounting evidence exploding the prevailing myth that people behave rationally, and when they do not it is because they have become unmoored by their emotions. Instead, available evidence suggests that belief comes quickly and naturally, and because humans have a low tolerance for ambiguity, skepticism about one's beliefs is slow and unnatural (Shermer, 2011). Second, developing skepticism in ways that lead to deep learning depends on an interaction between thoughts and feelings, cognition and emotion. Neither can lead to deep learning by itself. Third, critical reflection, both with oneself and with others, is the key to long-term behavioral change. Fourth, deep learning will often have political ramifications, requiring sensitivity to political dynamics. And fifth, aesthetic experience can be a powerful if often unrecognized source of deep learning. I end with some specific suggestions on steps we can take to facilitate deep learning, both for ourselves and for those with whom we live and work.

Here is a roadmap to the book.

The first two chapters discuss the challenges to deep learning in a world that is often hostile to it.

Chapter 1 describes why critical reflection is more important today than ever before, and yet harder and harder to do. I delve into this apparent paradox, why "facts" and "evidence" seem to have so little effect on rational behavior, and why this so often leads to bad decisions.

In Chapter 2 I review the basics of cognition, showing how old ideas about learning as storehouses of information, standing at the ready to address problems, have given way to much more complex notions about how our brains do not just take in information and store it, but make meaning of that information by attaching it – or not – to existing mental models. I discuss how this is not only vital to our survival as a species but also presents a challenge to our cognitive development. I also introduce the notion of *transformative learning*, arguably the most important theory on adult learning in the last half-century.

The next seven chapters describe and explain the keys for facilitating deep learning in the midst of turbulent social change.

Chapter 3 discusses "mindful learning." The central message here is Socrates' dictum, "know thyself first." We must know ourselves before presuming to think that we are in any position to influence others. I explore the now-bulging literature on personal and organization development and offer some integrating principles for understanding how deep learning can be developed in ourselves and others.

In Chapter 4 I discuss the power of what I call "constructive disorientation," and how it can lead to transformative learning as a tool for constructive change. Constructive disorientation is a sweet tension between curiosity, an innate human quality, and disquietude, a disturbance in our perceptual field that demands our attention. Neither alone is sufficient for deep learning, but powerful given the right balance.

In Chapter 5 I explore in detail the importance of critical reflection on human experience. Critical reflection is *not* an innate human quality and so must be cultivated. I discuss how critical reflection is important throughout all aspects of human learning, including the development of expertise and the incidental learning that happens every day, usually below our conscious awareness.

Chapter 6 takes on the importance of relational experience in learning. Despite our typical school experience, where the expectation is to learn alone and to demonstrate that learning alone, the research evidence is unmistakable: deep learning is most powerful, and often necessary, in social discourse. Learning in the presence of others allows us to understand the world as others see it, and to try on perspectives that we would not have known about otherwise. Learning with others is perilous, often leading to the hardening of beliefs and attitudes, and so I also discuss how social discourse can be most productive.

In Chapter 7 I acknowledge the power of politics (small "p") in making real change. If the core definition of politics is group conflict over scarce resources, leading to the use and manipulation of power, then how can politics and learning come together as a developmental force? Here I revisit philosopher John Dewey's ideas about a "learning democracy," presented more than a century ago, and recast them for the challenges we face today.

In Chapter 8 I look at the role of the arts as a compelling tool for social change: how the arts can serve to create just the sort of "constructive disorientation" that I write about in Chapter 4, in ways that probe our innermost values and bring them to the surface. The arts offer paths that are closed to logic and argument, and as such have enormous potential for promoting deep learning.

Chapter 9 explores "essential tensions" – paradoxes that are not resolvable but require constant attention if they are to remain in a useful balance. I argue that holding these tensions is vital for mindful – and hence deep – learning, and that they require a dialectical way of thinking and being.

Along the way in these chapters I present a model of the "deep learning mindset," piece by piece, displaying the complete version at the end of Chapter 9.

In Chapter 10 I offer an integration of the book's previous chapters, shifting from a review of prevailing theories and empirical evidence to a more practical set of recommendations. I address these two questions: How might I become a better deep learner? And, how might I encourage deep learning in others?

On a personal note: I have approached the writing of this book from the perspective of neither a neuroscientist nor a cognitive psychologist. My doctorate in educational psychology in the early 1970s is nearly useless today, except perhaps as a marker of just how far research on human learning has come. Most of my own learning has come through my work, much of which is represented here. Still, I am a nonexpert writing both for fellow academics and for those outside the academy, and thus risk appealing to neither group. I am however an expert pedagogue: I have spent most of my professional career working to make difficult and complex ideas accessible to others, both students and practitioners. I have tried to put these skills and decades of professional experience to use in this book, taking the now mountain of research on what helps and hinders deep learning and creating with it a guide to putting this research to practical use.

Note

1 The Troggs, 1966.

Acknowledgments

An essential part of deep learning is accessing the wisdom of others. I am indebted to, and have learned deeply from, the work of the more than 200 scholars cited here, some of them numerous times. These include Daniel Kahneman, most notable for his Nobel Prize-winning work on the frailties of human cognition, pulled together beautifully in his book *Thinking, Fast and Slow* (2011); Mihalyi Csikszentmihalyi for his groundbreaking work on flow theory (1990); Robert Kegan for his contributions to adult development theory (1982, 1994), and his and Lisa Lahey's ideas on "immunity to change" (2009) (a book that more than any other in recent memory changed the way I think about learning and change); Jack Mezirow, who revolutionized the world of adult learning with his transformative learning theory (2000); Peter Vaill, who coined the term "learning in permanent white water" (1996) nearly a quarter-century ago, and whose advice is even more pertinent today; and Ron Heifetz and his colleagues for their work on adaptive learning in organizations (Heifetz, Linsky, & Grashow, 2009). Most of all, I am indebted to the legacy of John Dewey. His deep and timeless thinking on learning, education, democracy, and the arts, is cited in nearly every chapter. One of my friends, having read a draft version of this book, teased me about having a "love affair" with John Dewey. Well, so be it.

For all of that, this book would not be what it is without the generous assistance of friends, colleagues, and former students. I trusted them to give me honest feedback on early drafts, and they delivered the goods. This group included colleagues Laurien Alexandre, Richard McGuigan, and Ron Cacciope, and dear friend and mentor of more than 50 years, Larry Braskamp. The group also includes a band of former doctoral students and Antioch alumni I called "critical friends" who read and commented on early drafts of chapters: Jane Alexandre, Shelley Chapman, Karen Geiger, Lisa Graham, Pat Greer, Sue McKevitt, John Porter, and Tayo Switzer.

Even if they may have taken the "critical" part a bit too literally once in a while, I benefitted from every comment and the book is immeasurably better for it.

I especially want to acknowledge the contributions of two very special and talented people.

First is Wendy McGrath, educator and visual design genius, responsible for the creative thinking that went into the diagram of the "deep learning mindset." Like many readers, I am easily exasperated by authors' attempts to "simplify" complex ideas with a maze of boxes and arrows going every which way. I have been guilty, too many times, of doing the same thing, disregarding philosopher Abraham Kaplan's (1964) classic advice that most conceptual models, instead of oversimplifying reality, do the opposite, namely *under*simplifying it. Wendy helped me break out of that box, so to speak, and I'm grateful to her.

The second is Norman Dale, friend, Antioch alum, editor, and keeper of intellectual wisdom. Norman is truly one of a kind, as anyone fortunate enough to know him will attest. He is an astute editor, spotting errors of fact and wording large and small. He is also insanely well-read, as evidenced by the number of times his suggestions have enriched these pages. Norman's droll sense of humor kept my spirits up during the dreaded but inevitable periods of sluggishness and self-doubt. How many authors can truly say that they look forward to feedback from their editors? His marginal notes were priceless. Here's an example. Reacting to a point about how social systems often need to be "nudged" into creative activity, Norman wrote this: "Popping into my mind here is a statement attributed to race car great, Mario Andretti: 'If everything seems under control, you're just not going fast enough.'"

I'm grateful to David Repetto, editor at Cambridge University Press, who saw potential in the book, and to Emily Watton, who with endless patience helped this needy author get the manuscript into publishable shape.

Finally I want to thank Maike Philipsen, wife, fellow scholar, and thought partner, who has changed my life, sometimes in small but profound ways. For example, she introduced me to the ritual of "sitting" twice a day, with or without an agenda. At first I would roll my eyes, try to glance at my watch without her noticing, and think about what I would do when the sitting was over. Now I sometimes have to remind *her* to "do the sitting." My life with her has helped me realize what it means to love deeply.

CHAPTER I

Why Deep Learning Is So Important ... and So Hard

So convenient it is to be a reasonable creature, since it enables one to find or make a reason for everything one has a mind to do.
Benjamin Franklin

1.1 Why Deep Learning Is So Important

One of the tectonic changes of the early twenty-first century has been the democratization of information. We are in an era unlike any before: instead of having access to information limited to libraries and media conglomerates, the Internet has made information from virtually every source available to anyone with a computer, smart phone, Wi-Fi signal, or data plan. At first, I applauded this development, and even wrote an article in the early 1990s about how expert knowledge that once was stored in university libraries had now transcended those physical boundaries. I predicted that this new "information democracy" would open up minds everywhere and transform how we learn.

A quarter-century later, it turns out that I was half-right. Learning indeed has transformed, but unfortunately in the wrong direction. The fact is that in many ways the Internet has increased closed-mindedness and made deep learning more difficult. Consider the unintended outcomes of Twitter. Originally designed as a way to convey brief messages to a network of followers, Twitter has become a form of "drive-by learning" in 240 characters. The US presidential election in 2016 spawned three new entries in our common lexicon: *fake news*, inaccurate information propagated by social media intended to solidify existing beliefs; *post-truth*, "relating to or denoting circumstances in which objective facts are less influential in shaping public opinion than appeals to emotion and personal belief," the *Oxford Dictionary* word of 2016; and *truth decay*, the blurred line between fact and opinion. This latest entry comes from a sobering report by the RAND Corporation (Kavanaugh & Rich, 2018). The authors write:

> Where basic facts and well-supported analyses of these facts were once generally accepted – such as the benefit of using vaccines to protect health – disagreement about even objective facts and well-supported analyses has swelled in recent years. In addition, a growing number of Americans view the U.S. government, media, and Academics with new skepticism. These developments drive wedges between policymakers and neighbors alike. (p. 3)

Researchers at RAND have identified four major causes of truth decay: (1) humans' proclivity to cognitive bias (which I discuss later in this chapter); (2) changes in the volume and dissemination of information, led by cable news and social media, leading to "self-reinforcing feeds of information"; (3) an educational system that has reduced the emphasis on civic awareness and critical thinking; and finally, (4) polarization of the electorate into isolated communities, each with its own narrative and worldview.

This is a toxic brew indeed. The worrisome implications of these trends for our body politic have been covered extensively by many others. The consensus opinion, held by social scientists, educators, and professional journalists, seems to be that we need to learn to become better critical thinkers (cf. Levitin, 2017), more skeptical of what we read and hear, and better able to discriminate between truth and falsehood, between the plausible and the implausible.

This all seems perfectly reasonable and it is backed up by some solid research. For example, Pennycook and Rand (2019) found that the propensity to think analytically – that is, rational assessment using accepted logic and objective facts – plays a key role in the ability to ferret out misinformation and biased reporting, regardless of one's political ideology. So far, so good. The question is, where does the ability to think analytically come from, and under what conditions are people motivated to use this skill – or not? A convergence of research has demonstrated that analytic thinking, while good for analyzing arguments, is of little help with what the authors have called "bull***t receptivity"[1] when the BS serves to strengthen one's own existing belief, and may in fact simply make us better at arguing our case and dismissing others' points of view (Mercier & Sperber, 2017). In other words, better analytic thinking does not necessarily lead to better learning, and *may even inhibit it*. The more important question is: what has to happen in order for critical thinking to lead to deep learning? The answers to these questions are complex and often counterintuitive, as we'll see shortly.

1.1 Why Deep Learning Is So Important

The stakes have never been higher. In his book *Thank You for Being Late: An Optimist's Guide to Thriving in the Age of Accelerations*, Thomas Friedman, columnist for the *New York Times*, argues that the three largest forces on the planet – technology, globalization, and climate change – are all accelerating at once (Friedman, 2016). Not just changing, not just developing, but *growing exponentially*, all at the same time. For technology he points to Moore's Law, which states that the power of microchips will double every two years. To date, the data bear this out and show no signs of leveling off. Friedman reports that as of 2017, Intel's latest microchip improves performance 3,500 times compared to the first one introduced in the early 1970s; improves efficiency by more than 90,000 times; and is 60,000 times cheaper!

Friedman (2016) defines globalization, the second of the accelerating forces, as "the ability of any individual or company to compete, connect, exchange, or collaborate globally" (pp. 126–127). Because technology has made it possible to digitize everything, Friedman argues, keeping up with the flow of information everywhere has become impossible.

Enter the spread of *mis*information. In 2016, shortly before the US presidential election, Aviv Ovadya, chief technologist at the Center for Social Media Responsibility, saw something fundamentally wrong with the Internet. Calling it the "Infocalypse," Ovadya warned of an impending crisis of misinformation. As reported by Buzzfeed: "Ovadya saw early what many – including lawmakers, journalists, and Big Tech CEOs – wouldn't grasp until months later: Our platformed and algorithmically optimized world is vulnerable – to propaganda, to misinformation, to dark targeted advertising from foreign governments – so much so that it threatens to undermine a cornerstone of human discourse: the credibility of fact" (Warzel, 2018, n.p.). Due to the combined effects of technology and globalization, the situation is likely to get worse: "ongoing advancements in artificial intelligence and machine learning … can blur the lines between fact and fiction … those things could usher in a future where, as Ovadya observes, anyone could make it 'appear as if anything has happened, regardless of whether or not it did'" (Warzel, 2018, n.p.).

Ovadya's alarmist predictions have been verified in a massive study conducted by researchers at the Massachusetts Institute of Technology. Soroush Vosoughi and his colleagues analyzed about 125,000 of what they called "rumor cascades" spread through Twitter. These were systematically sorted using various fact-checking devices into "true" and "false" categories. The researchers found that not only did false news reach many more people than factual news, it also diffused "significantly farther, faster, deeper, and more broadly" (Vosoughi, Roy, & Aral, 2018, p. 4).

More than a quarter-century ago Charles Handy (1994) predicted that the speed of technology would outpace our collective formation of values around how to use it, and his prediction has come true. The social implications of the "Infocalypse" phenomenon, namely continued "truth decay" and accelerating social polarization, are disquieting, to say the least. A particularly disturbing example is the recent Facebook scandal, during which the data of an estimated 87 million people were improperly shared with Cambridge Analytics for partisan political purposes. The scandal effectively erased the naïve assumption that if Facebook gave people tools, it was largely their responsibility to decide how to use them. It was "wrong in retrospect" to have such a limited view, Mark Zuckerberg later admitted: "Clearly we should have done more, and we will going forward ... Today, given what we know ... I think we understand that we need to take a broader view of our responsibility ... [namely] that we're not just building tools, but that we need to take full responsibility for the outcomes of how people use those tools as well" (BBC News, 2018).

The third of Friedman's three accelerating forces is climate change. Temperature and sea-level records are being broken every year. Wildfires in California during the summer of 2018 broke all records for damage and loss of life. As Friedman notes, while the power of information flow is "reshaping the workplace and politics and geopolitics and the economy, and even some of our political choices ... the acceleration in Mother Nature is reshaping the whole biosphere, the whole global ecological system" (Friedman, 2016, p. 173).

Friedman's advice on how to deal with these three accelerating forces might initially seem counter-intuitive: he suggests that we hit the psychological equivalent of a pause button – that we stop and reflect, question our assumptions, and entertain fresh questions that might lead to a change of perspective. Thus the title *Thank You for Being Late*, inspired by the author who realized he was given the gift of time while waiting for some friends who were late for a breakfast date.

His advice, while provocative, is hardly new. As I will show later in this book, making critical reflection a routine part of one's life is an idea that has been around for centuries. Socrates, in particular, source of the axiom that "the unexamined life is not worth living," believed reflection to be the most important value in life. Philosopher Immanuel Kant (1998) wrote in the eighteenth century that humans are distinguished from animals by self-consciousness and the ability to reason. (As we'll see shortly, this

1.1 Why Deep Learning Is So Important

Enlightenment notion of humans as rational creatures, for all its benefits, has led to some of the most enduring myths about our "specialness" as a species.) A quarter-century ago developmental psychologist Robert Kegan, in his book *In Over Our Heads: The Mental Demands of Modern Life* (Kegan, 1994), wrote that the complexity of modern culture is evolving faster than the capacity of our brains to deal with it. In other words, the failure of our society to encourage the development of higher levels of consciousness retards our ability to keep pace in any meaningful way with the complex roles of modern life, as workers and learners, parents and partners. To continue Kegan's metaphor, the best and in fact the only way to keep our heads above water, he argues, is to step back, adapt and reframe, and to see all of these life forces as part of a larger system. While Kegan's focus is on individuals' ability to cope with the larger social systems around them, parallels to organizations are easy to make.

A good example of this is the work of Peter Vaill (1996), a central figure in organization development, who popularized the metaphor "permanent white water" as the continual state of turbulence facing most modern organizations. Permanent white water has five characteristics, according to Vaill:

1. Permanent white water conditions are full of surprises.
2. Complex systems tend to produce novel problems.
3. Permanent white water conditions feature events that are "messy" and ill structured.
4. White water events are often extremely costly.
5. Permanent white water conditions raise the problem of recurrence.

In his book *Learning as a Way of Being*, Vaill asserts that the most important way to deal with white-water conditions is to become a more effective learner, because otherwise we experience "feelings of lack of direction, absence of coherence, and loss of meaning" (pp. 16–17).

Being effective in permanent white water requires, primarily, a different perspective about learning itself. The dominant educational model in Western society, what Vaill calls "institutional learning," is characterized by several dubious assumptions:

1. Learning is a means to a socially desirable end, not an end in itself.
2. Those in authority are in the best position to know what the means and ends should be.
3. A subject matter is "out there" to be learned, and this subject matter expands in predictable ways.

4. The major task for the learner therefore is to absorb this subject matter as efficiently as possible.

Recall my reference to Chris Argyris' article on "teaching smart people how to learn" (1991) from the Preface to this book: the very success leaders and other professionals have experienced with schooling helps explain the problems they have with learning! Permanent white water poses lethal challenges to the assumptions of institutional learning and requires a different kind of learning altogether. *Accelerating forces for change, causing the sensation of being "in over our heads" in "permanent white water," require a different perspective about learning itself.* Later on in this book I will describe this different perspective in detail. But first I need to make the case that getting there will not be easy.

1.2 Why Deep Learning Is So Hard

1.2.1 *Farewell to the Rationalist Philosophy*

Rationalist philosophers, going all the way back to Plato, then repopularized during the Enlightenment, believed that solving problems was a matter of employing rigorous logic and critical thinking. It turns out that rationalist philosophers simply had it wrong. Pure reason, that is, thinking logically and drawing conclusions based upon the principles of empiricism, is simply not how the brain works. We do not learn to understand the world that way. Contrarian Enlightenment philosopher David Hume ([1739–40] 1969, p. 462) had it right when he claimed that "reason is, and ought only to be, the slave of the passions and can never pretend to any other office than to serve and obey them." Hume believed that reason can be understood only within the context of studying human nature itself. Michael Shermer in his book *The Believing Brain* captures what we have learned from research on human cognition in the past half-century: "We form our beliefs for a variety of subjective, personal, emotional, and psychological reasons in the context of environments created by family, friends, colleagues, culture, and society at large; after forming our beliefs we then defend, justify, and rationalize them with a host of intellectual reasons, cogent arguments, and rational explanations. Beliefs come first; explanations for beliefs follow" (Shermer, 2011, pp. 261 ff.).

Realizing that most beliefs have a nonrational basis, and that rationality is introduced mostly to justify these beliefs, has been a hard pill to swallow for me personally. I spent much of my adult life convinced that beliefs are formed, and then revised, based upon facts and evidence. I believed tacitly in what Jonathan Haidt (2012) has called the "rationalist delusion"– the notion that reason and emotion are separate and incompatible, and that truth will be served only when passion becomes the servant of the logical mind. For years I took to heart John Adams' dictum that "facts are stubborn things." Sure, I thought, people can get things wrong based upon first impressions, but if you simply lay out the facts of the matter, minds will change. I spent a lot of time during the early years of my career doing evaluations of educational programs, and I learned about the limits of evidence the hard way, seeing how, in case after case, decisions were made that had little to do with the amount or quality of evidence presented. One particular case stands out in my mind. I was asked to be the external evaluator of a professional development program for university faculty. I followed all the usual procedures: pre-post surveys, observations of workshops, follow-up interviews of participants. I provided carefully worded feedback to the project team, which adopted some of my recommendations – the supportive ones – and ignored the recommendations suggesting that they ought to rethink some of the premises on which the program was built. Looking back, I realize today that team members were too invested in their ideas to change them in any significant way. "You're the evaluator," I remember one of them telling me, "not one of the creative people." It took me years to develop a significantly different and distinctly more nuanced view of the role of evidence in decision-making. It has been a difficult, even painful, learning curve.

1.2.2 Why Personal Belief Systems Are So Resistant to Change

Understanding why we so resist changing our beliefs is critical to our understanding of deep learning and how to effect it. The roots of this understanding go back to the mid-twentieth century and Leon Festinger's cognitive dissonance theory (1957). Through a series of experiments, Festinger demonstrated that we humans have a strong need to search for internal consistency, so that whenever we experience *inconsistency* – for example, discovering that the new car we just bought has been poorly rated by *Consumer Reports* – we are highly motivated to reduce the mental stress this causes by engaging in one of several adaptive responses. We don't like having the sneaking suspicion that we may have made a mistake, and so we ignore the report, or remember the time we followed the consumer agency's recommendation and purchased something we later regretted. Another example is smokers who routinely experience cognitive dissonance when they are exposed to information that reminds them just how dangerous smoking is to one's health – or when they are forced outside in freezing weather to take a smoke break. They might do the difficult thing and quit smoking. Or they might:

- Justify their behavior by downplaying the source of the dissonance, e.g., "it's ok to smoke once in a while."
- Justify their behavior by adding new conditions, e.g., "if I stop smoking I'll just gain weight and that's just as bad."
- Ignore or deny the dissonant information altogether, e.g., "my grandfather smoked like a chimney and he lived to be 95."

As anyone who has ever tried to quit smoking knows all too well, it is much easier to justify or ignore the behavior than to change it. In his best-selling book *Thinking, Fast and Slow* (2011), a masterful compilation of decades of research on human cognition, Nobel laureate Daniel Kahneman puts to rest the view held for centuries that humans will behave in ways consistent with their economic interest. Kahneman demonstrates the myriad ways we humans default to the "automatic," fast and easy ways of thinking – System 1 – rather than to the "effortful," slow, and difficult System 2. System 1 is innate and required for survival. It allows us to develop implicit understandings of the world around us, telling us what to notice, including potential threats, and giving us the capacity to respond without thinking. Imagine for example that you're driving along a busy street and notice out of the corner of your eye that the car approaching the stop sign on your right appears to be going too fast to stop in time. You do not construct a mental equation factoring in the car's velocity and distance to the intersection before you react – no, you realize instinctively that the driver may *not* stop in time and if you do not hit the brakes there is likely to be a collision. Your instincts keep you from potential harm. The problem is that *because* System 1 is automatic, fast, and easy, we do not let the effortful, slow, and difficult System 2 kick in often enough, and this can lead to foolish and even dangerous decisions. We act as if all decisions we face involve an impending crash. Moreover, as Kahneman (2011) points out, we often lull ourselves into a kind of seductive complacency: "We identify with System 2, the conscious, reasoning self that has beliefs, makes choices, and decides what to think about and what to do, [when in fact System 1] is where the action is" (p. 21). Contrary to our smug assumptions about how rational we are, the "conscious, reasoning self" that we are so proud of takes over only when we make a conscious effort. In the above example, someone might suggest to us that we may be

1.2 Why Deep Learning Is So Hard

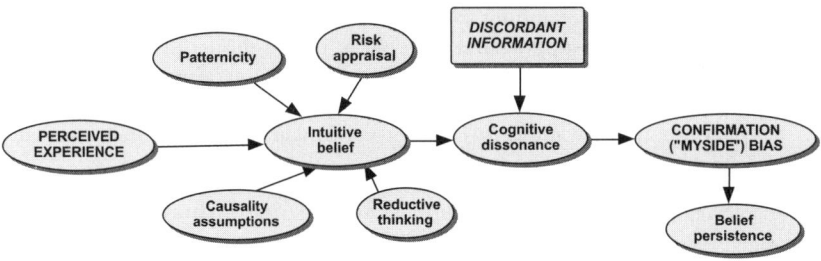

Figure 1.1 Sources and outcome of confirmation (myside) bias

stopping *too* suddenly and risking a rear-end collision. We are then forced into System 2, which considers whether we might be overreacting.

Kahneman and others have catalogued all of the cognitive mischief that can result when we do not step back and question what is happening at a subconscious, System 1 level. One source lists as many as 36 different variations (Shermer, 2011, pp. 261 ff.). Luckily, many of these overlap, and all are interconnected (see Figure 1.1). In the center is *confirmation bias*, "the mother of all cognitive biases" (p. 259). To the left are the enablers of confirmation bias and its underlying dynamics, and to the right are its effects, including its most pernicious, the polarization of group attitudes.

Confirmation bias is likely "the most widely accepted error to come out of the literature on human reasoning" (Evans, 1990, p. 41). The term was coined, most believe, by psychologist Peter Wason (1960) in an experiment testing the willingness of subjects to question their own hypotheses about the mathematical rule governing a series of numbers, such as "2–4–6." He found that when provided with additional information, subjects were able to build upon and complexify their initial hypotheses, but they hardly ever tried to *disconfirm* these hypotheses. Wason termed this phenomenon "confirmation bias." Defined by Michael Shermer (2011) as "the tendency to seek and find confirmatory evidence in support of already existing beliefs and ignore or reinterpret disconfirming evidence" (p. 259), confirmation bias is a term that 10 years ago almost no one other than cognitive psychologists had ever heard of, and now it is seemingly in everyone's vocabulary. (There's a joke about this, of course, along these lines: "Since I learned about confirmation bias I now see it everywhere.")

Like so many other deep insights about the human condition, the phenomenon of confirmation bias was recognized centuries ago. Back in the early seventeenth century, Sir Francis Bacon was an early pioneer of empiricism. In his book *Novum Organum* (New Instrument), he wrote:

> The human understanding when it has once adopted an opinion ... draws all things else to support and agree with it. And though there be a greater number and weight of instances to be found on the other side, yet these it either neglects or despises ... in order that by this great and pernicious predetermination the authority of its former conclusions may remain inviolate. (Quoted in Shermer, 2011, p. 294)

In an early and now-famous experiment on confirmation bias (Lord, Ross, & Lepper, 1979), researchers recruited American undergraduate students who either strongly supported or strongly opposed the death penalty and presented them with two fabricated studies of its effectiveness. One study showed the death penalty to be an effective deterrent, the other did not. Supporters of the death penalty found the study that was consistent with their belief to be convincing and well conducted; they judged the other one to be poorly designed and carried out. Students who opposed the death penalty had – you guessed it – the opposite reaction.

Numerous examples of confirmation bias exist in history. Among the best is the "Dreyfus Affair."[2] In the late nineteenth century French officer Alfred Dreyfus was accused, on the flimsiest of evidence, of giving military secrets to Germany, a rival power at the time. All it took was an incriminating note that appeared to have handwriting similar to his. The fact that Dreyfus was the lone high-ranking Jew in an anti-Semitic military culture did not help matters any. He was convicted of treason, stripped of his officer's rank, and sentenced to life on Devil's Island off the coast of South America. The espionage continued, however, and evidence uncovered later pointed to another officer, whose handwriting was a perfect match for the note. On appeal none of this mattered. Dreyfus, it was argued, had had the foresight to train others to carry on if he were caught, and had even coached them in how to mimic his handwriting! It took the persistence of a fellow officer who was willing to put aside his own anti-Semitism in search of the truth to finally exonerate Dreyfus, but only after Dreyfus had suffered in exile for more than four years, between March 1895 and June 1899.

Other historical examples of confirmation bias have been shown by people who are otherwise famed for their intelligence and creativity. Thomas Edison, for example, continued to argue the superiority of his invention, direct current (DC), well after alternate current (AC) had been shown to be more powerful and efficient. Even more striking is the case of Nobel laureate Linus Pauling. Pauling had long believed in the supposed power of vitamin C to treat a variety of health problems, including serious diseases (Mercier & Sperber, 2017), and he was persuaded by a study that seemed to show the effectiveness of vitamin C on cancer patients. Pauling's credibility as a scientist enabled a series of large-scale, tightly controlled studies, none of which found any evidence to confirm the findings of the earlier study. Nevertheless, instead of acknowledging that his initial hypothesis might have been wrong, Pauling instead attacked the methodology of these follow-up studies, and he and his wife continued to take high doses of vitamin C daily. Ironically, both eventually died of the very illness they were convinced that vitamin C could prevent.[3]

As the Linus Pauling story so graphically illustrates, pure intelligence and reasoning ability is no protection against confirmation bias. Neither is being a respected social scientist. Robert George (2019) cites several cases of studies where coding errors or outright fabrication somehow escaped the vetting process prior to publication of research articles, and even when discovered took years to retract. His culprit is confirmation bias:

> Confirmation bias – and its converse, the aggravated denial of unfavored results – flourishes when there is a lack of viewpoint diversity in scholarship. As such diversity has waned in the American academy, scholarly journals and federal funding agencies have too often become intellectually inbred. They sometimes constitute an academic version of interlocking directorates on corporate boards, in which decision makers who share the same outlook tend to view each other's work with an insufficiently critical eye. Research that pleases everyone in the club sometimes doesn't get enough scrutiny, even when its results are strikingly implausible. (George, 2019, p. A15)

Available evidence suggests that reasoning ability can make confirmation bias even *stronger* (Stanovich, West, & Toplak, 2013). This makes sense, because as we will see shortly, we use our reasoning skills to justify existing beliefs and to pick holes in those that differ from ours.

Hugo Mercier and Dan Sperber conducted a systematic review of the research on confirmation bias and concluded – convincingly, to my mind – that a more accurate term would be "myside bias":

> People have no general preference for confirmation. What they find difficult is not looking for counterevidence or counterarguments in general, but only when what is being challenged is their own opinion … Reasoning systematically works to find reasons for our ideas and against ideas we oppose. It always takes our side. As a result, it is preferable to speak of a *myside bias* rather than of a confirmation bias. (Mercier & Sperber, 2017, p. 218, emphasis in original)

Confirmation (or myside) bias helps us understand the persistence of belief, that is, holding onto one's original belief – such as avoiding vaccinations, purchasing guns for "protection," and drinking unpasteurized milk – in the face of overwhelming contradictory evidence. In their provocatively titled book *Denying to the Grave: Why We Ignore the Facts That Will Save Us*, Sara and Jack Gorman (Gorman & Gorman, 2017) cite these and many other examples. Why, one might rightly ask, are people so stubborn?

Consider the flow of Figure 1.1. An individual experiences cognitive dissonance; it is not just a mental puzzler but a gut-level sense of disorientation that leads to a desire for resolution and a return to homeostasis. I have given several examples already of cognitive dissonance; here is another. A young mother sees a posting on Facebook from a close friend that is linked to a website purporting to show the link between childhood immunization (specifically the vaccine for measles, mumps, and rubella, or MMR) and the development of autism. Alarmed by the mental image of her young son becoming autistic, she thanks her friend and clicks on a link to a video featuring a Hollywood celebrity who has a child with autism. The celebrity interviews other parents of autistic children, all of whom have been immunized, and points to a "scientific" study claiming to establish a cause–effect relationship. The video ends with a chart showing the profits pharmaceutical firms make from manufacturing the vaccines, darkly insinuating a conspiracy to suppress the evidence of harm. "That does it," the mother thinks, "I need to protect my children from Big Pharma." She now has an intuitive theory about the relationship between MMR and autism, made stronger by the desire to protect her son, setting her up for probable confirmation/myside bias. Some months later the child's pediatrician suggests that it's time for the boy to get the MMR vaccine. The mother declines, whereupon the physician warns her about the risks of these diseases, giving her data showing how dangerous and even life-threatening they can be. Immediately, the young mother experiences the same sensation she had when she saw the video of autistic children and recalls how she imagined her own son suffering the same fate. She does not have a similar image of her son with measles and holds firm to her decision. After the office visit she watches the video again, and does not look for any readily available materials challenging the validity of the video. The mother's fear speaks louder than data.

This vignette is an example of what has become known as the "Dunning-Kruger effect": the failure of those who lack expertise to accurately appraise their own knowledge compared to the expertise of experts (Dunning, 2011). A study reported in 2018 on the influence of the Dunning-Kruger effect on beliefs about the relationship between childhood vaccination and autism contains some illuminating findings (Motta, Callaghan, & Sylvester, 2018).

After surveying more than 1,000 US adults, the authors discovered that more than a third of respondents thought they knew as much or more than either doctors or scientists about the subject; those with the highest levels of overconfidence also knew the least about it! Researchers also found that overconfidence was related to opposition to mandatory vaccination policy and increased support for the role that nonexperts should play in determining such policies. The authors did not find that overconfidence was significantly related to a loss of confidence in experts, but rather that it tended to give more credence to the testimonies of celebrities and other nonexperts. Still, the researchers concluded that Dunning-Kruger effects should be "carefully considered in future research on anti-vaccine policy attitudes" (Motta et al., 2018, p. 274).

As Figure 1.1 indicates, intuitive theories can arise from a variety of sources. I have just illustrated one of these, the formation of causal assumptions. Humans specialize in reasoning about how the world works, about *causality*: why something happened, what caused it. Other sources include lived experience, patternicity, and reductive thinking. All of us experience seeing the sun "coming up" in the morning and "going down" in the evening; for some this leads to a mental model of the sun revolving around the earth, despite what we learned in elementary school. Our perceptual experience can easily override conceptual models.

Another contributor to intuitive theories is "patternicity," or "the tendency to find meaningful patterns in both meaningful and meaningless noise" (Shermer, 2011, p. 60). We are hard-wired to find patterns in incoming data. The idea that some things are random is hard to handle. And yet, the laws of probability make even unlikely events happen rather often. There's a clever little law called "Littlewood's Law of Miracles" (Lane, 2018). It goes this way: imagine the odds of something happening are a million to one; now imagine that we perceive one bit of information per second. If you calculate the number of seconds in a month, more than a million, this means that you will experience a "miracle" on the average of once a month! You run into someone from your high school graduating class 20 years ago on a street in Paris; you see the image of the Virgin Mary on a piece of toast; and so on.

Patternicity is often quite benign, as when we say a basketball player has a "hot hand," when in fact the laws of probability dictate that sooner or later that player will hit five shots in a row. Patternicity becomes more serious when the suggestion that an event is "random" creates the uncomfortable feeling that we lack control over our environment. We therefore have evolved to look for cause–effect relationships, even where none exist.

Given incomplete or unrepresentative data, we tend to jump to invalid conclusions. A common rule in statistics is that *correlation does not equal causation*. Some years ago, when teaching a research methods course, I decided to test the students' comprehension of this principle, and so brought in a newspaper article from the day before, stating that researchers had found a relationship between children's reading scores and whether they normally had breakfast in the morning. I casually asked the students, "So what are the educational implications of this finding?" You guessed it: Make sure kids have breakfast so they'll learn better! Now just imagine how many *other* explanations, how many potential intervening variables, there might be for this.

Our discomfort with the random and uncontrollable is why terrorism works: the fear that something that could strike anywhere at any time is more acute than the worry that we might be involved in a traffic accident, even though the latter is much more likely. In their book *Denying to the Grave*, the Gormans provide a number of examples of how we persistently overestimate small risks and underestimate large ones. One of these is the widespread concern over the Ebola virus, which posed a negligible risk to those living in the Western Hemisphere. One can almost feel their exasperation when they write, "How many people smoked a cigarette or consumed a sugary breakfast cereal while reading about the threat they faced in catching Ebola?" (Gorman & Gorman, 2017, p. 2).

Another contributor to intuitive belief is *reductive thinking*. The propensity to default to System 1 leads to the avoidance of complexity. As Steven Sloman and Philip Fernbach put it, "We ignore complexity by overestimating how much we know how things work, by living life in the belief that we know how things work even when we don't" (Sloman & Fernbach, 2017, p. 35). This leads to the Dunning-Kruger effect – the "illusion of understanding," tolerating complexity by failing to understand it – and thus, for example, the seductive appeal of Twitter, reducing complex issues to a series of sound-bites, not that hard to understand in this era of complexity and rapid change.

Again, Daniel Kahneman's research (2011) helps explain the pervasiveness of reductive thinking in our lives. Our natural drive to make meaning of the world around us (which I explore more fully in the next chapter) leads to forming mental models of how the world works. Inevitably, because these mental models represent our constructions of reality, they lead us to think in terms of categories: "chairs," "buildings," "planets." We get into trouble when we assume homogeneity within categories and ignore the diversity, which leads to stereotyping.

Intuitive beliefs, as Andrew Shtulman notes in his book *Scienceblind*, are a "double-edged sword":

> On one hand, they broaden our perspective of the phenomena they seek to explain and refine our interactions with those phenomena because holding an intuitive theory is better than holding no theory at all. On the other hand, they close our minds to ideas and observations that are inconsistent with those theories and they keep us from discovering the true nature of how things work … To get the world right, we cannot simply refine our intuitive theories; we must dismantle them and rebuild them from their foundations. (Shtulman, 2017, p. 11)

To review the chapter to this point: Intuitive beliefs arise from perceived experience. We attempt to make easy meaning of experience through patternicity, causal assumptions, and reductive thinking. When presented with information that is discordant with these beliefs we experience cognitive dissonance, which System 1 thinking encourages us to resolve through confirmation bias.

Confirmation bias is not, unfortunately, a one-off phenomenon. As suggested earlier in this chapter, and as indicated in Figure 1.1, confirmation bias promotes *belief persistence*, holding on to one's original belief in the face of overwhelming contrary evidence. In their fascinating book, *The Enigma of Reason* (2017), Mercier and Sperber explore what they call a "double enigma": why did human reason evolve to be so complex and different from other animals? And if evolution is the result of useful adaptations to the environment, then why did human reason evolve in such a flawed way? Mercier and Sperber, both cognitive scientists, argue that intuition and reasoning are not separate phenomena but that reasoning is a kind of "intuitive inference." "Reasons," they write, "play a central role in the after-the-fact explanation and justification of our intuitions, not in the process of intuitive inference itself" (Mercier & Sperber, 2017, p. 117). Reason, therefore, is intuition about reasons, used in interactions with others for the purpose of producing arguments in favor of "myside" and evaluating critically the reasons of the "otherside."

So how is this environmentally adaptive? Mercier and Sperber argue that humans are unique in how we have evolved complex forms of cooperation. Using what they call an "interactionist" perspective, they point to a body of research undertaken by them and many others to argue that human reasoning is ineffective, even counterproductive, when done alone. As we have seen already, solitary reasoning often fails to correct intuitive beliefs, and, due to various forms of confirmation bias, can even make matters worse. Reasoning works best when it takes place when interacting with others. "Take reason out of the interactive context in which it evolved," the authors note, "and nothing guarantees that it will yield adaptive results" (Mercier & Sperber, 2017, p. 10).

But how can "cooperation" emerge from interactions characterized by one side generating arguments for their own beliefs, while also criticizing the validity of beliefs on the other side – and while the other side is doing the same thing? Mercier and Sperber (2017) point to a substantial body of evidence that if a group has a common interest in finding the "truth," or has a shared interest in solving a problem, argumentation generally arrives at the "best" decision. But this, I would argue, is a big *if.* Jonathan Haidt, psychologist and expert in moral reasoning, has demonstrated how impervious moral judgments are to opposing arguments. No matter how strong they are, rebuttals of one's moral judgments by others will seldom change their minds (Haidt, 2012). As persuasive as arguments for the interactionist approach may be, they fail to account for how reason might deal effectively with intuitive beliefs that have a strong affective basis. When someone is emotionally invested in a belief, especially when that belief is part of one's identity, pure rationality fails to deliver.

Belief persistence is reinforced in two ways, according to Mercier and Sperber (2017): by the "lazy production" of supporting reasons and the "strong production" of opposing reasons. Just as we are not very good at acknowledging our own biases, we are very good at recognizing biases in others. We are able to come up with justifications for our beliefs quickly and easily. For example, if one opposes capital punishment s/he will be able to generate a list of reasons for that view with little trouble: it's not an effective deterrent; it costs the state more than life imprisonment; it systematically discriminates against those without means to hire quality legal representation; it forestalls the possibility of correcting a potential injustice; it is a barbaric practice that most civilized nations have foresworn long ago. (As an opponent of capital punishment myself, I generated this list in less than a minute.) I have a much harder time critiquing my position, and it takes longer. In the amount of time it took to generate all of the supporting reasons, I could come up with only one in opposition: that the state ought to have an ultimate penalty available for the most heinous of crimes. If, on the other hand, I were in a discussion with someone on the other side, I'd be able to shoot down virtually all of that person's arguments (at least to *my* satisfaction), and feel pretty good about doing so.

A point that I will make over and over in this book is that we overemphasize the role of cognition and downplay the role of emotion, both in how we learn and in how we change. Belief persistence is not just a function of a highly evolved ability to argue in a social context. It is also a function of psychological defense mechanisms that protect our egos from attack. One of these is what Ori and Ron Brafman have called "loss aversion" (Brafman & Brafman, 2008). Simply stated, "we experience the pain associated with a loss much more vividly than we do the joy of experiencing a gain" (p. 18). Loss aversion explains why casino owners make so much money: they count on customers chasing rather than cutting their losses. Loss aversion also accounts for what Zachary Shore calls "exposure anxiety," one of several reasons he cites for why otherwise-smart people make dumb – and in some cases disastrous – decisions. Shore explains: "Exposure anxiety is more than just a fear. It is a belief that the failure to act in a manner perceived as firm will result in the weakening of one's position" (Shore, 2008, p. 14). It is, in other words, fear of loss of face. I leave the reader to imagine just how many times this very fear has led political and military leaders to blunder into decisions that history has judged to be complete disasters.[4]

Developmental psychologists Robert Kegan and Lisa Lahey have done some groundbreaking research on the psychological mechanisms behind the emotional grip that irrational beliefs have on us. They call these mechanisms, collectively, "immunity to change (ITC)," arguing that real change is not just a matter of overcoming old beliefs but rather unearthing, naming, and facing what they call "competing commitments" (Kegan & Lahey, 2009). Kegan and Lahey chose the term "immunity" deliberately, intending to show that just as our bodies have complex immune systems designed to protect us from disease and other threats to our physical well-being, we also have psychological immune systems that serve to ward off anxiety. These immunities, Kegan and Lahey argue, are often dysfunctional, keeping us from making the developmental changes we sincerely want to make. Because immunities are subconscious, we are unaware of their existence and their power over us, and we thus experience anxiety, not just from change but also at the *thought* of change. Thus, when we engage in a self-improvement effort such as losing weight, we find ourselves unable to stick with the goal we have set for ourselves, ending up with frustration and self-blaming.

Kegan and Lahey demonstrate how these immunity systems can be changed, situating their model in constructive-developmental theory and sharing examples, both personal and organizational, from their own practices. They introduce a five-step exercise designed to uncover the unconscious immunities, make them conscious, and create experiences that mitigates their hold on us. I will be exploring this process as a tool for deep learning later in this book.

Kegan and Lahey's work, along with that of the other scholars cited in this chapter, should reveal the critical importance of paying attention to the role of emotion in learning. We need to become more critical thinkers, yes: in both school and in our adult experience we need to learn how to step back, evaluate facts, and form evidence-based conclusions. *But we also need to learn that we will not always behave that way in real life.* Much of what cognitive science has taught us over the years is what individual humans *can't* do – what our limitations are. Ignoring the power of these limitations leads to the sort of self-delusion that in turn leads to myside bias, belief persistence, and ultimately the pernicious effects of polarized attitudes, of the sort described at the beginning of this chapter. What we need are useful, research-based ways of dealing with and overcoming these limitations, the central focus of this book. First, however, I want to review how the brain works.

Notes

1 The authors reference Frankfurt's (*On Bullshit*, 2005) intriguing distinction between lying and bullshit: "Whereas lying involves a deliberate attempt at concealing the truth, which implies a concern for the truth, bullshit is constructed absent concern for the truth" (p. 9). The idea of doing something about the creation and spread of BS seems to be catching on, exemplified by a popular course at the University of Washington, "Calling Bullshit: Data Reasoning in a Digital World" (McWilliams, 2019).
2 The Dreyfus case has been cited in several sources as a dramatic illustration of confirmation bias. One of the most engaging is a TED talk by Julia Galef (2016).
3 Pauling did however live to be 93.
4 A good place to start would be Barbara Tuchman's classic, *The March of Folly: From Troy to Vietnam* (1984).

CHAPTER 2

How We Learn
A Short Primer

Education consists mainly in what we have unlearned.

Mark Twain

So far in this book I have argued that understanding deep learning and how to promote it is both important and difficult, especially in today's turbulent world and with the seductive appeal of drive-by learning. In this chapter I go back to the basics of human learning, focusing less on its flaws and more on the process itself. My goal is to lay the groundwork and provide an evidentiary basis for proposals I make later in the book.

In many ways, what we know today about how people learn has been a matter of rediscovering some old truths. Consider the following maxims:

Teachers open the door. You enter by yourself. Chinese proverb

What we have to learn to do, we learn by doing. Aristotle

You cannot teach a man anything; you can only help him find it within himself. Galileo

Tell me and I forget. Teach me and I remember. Involve me and I learn. Benjamin Franklin

Think about these for a moment. What do they have in common?

If you are like most people, you will observe that all four statements speak to learning as an activity that requires intentionality and action, and is best achieved when that learning is facilitated more than dictated. Recent research in human cognition has largely confirmed the ancient wisdom, but has also challenged it in two ways: first it has exposed the limits of rationalism, as we saw in the previous chapter; second and relatedly, it has demonstrated the critical partnership between cognition and emotion.[1] I will get to both of these shortly; first I need to provide a very brief foundation with some basic neuroanatomy.[2]

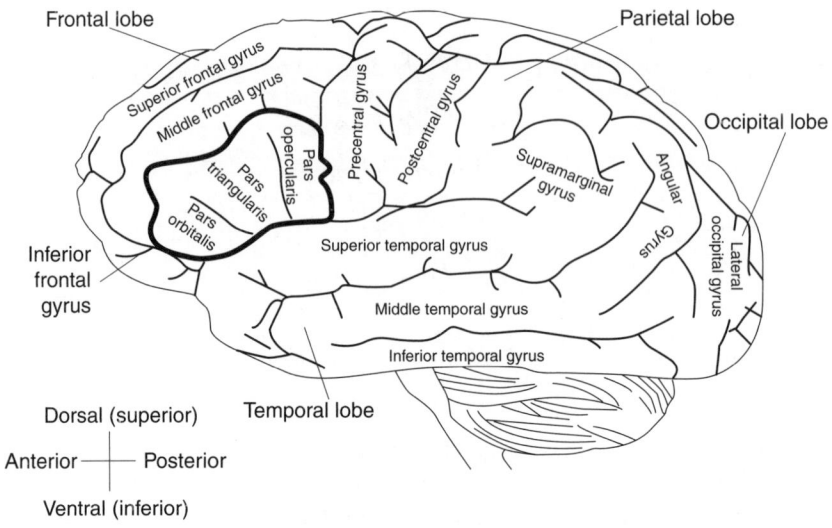

Figure 2.1 The human brain
Source: Blackbum and Hwozdek (2016). Licensed under CC0 1.0, creativecommons.org/publicdomain/zero/1.0/legalcode.

2.1 Inside Your Brain

For an organ that consumes so much energy, generates such enormous activity, and holds the keys to our individual identities, our brains are smaller than most people think: they weigh only about four pounds in the average adult, and are small enough to hold in the palm of your hand. Thanks to developments in positron-emission tomography (PET) and magnetic resource imaging (MRI), today's neuroscientists are better able to connect structure with function. The largest portion of the brain is the *cerebrum*, responsible for thinking, body movement, interpreting stimuli, and memory. The cerebrum has four regions, or lobes, each with a specific function. (See Figure 2.1)

The *occipital lobe*, at the very back of the brain, is where visual stimuli are processed; the *temporal lobe*, near the ears, deals with language, sound, and understanding speech; the *parietal lobe*, at the top of the brain and the back of the head, handles motor skills, movement, and orientation; and the *frontal lobe*, right behind the forehead, deals with intellectual tasks, planning, and decision-making. It is the last to develop, not fully

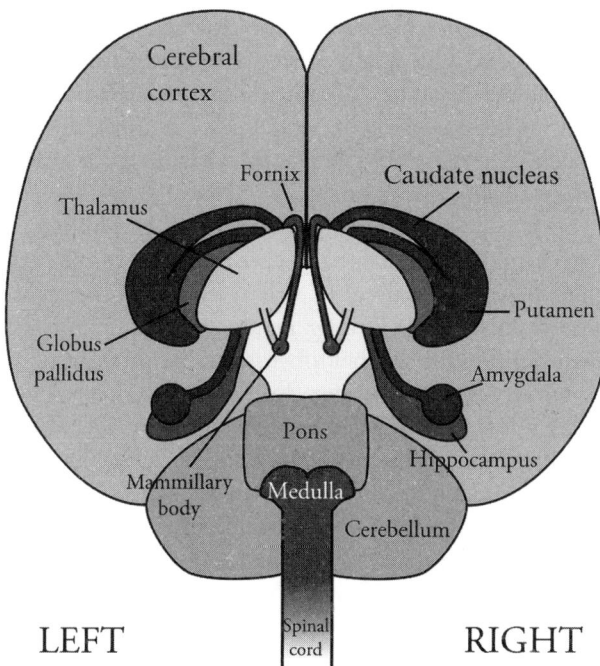

Figure 2.2 The limbic system
Source: Image courtesy of PublicDomainPictures, Pixabay.

until early adulthood. The thin outside surface of the cerebrum, about the thickness of a grapefruit skin, is the *cerebral cortex* containing about 100 billion neurons, which essentially manage the work of the brain.

Deep inside our brains is the *limbic system*, which manages emotions (see Figure 2.2).

Among the key structures of the limbic system, two are most responsible for learning. One is the *amygdala*, which seeks to make meaning of experience, mostly at an unconscious level. In situations of uncertainty it stimulates the frontal lobe to kick in, encouraging us to think it through. The other is the *hippocampus*, which is more concerned with memory. It takes in information from the senses, packages and processes the separate stimuli, and then sends them to the cortex where the information becomes part of long-term memory.

Finally, just below the cerebrum is the *cerebellum*, the primary source of motor control (Wright et al., 2016). The cerebellum is where somatic learning resides, the source of "muscle memory." When a behavior is practiced over and over again, the sequence of actions required becomes automatic, such as typing on a keyboard, driving a car with a manual transmission, or staying upright on skis.

This has been a drastically truncated tour of the brain, and here is why: While technology has enabled scientists to map various sensations to certain regions based on analyses of neural firings, as the technology has become more sophisticated, linking regions with functions has become murkier. For example, the cerebellum used to be thought of as almost a separate organ, representing more primitive evolutionary stages; now it appears to play a role in various aspects of cognition, including language. This makes understanding the interplay between sensation and meaning-making a more complex challenge. For example, where do emotions come from? How are they triggered? How are they regulated? The answers to these questions are still a matter of debate, and some of the evidence may seem counterintuitive. More on this shortly, but first I want to provide some further context.

2.1.1 *The physiology of learning*

Here are some amazing statistics about how we learn to make meaning of the world around us. A child is born with about 100 billion neurons, all he or she will ever have. If these neurons are energized they will become part of the brain's circuitry, but they will die if unstimulated. A newborn's neurons have relatively few connections, or synapses, between them, but these increase rapidly as a function of the child's experience with his or her environment. In the first years of life a child will have created many thousands of synapses with each neuron, so that by the age of 2 he or she will have already created the same number of synaptic connections as a fully-grown adult. Now here is the amazing part: by about age 6 our brains have created twice that number, and are twice as active; but then after age 8 or 10 or so, the number of synapses gradually decreases, until by about age 18 we've gone back to the same number we had when we were age 2.[3] (Not that we go back to thinking like a 2-year-old, of course: the adult brain retains a remarkable degree of flexibility, and if exercised, continues to mold its physical structure well into old age.) So, I ask, why is this? How does this happen? Why is so much synaptic pruning going on after early childhood? My guess is that the reader's first response is, "school!" Formal schooling indoctrinates us on what to think and how – basically what is important to know. And yes, there is certainly some truth to this. But there is a biological answer, demonstrated by a lot of cross-cultural research (Shatz, 1992). Consider for a moment the life of a 6-year-old. Everything is interesting, everything is important. Kids that age are veritable sponges of information, as every parent knows. Now imagine what it would be like if adults had the same synaptic connections they had at age 6, and imagine the mental chaos. Our brains use middle and late childhood to figure out how the world works by reinforcing some networks and letting others die out. Only those that are reinforced survive. We create individual mental models, the key to survival dating back to our earliest days as humans, to make meaning out of chaos.

Unfortunately, meaning making can take us in strange directions, as we saw in Chapter 1. Here are some more examples:

> In 2008 the International Center for the Advancement of Scientific Literacy at the University of Michigan put together a short quiz and administered it to a random sample of 2,500 US citizens. One of the questions was, "How long does it take for the earth to go around the sun?" The three choices were: "one day," "one month," and "one year." Only 67% of respondents had the correct answer. The clear inference here is that about one person in every three walking down the street doesn't know a basic fact about our solar system – that the earth is a planet taking a year to revolve around the sun – even though virtually every kid in school has to make a model of the solar system at one time or other. (King, 2015)

Now in case these researchers just picked an unusually dull group to survey, consider this: A researcher gets the bright idea of going around with a video camera after Harvard's commencement exercises, when new graduates are standing around looking smug, taking photos with their parents. She sticks the camera in their faces, asking common-sense questions like, "Why is it warmer in the summer than in winter?" Out of 23 randomly chosen graduates (plus some alumni and faculty), 21 were factually *incorrect*, most stating that seasons are caused because the earth is closer to the sun in the summer and further away in the winter. One of the students answering incorrectly had taken several physics courses at Harvard, including one in "planetary motion"! (Harvard Smithsonian Center for Astrophysics, 1987). These people learned the same stuff about the solar system in elementary school that the people in the Michigan survey did, so what is going on?

It turns out that when asked to reconsider their answers, most did in fact get it right; but they had seized upon the first mental model that came to mind, which is the simple principle that the closer an object is to a heat source, the hotter it will get. Retrieving a more complicated mental model, about how the earth is tilted on its axis, which affects the angle of the sun's rays, is harder. These people were, in essence, relying on System 1 thinking, when what they really needed to do was to pull up System 2 (Kahneman, 2011).

Here is a short thought experiment. Read through the following carefully. What is being described?

> A newspaper is better than a magazine, and on a seashore is a better place than a street. At first, it is better to run than walk. Also, you may have to try several times. It takes some skill but it's easy to learn. Even young children can enjoy it. Once successful, complications are minimal. Birds seldom get too close. One needs lots of room. Rain soaks in very fast. Too many people doing the same thing can also cause problems. If there are no complications, it can be very peaceful. A rock will serve as an anchor. If things break loose from it, however, you will not get a second chance.

Give up? The answer is in the endnote.[4]

Now it all seems obvious. The reason it was not so obvious right away is that a mental model did not exist in which to put the description.

The above example illustrates how important the process of meaning-making is. Every time we are presented with new information, we first attempt to fit it into an existing knowledge structure, a whole network of categories that our brains have organized for us. If a category immediately occurs to us, that is where the new information goes, and that is what Daniel Kahneman (2011) means by "thinking fast," or System 1. The same principle applies to recalling information, such as in the Harvard example above. Without any clues, however, our brains scramble to find a connection, and System 2 thinking kicks in. As Kahneman points out, System 2 makes our brains work harder, and so our usual preference is to default to System 1 whenever possible; therefore, he advises, we must learn to recognize situations in which mistakes are likely and try harder to avoid significant mistakes when the stakes are high.

Fair enough; but the problem is, how can we do that when our intuitive biases exist at a subconscious level? How do we keep from becoming ensnared by cognitive traps without even knowing it?

2.2 Experiential Learning Theories

Key to addressing these questions is the nature of human experience. The central role of experience in learning, as shown by the quotes that opened this chapter, has been appreciated for centuries. Paradoxically, however, the period known as the Enlightenment, ushered in by Galileo and others in the seventeenth century, also ushered in one of its more dubious achievements, what is known as "Cartesian thinking," named after philosopher Rene Descartes' notion of dualism, that "there is a great difference between mind and body, inasmuch as body is by nature always divisible, and the mind is entirely indivisible ... the mind or soul of man is entirely different from the body" (quoted in McNerney, 2011, pp. 1–2).

We have already seen in Chapter 1 the mischief this kind of purely rationalist thinking can cause. Some serious cracks began to appear in dualistic, Cartesian thinking in the late nineteenth century with the writing of philosopher William James, and later John Dewey, both pioneers of American pragmatism. In a landmark essay, "What Is an Emotion?" James debunked the thinking that emotion is simply a by-product of cognition:

> Our natural way of thinking about standard emotions is that the mental perception of some fact excites the mental affection called the emotion, and that this latter state of mind gives rise to the bodily expression. My thesis on the contrary is that *the bodily changes follow directly the **perception** of the exciting fact, and that our feeling of the same changes as they occur **is** the emotion.* (James, 1884, pp. 4–5, emphasis in original)

In other words, how we feel about something is not determined by how we think about it, but just the reverse. The sensation – the experience – comes first, followed by the brain's interpretation and meaning-making of that experience. With his anticipation of the function of the amygdala as the chief interpreter of sensation, James demonstrated in this essay a remarkable ability to foresee advances in neuroscience by nearly a hundred years. He also understood the key role of emotion in human judgment, and how it can often lead us astray. In the uniquely Victorian vernacular of his time he wrote, "peculiarly conformed pieces of the world's furniture will fatally call forth most particular mental and bodily reactions, in advance of, and often in direct opposition to, the verdict of our deliberate reason concerning them" (p. 4).

Later in the early twentieth century philosopher/educator/engaged citizen John Dewey laid out a comprehensive theory of experiential learning, first in 1916 (Dewey [1916] 1985) and revised 22 years later

(Dewey, [1938] 1997). Dewey, too, recognized the key role of emotion in human judgment, seeing it as the main entry into what he called "a life of thought." He envisioned the human mind not as a storehouse of ideas but as how humans make meaning of experience, and thus manage and lead lives of useful activity. Early in his career, spurred by such social upheavals as the Pullman Strike in 1893 – a widespread work stoppage and boycott of the railways that turned violent – Dewey turned to schools as democracy's best hope. Children's "inner nature," he felt, grows from within but must be completed through relationships, and thus schools must be a reflection of life. To the degree that schools are laboratories for living, society progresses toward greater democracy and social justice. Dewey's ideas were central to what became known as the "progressive education" movement (Martin, 2002). In the late 1930s, following attacks on freedom of expression in schools and universities in the United States, Dewey published *Experience and Education* (1938), a powerful restatement of the role of experience in learning. First he debunked the misunderstood notion that children, and people generally, "learn by doing." Some experiences, he averred, can be "mis-educative," that is, can be "unintelligent doing" that results in learning the wrong things. An "educative" experience, on the other hand, "arouses curiosity, strengthens initiative, and sets up desires and purposes that are sufficiently intense to carry a person over dead places in the future" (Dewey, [1938] 1997, p. 38). In this one sentence, Dewey encapsulates core ideas of deep learning, and I will be returning to his work extensively later in this book.

Part of what Dewey meant by "educative experience" is what has become known as *experiential learning theory*, introduced by psychologist David Kolb (Kolb, 1984). In his "experiential learning cycle," Kolb essentially turned formal education upside down: Instead of building knowledge by learning abstract concepts and then applying them, what radical educator Paulo Freire (1970) called the "banking model" of formal education, what the learner does in real life is to build knowledge by experiencing an event, reflecting on it, developing an abstract interpretation of it, and finally acting on this interpretation, thus generating further experience, reflection, theorizing, and action (Figure 2.3).

This model, probably because it is simple, plausible and easy to grasp, has been used and adapted thousands of times in every conceivable learning context over the years, and, inevitably, due to its simplicity and intuitive appeal, has also been the target of harsh criticism. Still, Kolb's learning cycle, with its clear connections to neuroscience research and to emerging models of adult development, has had an enormous impact on

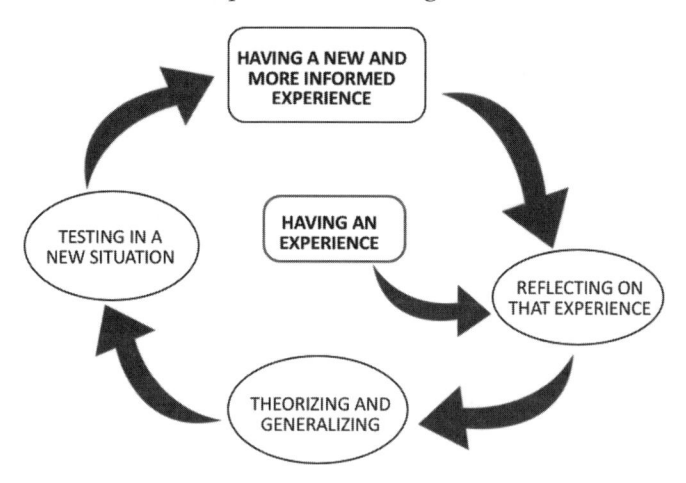

Figure 2.3 Experiential learning cycle

how we think about learning and about connecting learning with action, and has led to such paradigm-changing epistemologies as action research (cf. McNiff, 2017), and practice-based research (Jarvis, 1999).

One offshoot of the renewed interest in the interaction between action and cognition is research into *embodied cognition*, "the idea that the mind is not only connected to the body but that the body influences the mind" (McNerney, 2011). The key to understanding embodied learning that we do not just learn *from* experience, we also learn *in* experience. It is a felt reaction to experience that feels "right" or "wrong," and in adults this reaction can be quite nuanced. For example, the positive feeling created by the friendly behavior of a gracious hostess may lead someone who doesn't know her well to perceive her as "sincere," while in contrast, someone who has experienced her cordiality as superficial in prior experiences would think of the same conduct as "smarmy." Cognition that does not occur *from and in* experience will not create learning *for* experience. Sharan Merriam and her colleagues cite as an ironic example college courses that take on issues of social justice but only in an abstract, disembodied way, leading to students becoming quite sophisticated in critical social analysis but unable to apply these skills in real life – or even in simulations of real life (Merriam, Caffarella, & Baumgartner, 2007).

Aristotle understood the importance of embodied learning centuries ago, when he described three kinds of knowing: *episteme*, knowing *what* and *why*; *techne*, knowing *how*; and *phronesis*, knowing *when*. Quite simply, we may know a lot about issues of power and inequality, for example, and be skilled at knowing how to analyze them, but we may not know when and in what context to use these skills most effectively. One of the most dramatic examples of *phronesis* is the story of a nomadic tribe of "sea gypsies" in Thailand (Freiler, 2008). Most were able to survive the catastrophic tsunami of 2004, unlike thousands of others. When asked how they survived when so many others did not, they replied that they sensed a change in their environment, both in the sea and in other living things, that caused them to take higher ground before the tsunami actually struck. Another example is what is known in mining as "pit sense." In the dangerous setting of a coal mine, miners must learn to detect minute changes in their environment as a way of constantly assessing their safety; tellingly, this way of knowing depends not only on the miners' individual perceptions but also the senses of others in the mine (Freiler, 2008). Note how in both of these examples *knowing when* is triggered by a sensory experience, which is interpreted intuitively as a potential threat. Knowing when an experience feels "right" can be powerful as well. In baseball an experienced base-stealer will often know when to try for second base because it just "feels" right. An expert poker player will know when it is "right" to bluff with a weak hand. *Phronesis* is, in essence, practical wisdom, the ability to know when to rely on intuition (System 1) and when to make the effort to dig more deeply (System 2) (Kahneman, 2011). Practical wisdom is a topic I will return to later in the book.

Intuition, as I have pointed out numerous times already, is necessary for our survival; *and* it can also keep us from making wise choices. Given that intuitive biases exist at a subconscious level, what then has to happen in order for them to surface and be acted upon?

It turns out that we do have a solid theory about this, known as *transformative learning theory*, developed about the same time as experiential learning theory, and now arguably the dominant theory in adult learning. According to its originator Jack Mezirow, adults learn to become "critically aware of how and why our presuppositions ... constrain the way we perceive, understand, and feel about our world; of reformulating these assumptions to permit a more inclusive, discriminating, permeable, integrative perspective, and of making decisions or otherwise acting upon these new understandings" (Mezirow, 2000, p. 14). And what transcends the cognitive traps that block the critical awareness that Mezirow describes? What nudges us from System 1 into System 2? Mezirow (2000) asserts that adults can learn deeply only by experiencing what he calls a "disorienting dilemma," a problem that does not fit into existing mental models (or "meaning schemes," as Mezirow called them). You experience something that catches you off guard, off balance, something you can't quite make sense of, something you can't easily make meaning of. And it is too disturbing to ignore. The disorientation causes System 2 to kick in and you are forced to examine your assumptions and create, through reflection, a new mental model, thus transforming your set of knowledge perspectives. Mezirow suggests that while transformative learning can happen within the individual, it is most powerful in group dialogue, where people can try on the perspectives of others. Disorienting dilemmas can be small, like having to find your way around a strange city when your GPS isn't working, or they can be large, such as facing life-changing events like the loss of a job or a serious health or relationship problem.

Mezirow's theory has been exhaustively studied and criticized. Available empirical evidence does support the notion that changes in one's meaning perspectives are triggered by a disorienting dilemma, followed by a set of learning strategies that involve critical reflection and exploration of options in a social relationship (Taylor, 1994). Two criticisms are leveled most commonly at the theory. First is that his theory puts too much emphasis on rationality – that more intuitive and holistic views of learning are needed. In an exhaustive review of empirical studies of transformative learning, Taylor (1994) concluded that "transformative learning is not just rationally and consciously driven but incorporates a variety of nonrational and unconscious modalities for revising meaning structures" (p. 48). (Note the connection here to the role of emotion in creating and protecting beliefs, as discussed in Chapter 1.) The second criticism is that the theory pays insufficient attention to transformation in the service of social change, the focus of the great emancipatory educator Paulo Freire. Oppressed peoples, Freire believed, become empowered to change the world through critical reflection in a community of learners (Freire, 1970). Praxis, the combination of reflection and action, is the key to overcoming oppression. True education, according to Freire, is always a political act.

I will be covering transformative learning on both an individual and group level much more extensively in later chapters. For now, I want to make two points about how useful this theory is to our understanding of cognitive bias, and more importantly, how it might help us deal with the challenges that bias poses to deep learning.

First is Mezirow's emphasis on the importance of group dialogue. Recall from the previous chapter how private reflection on one's strongly held beliefs usually does not only *not* change these beliefs but can even make them stronger. With some exceptions, reflection and argumentation with others is what matters. I explore this in more depth in Chapter 6.

Second, we would not have a disorienting experience in the first place were it not for an emotional trigger. Without that an unusual experience is just a puzzle, one that we may be curious about and even want to explore. We may wonder, for example, how the magician David Copperfield could make the Statue of Liberty "disappear" in front of a thousand spectators, but our beliefs about the laws of physics are never at risk, because everyone knows that it's a trick. On the other hand, feeling "tricked" is bound to create disorientation. Recently I was waiting for a connecting flight at New York's Newark airport, browsing in a shop along the concourse. I was approached by a disheveled-looking young man who asked if I "traveled a lot." He then proceeded to give me a long story about how he was a recent college graduate who had been stranded overnight by a canceled flight to Pittsburgh and could not get on another flight until the next day. He showed me his original and "new" boarding pass as evidence, along with a driver's license and the business card of an executive in the company he was about to join. He was desperate for a place to stay overnight (and he certainly looked like he needed it), but he had no credit cards as yet and had to pay for everything in cash. Could I please loan him money for meals and hotel room? He took my address and promised to pay me back right away. I took pity on him, withdrew some money from an ATM and gave it to him, and he scurried away with lavish thanks for how I confirmed his belief that "there were still good people in the world." Now, I would not be relating this story if he had paid me back. Instead, the experience gave me a disorienting dilemma and led to a modest shift in my self-concept, from "generous person" to "easily duped person."

Much of the research on human learning, particularly in adults, supports the basic tenets of transformative learning, without necessarily acknowledging so. Here is an especially impressive example. Higher education researchers Ernest Pascarella and Patrick Terenzini conducted an exhaustive investigation into learning in college, covering 35 years of research and more than 5,000 books, journal articles, and miscellaneous reports (Pascarella & Terenzini, 1991). The product of this work was so massive that their students referred to it, with grudging admiration, as "Moby Book." The authors published an equally massive update, ten years later (Pascarella & Terenzini, 2005). Reflecting back on decades of research, Terenzini compiled a list of six "experiences that promote student learning" (Terenzini, 2014). Note how similar these six optimal learning experiences are to what has been reviewed so far on adult learning:

Experiences that promote student learning:

1. *Almost uniformly involve encounters with difference*, both with people different from themselves and with ideas different from those currently held. Because they challenge existing beliefs these encounters create cognitive dissonance.
2. *Require active engagement with these challenges.* Deep learning will not occur if the learner does not address the cognitive dissonance.
3. *Occur in a supportive environment*, offering opportunities for reasonable risk-taking without fear of failure.
4. *Emphasize meaningful and real-world activities*, including dealing with unstructured problems.
5. *Involve other people and interpersonal activities* that will spark a challenge.
6. *Invite and encourage reflection and analysis.*

2.3 The Role of Emotion in Learning

As should be evident by now, learning is not just a cognitive process. Most experts now agree that without emotion, deep learning is at best hit-and-miss. Unless learning has an emotional component it is not likely to last. If you want to be sure that learning will stick, you have to be sure that the learner cares about the learning.

A landmark book by moral philosopher Martha Nussbaum explores how emotions shape the "landscape of our mental and social lives" (Nussbaum, 2001, p. 1).[5] Emotions, she wrote, "involve judgments about important things, judgments in which, appraising an external object as salient for our own well-being, we acknowledge our own neediness and incompleteness before parts of the world that we do not fully control" (p. 19). Thus, far from having to be bottled up or pushed aside, emotions are essential if we are to engage the world and allow deep learning to occur.

This philosophical view has been backed up by recent research, captured beautifully by Lisa Feldman Barrett's pioneering work (2017) on how the brain creates emotions. From her research Feldman demonstrates that, contrary to conventional – and intuitive – thinking, sensations do not trigger certain "emotion centers" in the brain. Rather, emotions are *constructed* by the brain, in the same way that cognition constructs mental models of reality. Barrett defines her *theory of constructed emotion* this way: "In every waking moment, your brain uses past experience, organized as concepts, to guide your actions and give your sensations meaning. When the concepts involved are emotion concepts, your brain constructs instances of emotion" (p. 31). The brain constructs emotions in the moment, as part of the way it makes meaning of sensory stimuli. It makes meaning of a situation so that we will know what to do *in that moment*. The brain will make meaning of the same visual stimulus in vastly different ways. Approaching the first drop of a roller coaster will produce physiological responses similar to those when approaching the edge of a steep cliff; the former will be constructed as "excitement," while the latter will be constructed as "fear." Further, emotions are socially constructed and culture specific. Feldman states:

> [Y]our familiar emotion concepts are built-in only because you grew up in a particular social context where these emotion concepts are meaningful and useful, and your brain applies them outside your awareness to construct your experiences. Heart rate changes are inevitable; their emotional meaning is not. Other cultures can and do make other kinds of meaning from the same sensory input. (p. 33)

Today the key role of emotion in learning is clear and largely uncontested. Emotion does not only stimulate learning, it is part of the learning process itself. Emotion can be a force for deep learning, as when a disorienting dilemma leads to reflection and perspective transformation; it can also be a significant *barrier* to deep learning, as when someone encounters information counter to his or her belief system and reduces the anxiety this produces by resorting to myside bias.

So where, then is that sweet spot, that level of disorientation where people experience just enough discomfort with the status quo that they are able to reflect on what's going on and try something new? That point where we experience not just a felt need to change but also a desire to change? What is the right balance between the body's need to regulate stress and maintain homeostasis, as neurologist and neuroscientist Antonio Damasio (2018) has described it, and taking a creative risk that will upset that homeostasis, at least temporarily? To address these questions, I turn now to what we know about motivation to learn.

2.4 Motivation and Learning in Adults

I invite the reader to think for a moment about why you have chosen to read this far into the book. Is it because you are concerned about the amount of drive-by learning that goes on in the face of the accelerating challenges we face as a society? Because you are curious about the positive steps we might take to meet these challenges? Or, I hope, maybe both? Whatever the reason, you are demonstrating right now a motivation to learn (I am assuming that the motivation is intrinsic,[6] even if you're reading this as a required text!) As we've already seen, this simple question: why do people behave the way they do? leads to complex, often counterintuitive, and sometimes paradoxical answers.

Motivation is the link between emotion and action. It is purposeful behavior focused on accomplishing a goal. Part of the challenge in understanding motivation, as Wlodkowski (2008) points out in his comprehensive treatment of the subject, is that because motivation is an abstraction, a construct, we cannot measure it directly but must instead rely on observing someone's behavior. Nonetheless, the prodigious literature on human motivation over the years has led to some common understandings:

First, the drive for humans to make meaning of the world is innate (Chater & Loewenstein, 2016). "The brain has an inherent inclination for knowing what it wants ... We are compelled to pay attention to things that matter to us. Every moment of our lives is a competition among our senses to perceive what matters most" (Wlodkowski, 2008, pp. 17–18). Sensations accompanied by emotion get preferential treatment. Motivation is thus a complex interplay of sensations, emotions, and thoughts that are mixing and remixing in any given moment, in the body's constant attempts to achieve homeostasis (Damasio, 2018).

Second, motivation is not an inherent part of our character. Labeling someone as "unmotivated" is unhelpful and wrong (Ahl, 2006).[7] The culture we grew up in and the networks of which we are a part have a huge influence, as does the immediate context. A recent study found that one's identity – that is, the amalgam of what we understand about ourselves and understandings assigned to us through social position – is a major factor in motivation to learn, and is always socially negotiated. In their study of motivation to learn among novice teachers, researchers found that identification had two major consequences:

> First, as might be expected, when teaching practices resonated with novices' extant identities (i.e., they saw them as valuable and feasible), they engaged more readily and deeply in learning them ... Second, when teaching practices did not resonate with novices' extant identities – but messages in the environment linked them to desired identities – then novices overrode their initial concerns and persisted in learning them anyway. (Nolen, Horn, & Ward, 2015, p. 238)

Third, despite the importance of culture and social context, certain sources of motivation are, if not innate, certainly cross-cultural. These include curiosity about the world; the desire to belong and to feel valued; and to feel efficacious,[8] quite simply, the feeling that what we do matters, that we have had a desirable impact on the world around us. Each of these motivators has roots in other somatic-neurological processes. Curiosity arises from the need to make meaning, a drive that remains largely undiminished throughout the lifespan. The desire to belong and feel valued stems from an innate need to feel safe, in a community that accepts us and that will help protect us from harm. The need for efficacy stems from an innate disposition to not only make meaning of the world but to interact effectively with it. Together, these universal "motivators" help ease what Parker Palmer has called the "pain of disconnection" from the world around us (Palmer, 1998).

These universal sources of motivation will of course manifest themselves differently, depending on the social and cultural context. My own research on the factors that affect motivation among university faculty, for example, turned up four: autonomy, community, recognition, and efficacy (Wergin, 2001). "Autonomy" was closely related to curiosity: the freedom to experiment, to follow one's own leads wherever they may go, and to do so without fear of the consequences. "Community" was related to the need for belonging, to feel as if one is part of a professional community that cares about them. "Recognition" was the need to feel valued by that community, to know that others see their work as worthwhile. And, "efficacy" in an academic community meant that faculty had a sense that their work had an impact on their scholarly disciplines.

Fourth, motivation not only mediates learning but is a consequence of learning as well (Wlodkowski, 2008). The more motivated someone is to learn, the more enjoyable the learning, and the greater the motivation is to learn more. At the same time, no matter how high, motivation will not help someone accomplish a learning task that is significantly beyond their skill level or their ability to cope with the increasing complexity of modern life. In fact, due to the frustration and anxiety this causes, the likely result will be paralysis or a desire to escape. Finding examples of this in one's own life is, sadly, far too easy. I was clumsy and overweight as a youngster, but I wanted desperately to fit in with the other guys, so I went out for football. The coach used the daily practice as a way to act out his fantasies as an army drill instructor, and he made my life miserable. Not only did I stop going to practice, I developed an "unathletic" identity, one that lasted into early adulthood, and led me to avoid participating in competitive athletics of any kind.

Given this landscape, what then motivates adults to learn deeply? I have sprinkled a few clues throughout this chapter and will now make them more explicit.

Adults want to learn lots of things, for all kinds of reasons, related mostly to what is seen as practical and relevant to their lives. They want learning to be self-directed, not dictated by what others think they should learn (Knowles, 1984). They want to build new learning from life experience, to test this new learning, and to integrate it into their own lives. They want the learning to be enjoyable, but not necessarily easy: they seek competence but also value the challenge (Wlodkowski, 2008).

All of the above are necessary for deep learning to occur, but only the last one distinguishes deep learning from the others. Deep learning happens when existing beliefs are challenged, but only within the limits of a person's perceived ability to handle the challenge. To put it another way, *deep learning is achieved when an optimal tension exists: between a perceived challenge to one's existing belief system on the one hand, and a perceived level of confidence in one's ability to create new meaning in that system on the other.* Note the interaction of the "universal motivators" in this definition, how they are not independent and additive but intertwined and conflicting! A disorienting dilemma should make us curious, but not so curious that we put ourselves in a place that feels isolated and unsafe. We want to make meaning of and interact with the dilemma, but only within socially sanctioned limits. We need to feel that changing our belief system will make us more competent in dealing with our environment, as long as doing so will not threaten our important social networks (and our cherished self-images).

2.5 Conclusion

My goal in this chapter has been to lay the groundwork and provide an evidentiary basis for proposals I make later in the book. Whereas Chapter 1 focused on the challenges to deep learning, Chapter 2 has considered the necessary ingredients for deep learning to occur. They can be summed up this way:

Deep learning depends on how we make meaning of experience. Most of the time, this occurs at a level below conscious awareness, and most of the time this is appropriate and necessary. Using existing mental models, our brains interpret sensations based on prior experience, judge their importance, and when necessary construct an emotion that leads to a behavioral response. Small deviations from expected experience are handled smoothly. For example, while driving we constantly monitor other motorists' behavior, and have learned how to detect variations from "normal." Behavior that is interpreted as abnormal will lead to a response dictated by the emotion the brain constructs: say, either contempt ("where'd that idiot learn to drive"?) or fear ("that car isn't going to stop at the red light!"). The first leads to an action of (real or imagined) eye-rolling, the second to hitting the brakes. Sometimes, however, making meaning using existing neural networks and mental models is insufficient: something feels particularly discordant or "off"; something creates enough cognitive dissonance that it elevates an experience to a conscious disquietude. For example, while reading the op-ed page of the newspaper we glance at the headlines of various columnists. For the familiar ones we have formed mental models of their views. We read with pleasure the views consistent with ours, and with irritation those that are not. If, however, a cherished pundit expresses an opinion that is significantly different from our own, cognitive dissonance ensues, and depending on the valence of the emotion constructed around that dissonance, we either choose to examine our beliefs or stop reading and write off the essay as an aberration. This is easy to do if we are reading alone but harder if the piece becomes a topic of discussion with others and we are forced to explain why we dismissed the op-ed piece so quickly.[9] Our motivation to examine and possibly change our beliefs will then depend on the balance between the strength of the experienced challenge and the sense of our own competence in the moment. If the sense of challenge is too strong we experience anxiety and the motivation to escape the discussion. If the sense of competence is too strong we reinforce existing beliefs by constructing counterarguments. In either case the opportunity for deep learning disappears. If, however, the disorientation is experienced in a safe social space, safe enough to unlock our innate curiosity and allow us to imagine that changing our perspective will help us become more competent in dealing with our environment, the gate to deep learning opens.

In the seven chapters that follow I explore seven keys to opening that gate.

Notes

1 For more extensive accounts of the neuroscience of learning, cf. Changeux (2009) and Swart, Chisholm, and Brown (2015).
2 See Vanderah and Gould (2016) for a fuller treatment of neuroanatomy.
3 Much of the material in this section is adapted from Shatz (1992).
4 Flying a kite. Thanks to Dr. Shelley Chapman for the example.
5 Nussbaum takes her title from Proust, who called the emotions "geological upheavals of thought."
6 Defined as, "whenever people behave for the satisfaction inherent in the behavior itself" (Ryan & Deci, 2017, p. 4).

7 Ahl (2006) argues that motivation should not be regarded as something that lies within the individual; it is rather "a construct of those who see it lacking in others" (p. 385).
8 See Bandura (1977) for a full treatment of efficacy and learning.
9 A great example of this is the famous TV newscast by respected American journalist Walter Cronkite who, after a trip to cover the Vietnam War in the late 1960s, concluded that the war was at a stalemate, and unwinnable. Historians have pointed to Cronkite's announcement as a pivotal moment, leading millions who had supported the war to then have grave doubts about it.

CHAPTER 3

Mindful Learning

> There's something I must do first. I must educate myself.
>
> Henrik Ibsen, *A Doll's House*

Deep learning should not occur only when we experience a disorienting dilemma. It should not just be a passive process kicked off by an unexpected experience. Deep learning requires active, mindful agency of the sort that not only reacts to, but also *seeks out* new ways of being – ways that encourage us to step out of our comfort zones just far enough to allow our innate curiosity to take over. As I argued earlier, this is neither natural nor easy, but, rather, is a learned perspective on how we are to be in the world. And as I'll show in the chapters that follow, this capacity to learn deepens and becomes more complex. Hence, those who seek to facilitate deep learning in others, or to take on any leadership role for that matter, must follow Socrates' advice from centuries ago and learn how to know *themselves* first.[1] Any discussion of how to facilitate deep learning begins here. I will first set the stage with a brief discussion about the nature of the "self," followed by some adult development theory; I will then turn to research on developing oneself in an organizational context, starting with the now-classic works of Peter Vaill and Peter Senge. Then I loop back to the challenges facing deep learning and how research on adult development can help address them. And finally, I discuss *mindful learning* as one of the key linchpins of deep learning.

3.1 The Self and Development

If we are to take seriously Socrates' admonition to "know thyself," we first have to get straight what is meant by "self." Like many everyday expressions, "self" is harder to define than may at first appear. How to find one's "real" or "true" self has been a source of debate in both Eastern and Western cultures for centuries. Is it a unifying core of existence, our essential

3.1 The Self and Development 39

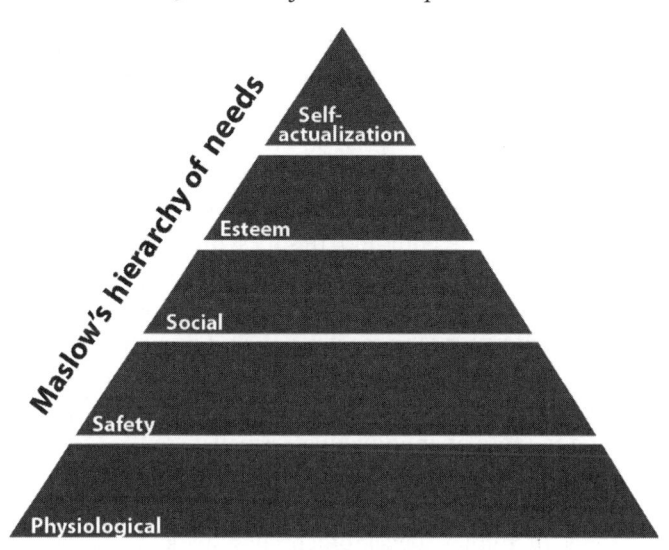

Figure 3.1 Maslow's hierarchy of needs
Source: Adobe Stock.

character, revealed by the narratives we tell ourselves and others? Or is it a self that, as Donna Ladkin put it, "mediates a relationship between an internal personal realm and the external world" (Ladkin & Taylor, 2010, p. 66)? As Morris Rosenberg (1979) observed drily: "In a scientific field generally undistinguished by the precision of its terminology, the 'self' stands as a concept foremost in the ranks of confusion" (p. 5).

3.1.1 *Essentialist Views of Self*

The essentialist view of self is rooted in psychoanalytic theory and humanistic psychology. The most well-known spokesman for this school is Abraham Maslow, whom most readers will recognize by his namesake, "Maslow's hierarchy" (1998). Maslow was concerned with the development of needs, also referred to as motives. In the familiar hierarchy shown in Figure 3.1, at the bottom are motives regulating the body's homeostasis by relieving hunger and thirst, seeking warmth and shelter, and so on.

These must be satisfied before other motives emerge, such as desires to discover and understand, to give love to others, and to push for optimum fulfillment of inner potential. All but the latter operate from a "deficiency" model, staving off disease or unhappiness. In contrast, fulfilling one's potential is a "being" motive and what Maslow called "self-actualization." After studying those few adults who seemed to have risen to the top of the hierarchy, Maslow concluded that complete self-actualization was quite rare and happened only relatively late in life.[2] He did, however, find many adults who had at least some of these qualities: an accurate perception of reality; acceptance of self and others; spontaneity and self-knowledge; problem centering (vs. self-centering); freshness of appreciation; and having peak experiences, deep and loving relationships, creativity, and a sense of humor. Those whose environments did not satisfy lower-level needs did not demonstrate a press for self-actualization and thus showed few of these qualities. In his final works Maslow described self-transcendence, going beyond any sense of separate self and merging with a higher purpose, a being without any sense of an individual, "smaller" self.

3.1.1.1 *Self-Development Theory*

Maslow's model of human development has sparked interest in recent years in what has been called the "positive psychology" movement,[3] moving away from a deficiency model of human motivation and development and toward a focus on satisfaction, optimism, and happiness. One of these applications is self-determination theory (Ryan & Deci, 2017). According to this theory, development of self is based on how well we have developed inner resources for growth and integration. In order for adults to experience *eudaimonia* – a sense of integrity and well-being – a state similar to Mazlow's notion of self-actualization, three needs, for *competence*, *autonomy*, and *relatedness*, must be met. "Competence" refers to a feeling of effectiveness in dealing with one's environment, roughly equivalent to Bandura's (1977) notion of self-efficacy. This does *not* necessarily mean that one must become constantly better at one thing; more important is having the agency to choose which activities to become better at, and being able to redirect one's resources accordingly. "Autonomy" refers to having the sense that what we do, we do voluntarily, under our own volition, not sticking doggedly to someone else's agenda. Even while in dependent states, such as illness or infirmity, it is important to be able to make independent choices. Finally, "relatedness" refers to the feeling of connection with significant others in one's life, people who care about you and "have your back," so to speak. (Note how similar these ego needs are to the sources of adult motivation discussed in the last chapter.)

Notable about research on self-determination theory is the amount of empirical research it has generated in the last few decades. Research has found that environments that do not foster all three needs will compromise a sense of well-being. For example, competence without autonomy – such as performing a task well only for the sake of external rewards, or to meet only the goals of others – does not lead to the development of self. Research has also demonstrated that the form of each of these basic needs changes with age. For example, regarding the need for relatedness, as one gets older the *quality* of contact with others becomes more important than the *quantity* of that contact (Kasser & Ryan, 1999).

3.1.1.2 *Reflected Best Self*

Another significant contribution of positive psychology has been to the work environment, notably research on how best to engage one's "best self" at work, conducted by Laura Morgan Roberts and her colleagues, scholars of positive psychology in organizations (Roberts, 2015). They have developed the concept of "reflected best self" (RBS), a subjective sense of well-being that one is performing at his/her best in a particular situation. The RBS "represents a fusion of the reality of lived experience (who I have been at my best) with the idealized sense of possibility for who one can be(come) when one fully embodies his or her best self" (Roberts, 2015, p. 3). RBS is fully situated in a social system, in which social experiences help define an individual's role in and contributions to that system. Thus, our sense of who we are when we at our best is not a fixed aspect of our personality but rather constantly changes and, one hopes, develops. Consciously refining one's understanding of these qualities is a necessary first step to making them accessible for use in the moment.

Aligning one's RBS at work consists of four pathways, all of which are grounded in research on human motivation. The first is *purposeful engagement*, connecting work-related tasks to one's own personal values, even if these tasks seem mundane or repetitive. For example, someone employed as a hospital janitor could see his job as helping to promote an environment conducive to healing. The second is *strength-based engagement*, which leads to a greater sense of vitality and contribution to the organization. The third is *authentic engagement*, "increasing the subjective experience of alignment between internal experiences and external expressions" (Roberts, 2015, p. 8). Authenticity depends on the alignment between one's culture and values and those of the organization. As Roberts notes, this is an especially critical element for people who differ from the dominant or majority culture of their organizations, who face the challenge of integrating their values and perspectives in ways that strengthen rather than subvert organizational effectiveness. The fourth and final pathway to enhancing one's reflected best self is *relational affirmation*, "the act of enhancing another person's sense of being known and understood for what he or she contributes to a relationship and to the social environment more generally" (p. 10). When people feel that others know and understand them, they are more likely to seek out feedback from others, which can include not only affirmation but also "jolts" that help develop more honest self-appraisal.

Putting these two "inside" views of self together – self-development theory and reflected best self – suggests that we reach optimal integrity when we feel that:

- we have the wherewithal to deal effectively with our environment;
- we have meaningful choices for how to do this;
- our dealings are consistent with our values; and
- we are recognized and valued for our contributions.

3.1.2 Interactionist Views of Self

While those aligned with the humanistic psychology tradition acknowledge the importance of one's environment for the development of self, others take a more "interactionist" view, that one's "true self" develops as we interact with an external context, mediated by our interpretation of experience (Wilson, 1988). As we experience the behavior of others toward us, both verbal and nonverbal, including the messages we get from families, cultures, and organizations, we develop a sense of who we are. This sort of "interactionist" view of self is critical, as it implies that our sense of who we are in the world evolves.

3.1.2.1 The Legacy of John Dewey

Most insights on the nature of human learning and development since the mid-twentieth century, whether philosophical, psychological, or biological, can be traced to the writings of John Dewey. Yes, that is an overstatement, but not by much. In his book *Experience and Education* (1938) he devoted an entire chapter to the "criteria of experience." Dewey proposed that in order for experience to be a source of learning (*deep* learning, in my terms), two criteria must be met, what he termed *continuity* and *interaction*. Regarding continuity, Dewey took what today would be described as an interactionist view of the development of self: "The principle of continuity of experience means that every experience both takes up something from those which have gone before and modifies in some way the quality of those which come after" (Dewey, [1938] 1997, p. 35). As not all experiences are of equal value, one must learn to discriminate among them. Experience must lead to growth, yes; but it must be growth of a particular sort: "Does growth create conditions for future growth, or does it set up conditions that shut off the person from … continuing growth in new directions?" (p. 36). That is, a quality experience "arouses curiosity, strengthens initiative, and sets up desires and purposes that are sufficiently intense to carry a person over dead places in the future" (p. 38).

Dewey's second criterion for experience is *interaction*: "An experience is what it is because of a transaction taking place between an individual and what, at the time, constitutes his [*sic*] environment [that is] … whatever conditions interact with personal needs, desires, purposes, and capacities to create the experience which is had" (p. 44). Interaction and continuity are, in essence, the immediate and longitudinal aspects of experience. A fully integrated person, Dewey suggested, is one who is able to integrate successive experiences with one another: he or she is able to use the learning from previous situations to deal more and more effectively with the situations that follow. Thus, the single most important attitude one can form, according to Dewey, is the *desire to go on learning*.

3.1.2.2 Constructive Developmentalism
Dewey's perspective has been expanded and articulated most clearly by those aligned with what is now known as "constructive developmentalism," pioneered by psychologist Robert Kegan. Beginning with his groundbreaking book *The Evolving Self* (1982), he built upon earlier developmental theorists – especially Jean Piaget – to argue that cognitive development (as well as social and emotional development) does not end with adolescence but rather continues throughout adulthood. In this book Kegan takes the interactionist view of self, suggesting that adults are faced with a constant struggle between two dialectic forces, *connection* and *independence*, a developmental oscillation of sorts. (Compare these terms with John Dewey's notions of "continuity" and "interaction": the continuity of experience encourages independence; the interaction of experience promotes connection.) As with self-determination theory, people need to feel accepted and nurtured by others who are important to them and by the culture in which they live; they also need a sense of autonomy and an ability to act successfully on their own. But Kegan adds this twist: Because the needs for connection and independence can never exist comfortably together, first one tends to dominate, then the other, in what Kegan called "fundamental alteration." Development occurs as individuals shift back and forth. Those who are most successful with this gradually appreciate

the importance of having a strong personal identity with connection – and independence surrounded by a nurturing community.

Kegan's view is that development is the expanding ability to make meaning of experience; thus, how people interpret a situation or event depends on their developmental level. In essence, Kegan takes Mezirow's theory of transformative learning (2000) and attaches a developmental perspective to it: we do not just create new schemes of meaning but do so in a way that these new frames of reference represent increasingly complex ways of knowing. As Kegan puts it, two processes are at the heart of transformative learning:

> The first is what we might call *meaning-forming*, the activity by which we shape a coherent meaning out of the raw material of our outer and inner experiencing. Constructivism recognizes that reality does not happen preformed and waiting for us merely to copy a picture of it. Our perceiving is simultaneously an act of conceiving, of interpreting …
>
> The second process … is what we might call *reforming our meaning-forming*. This is a metaprocess that affects the very terms of our meaning-constructing. We do not only form meaning, and we do not only change our meanings; we change the very form by which we are making our meanings. (Kegan, 2000, pp. 52–53, emphasis in original)

How does this happen? Kegan argues that one's current form of knowing is at least in part the result of moving from "subject" to "object":

> That which is "object" we can look at, take responsibility for, reflect upon, exercise control over, integrate with some other way of knowing. That which is "subject" we are run by, identified with, fused with, at the effect of. We cannot be responsible for that to which we are subject. What is "object" in our knowing describes the thoughts and feelings we say we have; what is "subject" describes the thinking and feeling that has us. We "have" object; we "are" subject. (Kegan, 2000, p. 53)

"Development" is the gradual process by which what was once "subject" becomes "object." What we were once controlled by, we are now able to step back from and see as part of a larger and more complex whole. Here is an example. "Beth" is a young woman who has been brought up to have an identity that is defined in large part by a set of strict social norms, including gender roles. Part of this culture scripting is that her worth as a woman will be determined by the social status of the man she marries. She meets and marries a young man from a wealthy family and almost immediately is subjected to verbal and physical abuse. She feels depressed and helpless, but with the help of others in her social network, including an insightful therapist, she begins to realize that her life does not have to be this way, that she has agency. Beth dissolves the marriage and builds a new life for herself. She is now able to look back, understand her earlier life choices, and see the world of relationships in a whole new light.

Constructive developmentalists would argue that navigating one's "life curriculum" is what "real" transformation is all about. The central developmental task of adolescents is to develop what Kegan calls a "socialized mind," building an identity by internalizing social norms and finding a place within the existing social structure so that one is able to live successfully as an adult. According to Kegan's research this is about as far as most people get. However, he argues, if we hope to cope with the "mental demands of modern life" (Kegan, 1994), with its multiple and often conflicting strains on us as parents, partners, workers, and life-long learners, we need to transform our socialized mind to a "self-authoring" mind. In the example above, Beth has found herself confronted with contradictory social expectations in her social network that are impossible to resolve. She is only able to escape from this by moving from a script written for her to one she writes herself.

What then is the catalyst for this developmental shift? Not all disorienting dilemmas lead to developmental transformations, even when they would make for more efficacious experience; not all examples of disequilibrium between "subject" and "object" lead to a more complex, more self-authoring developmental state. Sometimes the disequilibrium is resolved with no movement at all, as when various forms of confirmation bias kick in as a response to cognitive dissonance. Moreover, as Mezirow (2000) emphasizes, not all perspective transformations are of equal scope or consequence. Most of the time, perspective transformations are small movements from the status quo, and only after they have had a cumulative effect does one recognize a qualitative change. It would be ludicrous to suggest that one goes from a conventional, socialized mind to a postconventional, self-authoring mind in one giant leap. These are not pure states of existence and one does not become a self-authoring learner overnight.[4] Instead – and this is probably a familiar refrain to the reader by now – developmental steps are most likely to occur when the experience of disorientation is just enough to energize stepping away from our comfort zone and into a slightly more challenging space.

3.1.3 *Essentialist or Interactionist?*

The difference between these two perspectives is partly one of focus. Essentialists argue that our true selves are "in there," waiting to be shaped and molded by our environments, in the same way that Michelangelo noted that a sculptor's job is to take away that which prevents the sculpture from emerging. The degrees to which one experiences competence, autonomy, and relatedness (in self-determination theory terms) will determine the extent to which this happens. Interactionists argue that the self evolves, constantly changing and transforming itself in an oscillation between the self and its environment. My position leans toward the interactionists, namely that knowing oneself is less a matter of congruence between one's "true self" and his/her environment than a constant tension between the two, out of which development takes place. I also like what Ladkin and Taylor (2010) say about how one's self is best revealed, not by what goes on in our heads but by what happens in our bodies:

> The ground for a person's awareness of self ... is negotiated, made sense of, and then expressed through the body. Enacting that self is dependent on awareness of the somatic clues the body gives us about how we are experiencing a given situation ... Our kinesthetic sense of ourselves is our most primordial, [and] this would suggest that the body is a more trustworthy ground for revealing individuals' deeper, perhaps "truer," motives and emotions. (p. 66)

3.2 Self-Development in Organizations

3.2.1 *Action Inquiry*

Some psychologists, such as Kegan, have made extensive use of their work in organizational settings. Others have taken the basics of constructive-developmental theory and embedded it entirely in organizational contexts. Probably the best known of these is the work of Bill Torbert and his model of "action inquiry" (2004) as the key to learning and development in organizations. Torbert defines action inquiry as "a way of simultaneously conducting action and inquiry as a disciplined leadership practice that increases the wider effectiveness of our actions" (p. 1), viewing it as a form of transformational learning and development, and from a perspective that is very similar to Kegan's. Torbert views action inquiry as a disciplined way of gradually learning how to take advantage of the present moment as an opportunity to "learn anew, in the vividness of each moment, how best to act now" (p. 2). In the spirit of those who preach the importance of mindfulness as a way of "waking up" and engaging in fully conscious living (for example Tart, 2001), Torbert (2004) urges that we "carefully attend from the inside-out to the experiences we have, hoping to learn from them and modify our actions and even our way of thinking as a result" (p. 4). Like Kegan, Torbert sees deep learning in adults as a process through developmental stages, which he calls "action logics," embedded and largely subconscious aspects of self for dealing with the world around us. "Conventional" action logics correspond roughly to Kegan's "socialized mind"; these are, in order of complexity, the *opportunist*, the *diplomat*, the *expert*, and the *achiever*. Each relates to ways in which we make meaning of experience:

- *opportunist*, how to manipulate our environment to our own advantage;
- *diplomat*, how to curry favor with others;
- *expert*, how to master a world of thought; and finally
- *achiever*, how to put these first three action logics together to accomplish something useful within existing social norms.

According to Torbert's research (2004) more than 90 percent of organizational managers hold one of these action logics and only 7 percent operate from "postconventional" action logics beyond these four, or in Kegan's terms, have developed beyond the socialized mind. Whereas those holding conventional action logics are motivated by similarity and stability, those with postconventional action logics are motivated increasingly by difference and creative experimentation. People at these levels are more likely to see their environments as complex, changing systems presenting complex problems for which there are no clear solutions; they recognize the importance of collaboration with others; and they actively seek out both confirming *and* disconfirming feedback on their actions. While Torbert does not put it this way, deep learning is a particular challenge for those operating out of conventional action logics, because they prefer order and stability over uncertainly and disorientation.

3.2.2 *Permanent White Water*

In Chapter 1, I introduced my former Antioch colleague Peter Vaill, a leading scholar in organization development for nearly the past half-century. In his book *Learning as a Way of Being* (1996) he popularized the term "permanent white water" as the continual state of turbulence facing most modern organizations. Because Vaill understood and foresaw this turbulence a quarter-century ago, and because his ideas on learning in organizations are among the pillars on which this book rests, I will cover his work in some detail here.

As I noted earlier, Vaill asserts that the most important way to deal with white-water conditions is to become a more effective learner. What makes the phenomenon of permanent white water so important for learning? Vaill (1996) sums it up this way: "Permanent white water is the meaning we attach to our experiences. We experience both surprising, novel, messy, costly, recurring and unpreventable events and feelings of lack of direction, absence of coherence, and loss of meaning" (pp. 16–17). Note the similarity of Vaill's ideas to Mezirow's and Kegan's: organizations confronted with continual white water are presented with one disorienting dilemma after another, which, if not handled in a way that makes meaning of them, puts those in the organization at risk of feeling overwhelmed and paralyzed.

Being effective in permanent white water requires, primarily, a different perspective about learning itself. As I noted in Chapter 1, what Vaill calls "institutional learning" is the dominant educational model in Western society (similar to what Freire (1970) called the "banking model," which assumes that learning is simply a matter of depositing information in the brain). Institutional learning[5] is simply inadequate to deal with perpetual white water, which requires a different kind of learning altogether. Vaill maintains that learning in perpetual white water should have seven qualities, each building on the previous ones:

- *It should be self-directed.* Self-directed learning is the antithesis of institutional learning. One cannot be effective in creating environments conducive to deep learning in others without self-direction.[6]
- *It should be creative,* characterized by a spirit of experimentation and exploration and driven by a sense of both freedom and competence to try new things. A creative spirit, Vaill notes, also requires that we self-impose a sense of discomfort with the status quo – in a way to create our own disorienting dilemmas.
- *It should be expressive,* interacting actively with one's environment and linking experience to what has come before and to what will come next. This relates directly to John Dewey's principles of continuity and interaction as criteria for deep learning. As I have noted earlier in this book, experience can also be a barrier to deep learning, what Dewey ([1938] 1997) called "mis-education." The meaning-making schemes that develop to help us make meaning of experience can also block incoming information that is dissonant with these schemes. Dewey called this "routine action," and it narrows the usefulness of new experience. Dewey warned that routine habits can possess us and prevent "intelligent action." He could have been foretelling the challenges of permanent white water!

- *It should include both thinking and feeling*, recalling the central theme of Chapter 2, namely that reflective cognition leading to deep learning is always stimulated by emotion. Material that has no emotional resonance for us is a signal that at an intuitive level we do not have a strong need to know about the subject of that material. Unless something piques our curiosity or knocks us off balance and creates disorientation, we are unlikely to pay much attention to it. Vaill (1996) implies that we must develop a consciousness about feeling: "Probably none [of the three previous qualities] are possible for us if we are not able to feel learning happening within ourselves and honor it, respond to it, build on it" (p. 73).
- *It should occur in the moment*. Vaill (1996) avers that learning in permanent white water requires that we "find ways for as much learning as possible to occur on the job and in all other aspects of a learner's life" (p. 76). One should, in other words, cultivate Torbert's (2004) habits of "action inquiry." Peter Jarvis provides some details on how to do this in his book *The Practitioner-Researcher* (1999). Jarvis holds that professionals learn by reflecting on practice and by "incorporating into their reflection any professional updating or reading they have undertaken" (p. 133). They use this synthesis to then develop their own theories, which they test in the next practice situation, and so the loop repeats. (Recall my discussion of the experiential learning model from the preceding chapter.) This process embodies Freire's (1970)concept of *praxis*, an interaction between action and reflection; Donald Schön's (1983) "reflection in action"; and his and Chris Argyris' notion of "double-loop learning" (Argyris & Schön, 1978): that is, not just solving problems but also assessing the assumptions we make about what the problem is. I will have more to say about each of these writers in coming chapters.
- *Learning should be continual*. Continual learning is more than "lifelong learning," a term that has become a vacuous cliché. Vaill's (1996) provocative point is that permanent white water "makes perpetual beginners of us all. Almost nothing we have learned is immune from challenge and change … We do not need competency skills for this life. We need *incompetency* skills, the skills of being effective beginners" (p. 81, emphasis in original). Vaill's point is much like Torbert's urging to use the "vividness of each moment" to "learn anew," as quoted above. Vaill suggests that leader/learners in permanent white water adopt the persona of a "reflective beginner": someone who is able to check his or her ego at the door, seek the advice of others, and accept failure as a learning opportunity.

- And finally, *reflexive learning* for Vaill incorporates all of these qualities because reflection permeates everything a leader/learner does in permanent white water. Vaill promotes continuous reflection on each of the six qualities, asking honest questions about each: Are we directing our own learning or are we depending on others? Are we absorbing the learning of others or are we exploring new territory? Are we just "sitting there" or are we taking in what is to be learned in the moment? Are we ignoring our feelings as clues to what is important, or are we infusing them into our learning? Are we isolating ourselves from learning opportunities in our immediate environment, or are we taking good advantage of these opportunities? Do we view learning as a series of disconnected challenges, or do we seek growth with an appropriate mixture of challenge and support?

3.2.3 Senge and The Fifth Discipline

Management guru Peter Senge, in his now-classic book *The Fifth Discipline* (2006), includes "personal mastery" as the first of five "disciplines" that must be mastered by any organization that aspires to be a "learning organization": "Organizations learn only through individuals who learn. Individual learning does not guarantee organizational learning. But without it no organizational learning occurs" (p. 129). Despite making few if any references to the developmental psychology literature or adult learning theory, Senge promotes the notion of personal mastery in ways faintly reminiscent of Dewey's "fully integrated person" ([1938] 1997), Kegan's "self-authoring mind" (1994), Torbert's "postconventional action logics" (2004) and particularly Vaill's (1996) seven principles of "learning in perpetual white water": "'Personal mastery' is the phrase we use for the discipline of personal growth and learning. People with high levels of personal mastery are continually expanding their ability to create the results in life they truly seek. From their quest for continual learning comes the spirit of the learning organization" (p. 131).

By "discipline" Senge means an activity that we integrate into our daily lives in such a way that becomes *habitus* as Bourdieu (1977) explained the term, that is, part of the values and dispositions acquired through the activities and experiences of everyday life. Personal mastery has two components. The first of these is regular clarification of what is important to us, that is, a vision of what we are trying to accomplish, without getting sidetracked by the inevitable daily problems. It is a matter of focus. (As

I write these words I find myself getting distracted by political news popping up on my computer. I make a note to turn these off.) The second component of personal mastery is "continually learning how to see current reality more clearly" (Senge, 2006, p. 129). This part, I would assert, is much harder. Our reaction as humans to cognitive dissonance is to reduce the dissonance with a minimum of effort, resulting in all of the varieties of self-delusion I described in Chapter 1. Here is a common organizational example. Once upon a time, strategic planning was all the rage, and still is in some quarters, despite mounting evidence that it does not work very well, and in fact is often counterproductive (cf. Buller, 2015). Strategic planning is based on three shaky – at best – assumptions: first, that change is predictable; second, that change is linear; third, that change occurs as a result of rational rather than political decision-making. Each of these assumptions is demonstrably false. This does not mean that strategic planning is inherently a bad idea; the problem is that once a plan is in place there is every incentive – if you hold one of Torbert's conventional action-logics – to stick with it and not, in Senge's terms, make regular assessments of the current reality and change course accordingly. I have seen this repeated over and over again in higher education: a lot of planning – and no change.

Those with high levels of personal mastery share several qualities, according to Senge: they have a strong sense of purpose, they are "deeply inquisitive" about the current reality, they feel deeply connected to others, they "live in a continual learning mode," and – especially reminiscent of Vaill's (1996) notion of the "reflective beginner" – they are acutely aware of how much they have to learn.

Now here is where Senge's ideas intersect with a key theme threading throughout this book. Senge (2006) argues that juxtaposing vision ("what we want") with a clear picture of current reality ("where we are relative to what we want"), results in what he calls "creative tension, a force to bring them together, caused by the natural tendency to seek resolution." "The essence of personal mastery," he notes, "is learning how to generate and sustain creative tension in our lives" (p. 132). Why, one might ask, would someone want to be in a constant state of creative tension on purpose? Senge's response, somewhat unhelpfully, is, "We want it because we want it" (p. 135), presumably because we are operating at a post-conventional stage of development. There is a better answer to the question of why one would want to seek out creative tension and I will explore this apparent paradox in the next chapter.

3.3 Integrating Principles

For now I will pull together what I have discussed in this chapter into a set of principles on what it takes to develop one's "self" into a deep learner. Each point is backed up by the science of learning presented in Part I of this book.

- Developing a disposition to learn deeply is a process. It is not learning "what" (which Aristotle called *episteme*, or learning content); it is not learning "how" (which he called *techne*, or learning a skill); and it is not even learning "when" (which he called *phronesis*, or learning the appropriate times to employ knowledge and skills, often used as a definition of wisdom). Deep learning is not bound by time or circumstance. Deep learning is instead a disposition driven by a sort of humble curiosity that there is always more to know, and that the result of that knowing will make for a more satisfying and efficacious life.
- Deep learning requires a certain level of consciousness that routinely pays attention to feelings, especially feelings of disorientation. Those who learn deeply have learned to follow that disorientation.
- Deep learning occurs as the result of opposing forces or dialectics, always in tension. How someone lives with, acknowledges, and manages these tensions will determine in large measure how he or she develops the capacity to live effectively in the world. (I develop these ideas more fully in Chapter 9.)
- Becoming one who learns deeply is not just a solitary process. Deep learning happens through interaction with others, with enough confidence in oneself that others' perspectives are valued as tools to one's own development.
- A deep learner accepts the reality that making meaning out of chaos is only temporary and that turbulence is ongoing and inevitable. A deep learner finds forming and reforming meaning perspectives to be a creative challenge and thus intrinsically rewarding.
- The key to all of the above is to develop a spirit of reflexivity as *habitus*: pausing regularly to ask ourselves fresh questions about our experience, and entertaining other ways of making meaning of that experience.

3.4 Mindful Learning

Deep learning faces deep challenges. I have stressed the great difficulty of changing our worldviews (see Figure 1.1 in Chapter 1). A firmly held

3.4 Mindful Learning

intuitive belief, when confronted with discordant information, produces cognitive dissonance and disquietude, and we are tempted to take the easy course of engaging in confirmation/myside bias, which serves to make the intuitive belief even more persistent. We are more likely to do this than not: even those at post-conventional levels of development will find themselves experiencing cognitive dissonance that is distinctly aversive. If the dissonance is powerful enough we experience a true disorienting dilemma; resolving the dilemma depends on how we make meaning of the disorientation, and this in turn depends on our level of cognitive and emotional development. If we are perceiving the world in a manner consistent with the "socialized mind" or "conventional action logics," we are likely to fall back on internalized social and cultural norms, finding safety there. If we are perceiving the world in a manner consistent with the "self-authoring" or "post-conventional" mindset, on the other hand, we are more likely to follow the disorientation, treating it as "object" rather than something we are "subject" to.

In this book I argue for a proactive approach to deep learning, one that does not depend on having to respond to a disorienting dilemma powerful enough to breach our usual cognitive defenses. I call it *mindful learning*, borrowing from Ellen Langer's book of the same name (Langer, 2016). In her view, mindful learning has three characteristics: "the continuous creation of new categories; openness to new information; and an implicit awareness of more than one perspective" (p. 4). While my conception of it is consistent with hers, my take is based more on East Asian philosophy, namely that mindfulness is a state of heightened alertness, one that is conscious of body sensations, accepting these without judgment, and focused more on the present moment than ruminating about the past or worrying about the future. Buddhist teacher Bhante Gunaratana captures it well:

> Mindfulness registers experiences, but it does not compare them. It does not label them or categorize them. It just observes everything as if it [were] occurring for the first time. It is not analysis [that is] based on reflection and memory. It is, rather, the direct and immediate experiencing of whatever is happening, without the medium of thought. It comes before thought in the perceptual process. (Quoted in Davis & Thompson, 2015, p. 48)

Ponder this last sentence for a moment: that mindfulness "comes before thought." How does that square with one of the key points in this book, namely that deep learning requires us to think and reflect, not just to react?

The answer is that mindfulness allows us to *interrupt* knee-jerk reactions to stimuli that might lead to the assortment of cognitive biases that stand in the way of deep learning. One of the best illustrations of this is the nascent practice of using mindfulness as addiction therapy. Judson Brewer and his colleagues have extensively studied ways of using mindfulness training to help those with addiction disorders (including alcohol, smoking, and drugs) overcome their cravings. They assert that, for example, a smoker's craving for a cigarette is a form of "affective bias." They write,

> Affective bias underlies emotional distortions of attention and memory, preventing individuals from accurately assessing what is happening in the present moment and acting accordingly. Mindfulness functions to decouple pleasant and unpleasant experience from habitual reactions of craving and aversion, by removing the affective bias that fuels such emotional reactivity. It is the absence of emotional distortions, we suggest, that allows mindfulness practitioners to "see things as they are." (Brewer, Elwafi, & Davis, 2014, pp. 74–75)

So, when a smoker gets a craving for a cigarette, whether that craving has a positive affect, such as looking forward to the pleasure of a cigarette after a meal, or a negative affect, such as stress or irritability, s/he associates smoking with satisfying that craving: it is in essence an intuitive belief, that the way to respond to the craving is to light up. Breaking the pathological chain works like this:

> Mindfulness training teaches individuals to instead step back and take a moment to explore what cravings actually *feel* like in their bodies, however uncomfortable or unpleasant they may be. Two important insights can be learned from this process. First, individuals learn that cravings are physical sensations in their bodies rather than moral imperatives that must be acted upon. Second, they gain first-hand experience with the impermanent nature of these physical sensations. (p. 78)

Patients therefore learn to make new associations with body sensations, so that instead of thinking, "I need a cigarette to settle my nerves," they think, "I'm feeling anxious; what do I do about it?"

Imagine how mindful learning can serve similar purposes for the quotidian matters of everyday life, unrelated to addictive behavior. Here are some examples:

- You read that a habit of grabbing a daily latte from a coffee shop can add up to a cost of about $1,000 per year. You realize that getting a daily latte is exactly what you do. Your intuitive belief has been that, in the larger scheme of things, spending a couple of dollars on a latte is a pittance. Still, you experience some cognitive dissonance. You could brush this

3.4 *Mindful Learning*

off as a minor annoyance, rationalizing that you could be engaging in much more expensive indulgences than this; or you could recognize this sensation as a signal that you might want to consider how you might otherwise spend that $1,000 if you made your lattes at home.
- You are meeting with your primary care physician for your annual checkup. She asks about alcohol consumption. Your answer is, "about two drinks a day." You experience a pang of guilt, knowing that you are fudging a bit, given that your physician told you at your last visit about recent research tying even moderate alcohol consumption to increased risk of stroke for those over 50 (and you are well past that). You could react silently with, "everyone has a small vice and this one is mine," or you could interpret the "guilt" emotion as something you need to pay attention to.
- You are in a business meeting and a close associate, one with whom you have a valued relationship, makes a comment that could be interpreted as racist. Something about the remark is disturbing. You could interpret it as a one-off exception and dismiss it; or you could recognize that the disturbance you felt is telling you something, and that you may want to speak to the colleague about it.
- You are attending a soccer game and the goal keeper on your favorite team has successfully blocked a succession of shots on goal. You think, wow, this guy is really on his game today – and then he fails to block the shot that wins the match. In your disappointment you could be upset with the goal keeper for failing to come through at a critical moment, just when he was playing so well. Or you could stop to wonder where your anger came from: could it be a case of expecting what is likely a random streak of saves to continue?
- As an administrator of a small college you become embroiled in a dispute with faculty members over a proposed institutional initiative. You could fume about how "faculty are always resisting change," or you stop and wonder whether you are engaged in reductive thinking, that possibly more complex dynamics are at work.

All of these examples, and countless others, *may or may not* lead to the kind of disorientation that could result in transformative learning. They may or may not, in other words, rise to the level of disorienting dilemmas. Getting them into that space requires a conscious, *mindful* awareness that broadens the potential for deep learning. I explore what that potential might look like in the next chapter.

Notes

1 As my friend and colleague Ron Cacciope reminded me, the phrase "know thy self" comes from the inscription on the temple at Delphi, the spiritual retreat outside of Athens.
2 More recent research suggests that these numbers may be higher than Maslow thought, depending on the cultural context. See Chapter 9.
3 See for example Seligman's book, *Learned Optimism* (1991).
4 This is the problem I have with "andragogy" as espoused by Knowles (1984) and others, that adults are "self-directed learners": sometimes they are and sometimes they aren't, depending on both the learning context and their own developmental stages.
5 Thanks to my friend and colleague Richard McGuigan, who pointed out that "institutional learning" assumptions are not reflective of current approaches to adult education. Vaill was referring to typical curricula in professional schools, and professional development programs in organizations.
6 The reader may notice an apparent contradiction with a previous note about "andragogy." While it's a mistake to assume that all learning in adults should be self-directed, developing oneself to *be* self-authoring and thus self-directing is a requirement for deep learning.

CHAPTER 4

Constructive Disorientation

There is no right not to be offended.

Lynn Davies

In this chapter I develop in detail a theme I have been alluding to in previous chapters: that the path to deep learning begins with tension, but tension of a positive sort. I call it *constructive disorientation*, a feeling of arousal brought about by a perceived disconnect between the current and a desired state, accompanied by a sense of efficacy that one is capable of dealing with that disconnect. I make no claim that the concept is at all new. It goes back at least as far as John Dewey ([1938] 1997), who wrote that successful learning for life is a function of both curiosity and disquietude, neither one of which alone is sufficient. Solving the Sunday crossword puzzle in the *New York Times* may satisfy a temporary desire to figure it out and it might provide a momentary sense of accomplishment, but it is not likely to affect your ability to navigate your world in any significant way (aside, perhaps, from keeping your mental faculties sharp). Feeling uneasy about a personal relationship does not by itself create energy to resolve that unease. Interpretation of experience must have an awareness of both an interruption in homeostasis and confidence that, despite having been pushed beyond the comfort zone, one is capable of making new meaning of that experience. This is the wonderful way in which Dewey uses the term "curiosity," as an inherently positive drive to learn.

Dewey is not the only one to have described this phenomenon. Here are some others: In the last chapter I described Peter Senge's (2006) notion of "creative tension," what he referred to as a natural tendency to seek resolution between what we want and the current reality. What Senge did not do was to go deeper into the literature on human learning to explore what optimal creative tension looks like and how to stimulate it. Similar to Senge's "creative tension" is a key element of what Ron Heifetz (1994) calls "adaptive learning." Individuals and organizations like to stay in their comfort zone, but:

> When you raise a difficult issue or surface a deep value conflict, you take people out of their comfort zone and raise a lot of heat ... Your goal [as a leader] should be to keep the temperature within what we call the *productive zone of disequilibrium (PZD):* enough heat generated by your intervention to gain attention, engagement, and forward motion, but not so much that the organization (or your part of it) explodes. (Heifetz et al., 2009, p. 29, emphasis in original)

I will have more to say about adaptive learning and its relationship to deep learning later on; for now, I will make this distinction between PZD and constructive disorientation: the former refers to the management of system disruption, the latter to individual experience. Trying to create a productive zone of disequilibrium in an organization will fail if individuals in that organization do not *themselves* experience constructive disorientation.

A third term similar to constructive disorientation is the "zone of proximal development," coined by developmental psychologist Lev Vygotsky in the 1930s (Vygotsky, 1978). Something of a pariah in his country's educational establishment because of his progressive views, Vygotsky argued that the most effective means of educating children is not to load them up with information but rather to identify the difference between what they are able to learn on their own and what they are able to learn with adult help, and then create the appropriate pedagogical structure or "scaffolding." Like Dewey, Vygotsky maintained that deep learning is a function of experience and supportive interaction with one's social environment. While Vygotsky's focus was on young children, we can readily apply his thinking to adult learning: individuals need an appropriate mix of challenge and support if they are to learn effectively.

Enter *flow theory*, one of the most important concepts in human motivation and learning to emerge in the past few decades, developed through the research of Mihaly Csikszentmihalyi (pronounced, roughly, "chick-sent-me-high-ee") (1990). Based on a fascinating series of studies of intrinsic motivation, Csikszentmihalyi discovered an optimal state of being, which he called *flow*. A person in a state of flow is completely focused on the task at hand, enjoys a sense of competence and control, and often loses track of time. Csikszentmihalyi discovered that flow experiences have eight essential components: a succession of clear goals, immediate feedback to one's actions, an alignment between challenges and skills, a merger of action and awareness, intense concentration and a focus on the here and now, loss of self-consciousness and fear of failure, a sense only of a "continuous present," and activity that becomes "autotelic," that is, doing something that becomes an end in itself. Csikszentmihalyi also discovered something counterintuitive: that even those doing work many would consider to be repetitive and boring, such as working on a factory assembly line, would report experiencing flow in their jobs. They would approach their work as a process of discovery, finding new ways to fine-tune their skills and contribute to the larger whole. In short, it turns out that it is not *what* people do that counts, but *how* they do it.

Csikszentmihalyi (1997) hypothesizes that the drive to discover and create is a product of our evolution as humans. We have evolved not only to learn from the past but also to prepare ourselves to deal with unpredictable change. This impulse, however, exists in tension with what Csikszentmihalyi calls the "effort imperative," the need to wind down and conserve our energy to face the unexpected. Too much of a focus on discovery leads to exhaustion; too much focus on conserving efforts leads to listlessness and entropy.

Most of us have experienced flow: we are working on a project and everything seems to click; we are playing tennis and at the top of our game, seemingly able to anticipate where the next shot is going; we are so engrossed in a book that we suddenly realize that we have been up half the night. Not surprisingly, we are most able to learn deeply when in a state of flow. The obvious question then becomes, what can we do to make the experience of flow more likely? The answer, according to Csikszentmihalyi, is to imagine flow as a state of balance between the challenge of a task, on one hand, and a sense of competence, on the other. Flow results when an optimal balance exists between the two, when the challenge is just beyond the reach of a person's competence, but close enough to grasp with effort. Flow is also a developmental state: A novice piano student might experience flow by being able to play a "C" scale perfectly for the first time; but maintaining flow requires another and slightly and increasingly more difficult challenge. (Note the similarity here to Vygotsky's zone of proximal development.)

Flow is difficult to maintain, and so we spend most of our days in less optimal states. We find either that the tasks we are performing lack appropriate challenge, resulting in boredom, or that the challenge is perceived to be too great, resulting in anxiety, or at worst, the impulse to escape the situation altogether. Being in flow, however, is not "good" in an absolute sense. Imagine how annoying it would be to be around someone who was "in flow" all of the time: this person would be completely and continuously self-centered, focused on fulfilling current goals, oblivious to the need for new learning. Csikszentmihalyi (1990) himself recognizes the danger of flow's "addictive potential" (p. 62). A self-centered self cannot become more complex, and thus a slide back into a "normal" state of consciousness is necessary in order to allow for other constructive disorientation opportunities.

4.1 What Makes Disorientation "Constructive"?

Just as flow states are not sufficient for deep learning, not all disorientation is constructive. A mild state of cognitive disorientation may simply be experienced as irritation, and easily swatted away. An extreme state of disorientation will not lead to deep learning, either. So what, then, defines that sweet spot, that space most conducive to constructive disorientation and deep learning in an organization? Necessary criteria include a situation requiring "adaptive learning" and three interacting sources of intrinsic motivation – autonomy, efficacy, and relatedness, terms I have modified slightly from self-determination theory (Ryan & Deci, 2017). I describe each of these four criteria in turn, below.

4.1.1 *A Situation That Requires Adaptive Learning*

A term first introduced by Ron Heifetz (1994), adaptive learning is the learning required when a gap exists between the values people stand for (those that constitute thriving) and the reality that they face (their current lack of capacity to realize those values). The challenge is such that neither the problem nor its solution is clearly defined, and thus there are no easy answers or singular solutions. As tempting as it might be to hope that existing perspectives will lead to a solution, addressing the challenge is possible only through changes in people's priorities, beliefs, habits, and loyalties. Achieving agreement on a course of action means that participants must suspend assumptions, entertain fresh questions, and try on the perspectives of others. They must realize that a solution is not a matter of applying technical solutions more expertly, but rather one of framing problems differently. In other words, space must exist for deep learning to occur.

Creating this space is not easy. The tendency will always be to default to technical solutions, what Donald Schön (1983) called "technical rationality." Why is this so? Consider the insidious influences of cognitive bias, explored in Chapter 1 of this book. When faced with cognitive dissonance, in this case the disorientation produced by an adaptive challenge, continuing the tried and true is far more comfortable than leaping into the unknown. Back in 2000 the now defunct Blockbuster video rental chain scoffed at a proposal from then start-up Netflix to integrate their services within the Blockbuster model. It would have cost the company about $50 million then; Netflix is worth about $10 billion now (Lucas, 2012). More recently, the traditional hotel industry mostly ignored the threat of Airbnb. I can only imagine the dismissive attitude of corporate executives: "People staying in a stranger's bedroom, rather than enjoying all the benefits of a hotel? A cottage industry at best, catering only to a niche clientele." Thus, rather than understanding the adaptive threat, the hospitality industry focused on improving their "hotel-ness" rather than understanding the emergent market appeal of homey, low-cost accommodations and adapting accordingly.

But even when the threat becomes consciously real, adaptation may still not occur. Heifetz and his colleagues (2009) maintain that the common thread explaining failure to adapt is fear of loss. Organizational leaders may recognize the need for adaptive change and even set strategic goals accordingly, and still nothing substantial happens. Adaptation is not a normal response for most organizations, which have structures that optimize production, not innovation. Recall the concept of "immunity to change" (Kegan & Lahey, 2009) introduced in an earlier chapter. Forces for stability in the face of pressures for change lead to immunities kicking in at both the individual and organizational levels. Imagine the competing commitments: protecting an organization's identity and one's role in it, holding on to a carefully cultivated skill set, having the security of a known culture, and so on. The "big assumption," namely that major adaptive change will upset and destabilize and lead to an organizational landscape littered with victims, is simply too hard to face.

Loss aversion, and the desire of most organizations to keep turbulence under control in order to maximize productivity, leads to what complexity theorist Mary Uhl-Bien (2018) has called the "order response," in the form of structures we know as "bureaucracies." Organizations are set up for stability, and disturbances to that stability are met with pressure to return to order. Uhl-Bien and her colleagues argue that while an administrative lattice of some kind is necessary, adaptive learning should coexist with it. Complexity theory holds that organisms, including organizational systems, are "complex adaptive systems" with rich patterns of interaction. These interaction patterns create a constant state of disequilibrium in the system, which leads to "nonlinear, emergent dynamics" (Uhl-Bien, Marion, & McKelvey, 2007, p. 293). Rather than suppress these dynamics, healthy organizations should strive to "structure and enable conditions such that complex adaptive systems are able to optimally address creative problem solving, adaptability, and learning" (p. 293). These complex systems are kept healthy by fostering interaction and interdependency, while also injecting tension sufficient to keep the energy going. As counterintuitive as it may seem, without what Lynn Davies (2015) calls "educative turbulence," organizations and other complex systems will die. Turbulence, therefore, is a productive force. To evolve and thrive, she writes, "a system has to experience turbulence, to get to the edge of chaos, before settling into a new fitness landscape. Simple perturbations can nudge a system into creative activity" (p. 451). Note Davies' choice of words here: *simple* and *nudge*, not *overwhelming* and *force*. As would be predicted by flow theory, turbulence is most likely to be a force for positive change when it is perceived as requiring a series of incremental moves from the status quo, in an atmosphere that values experimentation and learning. Sources of healthy turbulence can come from both internal and external sources. External sources would include information about the organizational environment and how it is changing. Internal sources would emerge from a culture that creates a welcoming environment for diversity of ideas, honest dialogue and conflictual conversation, leading to what Young calls "enlarged thought":

> If dialogue succeeds primarily when it appeals to what the participants already share, then none need revise their opinions or viewpoints in any serious way in order to take account of other interests, opinions or perspectives. Beyond this, even if we understand that we need others to see what we all share, it can easily happen that we each find in the other only a mirror for ourselves. (Young, 2000, quoted in Davies, 2015, p. 453)

I will come back to the power of dialogue in deep learning in Chapter 6, and the role of conflict in Chapter 7.

4.1.2 *Intrinsic Motivation*

As I have described in previous chapters, humans have evolved to be curious, active, deeply social creatures. We have an intrinsic drive to be deeply interested in and to have control over our internal and external worlds. When these needs are met we have the potential to develop increased complexity and more integrated functioning. When these needs are *not* met, development is stalled, defensive and other dysfunctional behaviors emerge, and human flourishing is compromised. More directly to the point of this book, *people will select optimal challenges leading to deep learning when, and only when, they are intrinsically motivated*. Decades of research point to these three determinants of intrinsic motivation, all interrelated:

4.1.2.1 *Autonomy*

Situations leading to the potential for adaptive learning will go nowhere without both individuals and groups experiencing autonomy. Autonomy, the first of three necessary elements in self-determination theory (Ryan & Deci, 2017), is having the sense that what we do, we do voluntarily, under our own volition, and not under external control. Without autonomy, individuals feel powerless to do anything about what is happening to them, a mere cog in a wheel, reminiscent of Charlie Chaplin's hapless character on the assembly line in *Modern Times*. In their book on self-determination theory, Ryan and Deci (2017) describe an autonomy-control continuum. At the pure autonomy end, individual volition is total, behavior emanates from one's sense of self, and motivation is purely intrinsic, a situation reminiscent of flow. At the other end is pure control, wherein the individual is forced to act in a manner incongruent with self, and so the motivation is purely extrinsic. A great deal of research over the years has extolled the virtues of intrinsic motivation as a means to personal development and wellbeing. In self-determination theory the matter is more complex: extrinsic motivators can, over time, become internalized and integrated with one's own sense of self, and thus become intrinsic. Religious beliefs, for example, begin as extrinsic values taught by parents and/or the larger society, but over time can become so integrated into one's belief system that the motivation for their expression becomes intrinsic. (Consider the satisfaction experienced by religious missionaries as they deliver the Word around the world.) Thus, in self-determination theory, optimal motivation is "autonomous motivation," a combination of one's intrinsic motivation, driven by innate curiosity about the world, and well-integrated extrinsic motivation.

Autonomy, Ryan and Deci (2017) note, adds an important variable to flow theory. Flow is not just the optimal balance of challenge and competence: one could be presented with a situation having exactly this balance and still not be motivated to act. I might be invited to play a video game, something I am perfectly capable of doing, and still not be motivated to participate. I need to feel curious, and that I am playing of my own volition, not because of social expectation.

In my research on motivation in university faculty (Wergin, 2001), I found professional autonomy – the freedom to experiment, to follow one's own leads wherever they may go, and to do so without fear of the consequences – to be the single strongest predictor of faculty productivity.

I also found, however, that when the value placed on autonomy is taken to an extreme, it becomes more a matter of personal privilege rather than social obligation. When John Dewey (1981) defined freedom as "the power to grow," he did not include the power to be accountable only to oneself. In any professional context, therefore, the responsible expression of autonomy is the freedom to contribute to the common good.

4.1.2.2 *Efficacy*

Efficacy is universally regarded as a core element in motivation. The term is closely related to competence, one of the two key elements leading to flow, and the second of three key elements in self-determination theory, where competence is defined as "our basic need to feel effectance [*sic*] and mastery. People need to feel able to operate effectively within their important life contexts" (Ryan & Deci, 2017, p. 11). Those who have a sense of efficacy, in addition, not only feel that they are able to operate effectively, they also feel that they are having a significant effect on their environment (Bandura, 1977). In other words, while competence refers to confidence in the doing, efficacy refers to a sense of confidence in the *effect* of the doing, and is therefore more powerful. Competence is necessary for efficacy, but not vice versa. In my research on university faculty, efficacy was another key motivational driver. Even faculty members with long lists of publications did not always feel efficacious: there also had to be the satisfaction of believing that they were having an impact on their disciplines. In an organizational context, efficacy is what gives our work meaning; it is a feeling that what we do matters. Efficacy is the difference between coming home from work and asking yourself, "just what did I accomplish today?" and knowing that something you did that day made a difference for the better. Just as volitional action is necessary for deep learning, so is the feeling that such action will have a tangible result.

4.1.2.3 *Relatedness*

The third key element in self-determination theory, relatedness means feeling socially connected and cared for by others. But in addition, "relatedness is also about belonging and feeling significant among others ... [thus] experiencing oneself as giving or contributing to others. Relatedness pertains, moreover, to a sense of being integral to social organizations beyond oneself" (Ryan & Deci, 2017, p. 11). This last point is critical, as it ties relatedness with efficacy. One feels not only cared for but also impactful. More than 30 years ago, researcher Barry Staw (1983) identified two key factors that lead to what he called "organizational motivation." He suggested that individuals are motivated to behave in ways befitting the interests of their organizations when two conditions are met optimally: when they identify with their organizations (having a sense of "community") and when they see tangible evidence that they are contributing to their organizations in meaningful ways ("efficacy"). Note how community and efficacy together become "relatedness" in self-determination theory.

Back in the late 1980s, several of my colleagues and I did a study of career satisfaction among senior faculty members in five diverse institutions (Caffarella, Armour, Fuhrmann, & Wergin, 1989). We wanted to know which factors most contributed to satisfaction among these faculty. What proved to be the most important factor separating high- and low-satisfaction groups across all institutions was what we called a sense of "niche," a perception that individual faculty had a place in their academic community that was theirs and no one else's. A niche has two characteristics: it is connected to a larger whole, and it is constantly evolving. We examined the difference between a niche and a "rut": the former has a warm, comfortable, three-dimensional feel, defined by a larger space. A rut is something one gets stuck in. A niche promotes growth and change; a rut does not. Looking back on that research today, I am struck by how closely our findings parallel self-determination theory: "niche" communicates autonomy, it requires a community context, it provides a tacit recognition of worth, and it is a mark of efficacy. What was missing from our discussion of niche 30 years ago, was the importance of disorientation as a force for growth and development. Now it is clear, even if counterintuitive, that being comfortable in a niche requires being amenable to change. We need to know that our organizational niche will, sooner or later, require redecoration, renovation, or even relocation – but we also need to know that change will at least in part be on our own terms, that we have a sense of autonomous motivation.

4.2 How to Enable Constructive Disorientation in Others?

As I noted earlier in this chapter, two organizational theorists, Ronald Heifetz (Heifetz et al., 2009) and Peter Senge (2006), have introduced concepts similar to constructive disorientation, namely "productive zone of disequilibrium" and "creative tension," respectively. Each of these concepts is based on practice experience, and both have resonance with organizational leaders, what psychometricians call "face validity." Both also have serious limitations. First, they focus on organizational conditions, not individuals' *experience* of disequilibrium or tension. Second, both authors provide limited advice on how to stimulate these conditions. And third, neither has situated his concept in learning theory or informed it with existing empirical evidence. In the remainder of this chapter I will address these limitations with suggestions that are grounded in motivation theory and backed up by empirical research – not just from a few isolated studies but from a convergence of findings that cut across cultures and organizational settings.

In order to achieve a state of constructive disorientation one must be confronted with an experience that creates cognitive dissonance, perceived as a slight imbalance of challenge over support (Csikszentmihalyi, 1990), leading to a "creative tension" (Senge, 2006), a "productive zone of disequilibrium" (Heifetz et al., 2009), or "zone of proximal development" (Vygotsky, 1978) fueled by autonomous motivation (Ryan & Deci, 2017) and one's belief that the effort will be efficacious (Bandura, 1977). This is about as close as it gets to theoretical and empirical consensus. We should be able to recognize constructive disorientation in ourselves. But how do we promote it in others? The evidence points to four key enablers:

4.2.1 *A Clear But Manageable Challenge*

This is the essence of constructive disorientation. There must be a clear sense of disconnect between the current and a desired state. In order for this disquietude to be constructive it must be accompanied by the belief that the challenge is manageable, that one has both the competence and the social support needed to meet the challenge. Recall that in flow theory (Csikszentmihalyi, 1990), the challenge must be balanced by support in order to have the optimal conditions for "flow." When these are out of whack, when the challenge is perceived as too great, anxiety reduces efficacy and the desire to learn. One of the common mistakes made by corporate trainers is to assume that all performance problems are "training problems" (Mager & Pipe, 1983): that is, if individuals are not performing at a level appropriate to the task, then what is needed is a training program to fill the learning gap. While this may make intuitive sense, the problem is that at any more than a moderate level, anxiety is detrimental to learning. Under these conditions the impulse is to do whatever is necessary to reduce the anxiety, and this takes priority over the desire to learn, even if in the long run learning will increase competence and restore an optimal balance.[1] Just as in trauma surgery, where the first priority is to stop the bleeding, in adult learning the first priority is to reduce the learner's anxiety to manageable levels and *then* focus on building competence. This point leads to the second enabler:

4.2.2 A Flexible Structure

Consistent with self-determination theory and autonomous motivation, constructive disorientation is enabled when participants have the ability to increase or decrease the level of challenge so as to match skills with requirements for action. A flexible structure is one of the cornerstones of self-directed learning (Knowles, 1984) and is also a key feature of both problem-based learning, which originated in medical education and now enjoys widespread use in other academic disciplines (Fredrickson, McMahan, & Dunlap, 2013), and action learning, developed initially for the workplace (Scott, 2017). The two approaches, while developed independently, have so much in common as to be nearly indistinguishable. Each one follows a similar process. Small groups are formed and presented with a complex, ill-structured problem taken from real life, for which the solution is unknown. With the help of a coach or facilitator, the group sets learning goals, defines the problem, identifies information needed to address the problem, engages in self-directed learning both individually and collaboratively, meets together to ask questions and challenge assumptions, revisits how the problem has been defined, and identifies solutions. Participants then reflect on their actions and what they have learned, and receive feedback from the coach or facilitator (or in the case of action learning, other members of the organization). Note how this process incorporates the principles of adaptive learning (by focusing on complex, ill-defined issues), Vygotsky's (1978) notion of proximal development (by having a facilitator help identify what people are able to learn on their own and where they need help), Kolb's (1984) experiential learning (by beginning with real-world problems the learner can identify with), and Dewey ([1938] 1997) and others' insistence on the importance of drawing upon the learner's innate sense of curiosity as a driver of deep learning. Further, the evidence about the effectiveness of problem-based learning and action learning suggests that the process works best when problem difficulty is balanced by prior knowledge (as per flow theory) (Csikszentmihalyi, 1990), and when intrinsic motivation is blended with internalized extrinsic motivation, leading to autonomous motivation experienced both by the individual (Ryan & Deci, 2017) and the team (Yeo & Marquardt, 2010). This last criterion may be the most important of all. The team must perceive an organizational climate supportive of team control over its learning and problem solving.

4.2.3 A Setting for "Deep Work"

Coined by Cal Newport (2016) in his book with the eponymous title, deep work refers to "professional activities performed in a state of distraction-free concentration that push your cognitive capabilities to their limit. These efforts create new value, improve your skill, and are hard to replicate" (p. 2). Newport recounts how some of the most productive figures in history, from Emily Dickinson and Mark Twain to Carl Jung and Bill Gates, carved out and made space for long and uninterrupted chunks of time. In modern terms, this means being able to fight off the temptation to check one's email or access social media – something many people find very difficult to do. As Newport notes, "the rise of [internet tools], combined with ubiquitous access to them through smartphones and networked office computers, has fragmented most knowledge workers' attention into slivers" (p. 5). This gives rise to "shallow work: noncognitively demanding, logistical-style tasks, often performed while distracted. These efforts tend to not create much new value in the world and are easy to replicate" (p. 6). Shallow work can be extraordinarily seductive. Situations requiring adaptive learning are by definition unsettling, and as Heifetz and his colleagues (2009) point out, can lead to "work avoidance." Think for a moment about how on almost a daily basis we are "thinking fast" when we should be "thinking slow," in Kahneman's (2011) terms. About how, when faced with a challenging task, we check our email inbox one more time … and then again. (In terms of my own behavior when doing the deep work of writing this book, I reserve the right to remain silent.[2]) A point I have made earlier in this book is that drive-by learning encouraged by network tools, a sort of "Twitterized" learning, is an impediment to deep learning. So are the new power dynamics in organizations, introduced when managers "ping" their employees and expect an immediate response. What is needed are more opportunities for deep work, and as Newport (2016) points out, in our postindustrial and knowledge-based economy, these opportunities have become both increasingly rare and increasingly valuable. Settings conducive to deep work cultivate the kind of deep concentration that produces flow – stretching just beyond one's comfort zone and losing oneself in an activity – and, therefore, conditions that lead to deep learning.

4.2.4 Clear Criteria for Performance, Concrete Feedback, and "Freedom to Fail"

Recall that clear criteria for performance, concrete feedback, and lack of fear of failure are three of the common markers of flow (Csikszentmihalyi, 1990). An individual or working group must believe that failure is not only permissible but is also an essential aspect of learning. I have done a lot of work over the years in program accreditation and evaluation in higher education, and one of the persistent myths is that "accountability for results" should be a hallmark of program assessment. I recall giving a talk on the nature of quality at a professional conference in 2006, suggesting that holding a program accountable for results *was exactly the wrong thing to do* – and seeing the aghast expressions on the faces of people in the audience! I hastened to add that paying attention to results is, of course, important, but what programs should be held accountable for is *learning* from results in ways that lead to program improvement. Persistence in valuing accountability for results has, in my experience, led to a lot of stifled creativity and many missed opportunities. The evidence discussed in this chapter suggests why this is so: under conditions of overemphasis on accountability for results, autonomous motivation disappears and is replaced by "goal displacement" (Welner, 2013): replacing a shared goal with quantitative, externally imposed indicators purporting to measure goal achievement. This is what happens when schools are held accountable for improving children's performance on standardized test scores, or when a nonprofit's effectiveness is defined by financial contributions or number of people served. Should we then be surprised when schools reduce emphasis on the arts and physical education, or when a nonprofit hires a chief executive with little experience related to the mission of the organization but is known for fund-raising skills? One of the most egregious examples of accountability for results run amok is the knee-jerk embrace of strategic planning as a management tool, despite the mounting evidence of its ineffectiveness (Buller, 2015). As I argued in the previous chapter, strategic planning is based on three dubious assumptions: that the future is predictable, that change is linear, and that decisions are made rationally. The future is in fact highly unpredictable and nonlinear – leading to the need for adaptive work (Heifetz, 1994) – and organizational choices, especially the most important ones, are made for political and not solely empirical reasons.[3] Let me emphasize that nothing is inherently wrong with strategic planning as long as the organization does not fall into the trap of reifying the process and holding units accountable for achieving strategic goals.

Instead, strategic planning can be helpful if and only if it is undertaken as an organic process within a larger strategic vision, encouraging a culture of reasonable risk-taking and staying alert to serendipitous opportunities.

4.3 Conclusion

In this chapter I have made the case for constructive disorientation as a condition necessary for deep learning. Learning that does not stem from disorientation deepens one's knowledge perspectives and increases technical competence, and I do not mean to make light of this kind of learning: it is not the same as what I have referred to dismissively as "drive-by learning" or, in Newport's (2016) terms, "shallow learning." Just as being in a constant state of flow is not an altogether good thing, neither is it possible or desirable to be in a constant state of deep learning. Learning *what*, *how*, and *when* (Aristotle's *episteme*, *techne*, and *phronesis*) must of course occur; otherwise constructive disorientation would never lead to anything constructive. My point, made repeatedly in this book, is that the increasingly complex nature of the challenges we face as a society requires going beyond technical rationality to engage in deep learning. And for this we must recognize and create opportunities for constructive disorientation, a perceived disconnect between where we are and where we need to be, accompanied by a sense that we are capable of dealing with that disconnect.

In order for disorientation to be constructive it must have four essential qualities.

First, the situation must be one that makes this disconnect clear, one that requires adaptive learning (Heifetz, 1994). Whether it relates to an individual or a group, there must be a perception of a gap between what is valued and the reality that what is valued is not being realized in the current environment. This is exactly what Mezirow (1990) meant when he conceived of a "disorienting dilemma" as the key to transformative learning. The disorientation must be strong enough to encourage suspension of assumptions and beliefs and the willingness to entertain fresh perspectives, but not so strong that a response to the preexisting order is triggered, as well as various immunities to change (Kegan & Lahey, 2009), all of which relate to fear of loss.

Second, the situation must be conducive to autonomous motivation, an amalgam of intrinsic motivation and extrinsic motivators that have become internalized and integrated. Being aware of an adaptive challenge is not sufficient for constructive disorientation and, eventually, deep learning. As important as flow theory (Csikszentmihalyi, 1990) has been to our

4.3 Conclusion

understanding of intrinsic motivation, one is not necessarily motivated to engage in learning when faced with an optimal balance of challenge and support: the learning must have a volitional quality, driven by curiosity, an innate human need to explore.

Third, the situation must empower a sense of efficacy, a feeling that not only is one competent to engage in a learning task but also that the effort will have a tangible result of value to the learner.

And fourth, the disorientation must occur in an environment where one feels socially connected, cared for by others, and confident that they are contributing to their social or organizational environment in healthy and valued ways.

Promoting constructive disorientation in others also has four necessary and distinctive features.

First is a clear but manageable challenge, the essence of constructive disorientation. One must experience a sense of disquietude, accompanied by the belief that one has both the competence and social support needed to meet the challenge. The key to maintaining this balance is not to attempt to reduce the disorientation through increasing competence, but rather to manage the inevitable anxiety. Anything beyond a moderate anxiety inhibits motivation to learn.

Second, building upon the previous point, individuals – and groups – must be able to increase or decrease the level of challenge so as to match skills with requirements for action. These learning strategies use models embedded in problem-based learning and action learning: small groups define the presenting problem, identify learning needs, set learning goals and strategies, meet together regularly to share and reflect on what has been learned, seek feedback, discuss how the problem should be redefined, and continue the process, all under the guidance of a facilitator who keeps the process going and the disorientation at a constructive level.

Third, the learning should be in an environment free from distractions, one conducive to "deep work" (Newport, 2016) and "thinking slow" (Kahneman, 2011).

Fourth and finally, consistent with flow theory (Csikszentmihalyi, 1990), the learning activity should have clear criteria for performance, concrete feedback, and freedom to fail. The first two of these criteria are commonly understood; the third is not. The trend toward holding individuals and groups accountable for measurable results, and the ubiquity of strategic planning in organizations, left unchecked, stifles creativity, ignores serendipitous opportunities, and leads to the displacement of valued goals by quantitative benchmarks. In order for constructive disorientation to occur the organizational culture must support experimentation and reasonable risk-taking.

Constructive disorientation must go somewhere: one must know how to follow it and what to do. In the next chapter I turn to the third key to deep learning, critical reflection on experience.

Notes

1 The deleterious effects of anxiety on learning are well documented (cf. Sogunro, 1998).
2 A humorous if unsettling diversion about such pains is Edward Gorey's *The Unstrung Harp: Or Mr. Earbrass writes a novel* (1999). Thanks to Norman Dale for the reference.
3 See Chapter 7 for a full elaboration of this point.

CHAPTER 5

Critical Reflection

> In searching for the truth, it may be our best plan to start by criticizing our most cherished beliefs.
>
> Karl Popper

In this chapter I explore the importance of critical reflection to deep learning. Knowing oneself and facilitating constructive disorientation are both necessary but insufficient conditions. Who would want to be in an organization full of people who spend their days as learning dilettantes, flitting from one moment of intellectual curiosity to the next, without ever pausing to do the deep work of challenging existing ways of thinking and potentially integrating new insights? As Kahneman and Renshon (2007) pointed out, even in a healthy state of disorientation we scramble to find a connection with existing perspectives, and because "System 2" thinking makes our brains work harder, we have to make a conscious and deliberate effort to resist defaulting to System 1 thinking. Thus, the necessity for critical reflection. In Chapter 2, I wrote about the importance of reflection on experience as a way to develop *phronesis*, or the ability to know when to rely on intuition (System 1) and when to make the effort to dig more deeply (System 2). Deep learning, therefore, depends on how humans make meaning of experience – on whether or not that experience will become, in John Dewey's ([1938] 1997) terms, "educative."

Reflection, a "turning back on experience," can take many forms: "Simple awareness of an object, event or state, including awareness of a perception thought, feeling, disposition, intention, action, or of one's habits of doing these things. It can also mean letting one's thoughts wander over something, taking something into consideration, or imagining alternatives. One can reflect on oneself reflecting" (Mezirow, 1998, p. 185)

John Dewey ([1938] 1997) was one of the first to affirm the importance of reflection on experience in human learning, separating "intelligent action" from "routine action." For Dewey, "true" reflection meets four criteria (Rodgers, 2002):

First, reflection is a meaning-making process that moves a learner from one experience to the next with deeper understandings of its relationships with and connections to other experiences and ideas. Recall from Chapter 3 that for Dewey, *experience* is more than just participating in events; it is active interaction with one's environment in a sort of dialectic that results in change on both sides. As I have argued throughout this book, while experience is the basis of learning, it can also be a barrier to learning: the schemes that help us make meaning of experience can also serve to block incoming information that is dissonant with those schemes. Reflection is the thread that makes continuity of learning possible, ensuring the progress of the individual and, ultimately, society. It is a means to socially desirable ends.

Second, reflection for Dewey is a systematic, rigorous, disciplined way of thinking, with its roots in scientific inquiry. Reflection on experience is not "spontaneous interpretation" (Dewey, [1938] 1997), which leads one to interpret experience based on existing schema and then to act accordingly (Kahneman's System 1 [2011]). Instead, two other elements are necessary: a sense of disequilibrium causing a need for resolution, and a sense of curiosity, both of which are essential to constructive disorientation. Dewey's suggested process for inquiring into experience looks a bit linear and overly rational today, as he based his approach on the traditional scientific method: that is, identifying the problems that arise from experience, generating possible explanations for the problem(s), converting these into hypotheses, and testing the hypotheses using objective scientific methods. Dewey did not assume that the results of inquiry would settle the matter, but rather would lead to "intelligent action," which in turn would lead to further reflection.

Third, reflection needs to happen in community, in interaction with others, a point I have made throughout this book and explore in greater depth in Chapter 6.

Fourth, and finally, reflection requires attitudes that value the personal and intellectual growth of oneself and others, a value Dewey considered critical for a democratic society. Reflection that is truly useful should be determined by public inspection and criticism, and should be used as a means to essentially moral ends.

Dewey largely ignored the power of emotion in learning (except when writing about the arts) and the pernicious effects of cognitive bias. He also downplayed the role of politics in learning. Dewey's thinking is criticized today mostly for its optimistic, even naïve, assumptions about the power of education alone to bring about social change. Dewey, and other progressive educators like Eduard Lindeman (1961), who took Dewey's ideas on the education of children and applied them to adults, rarely mentioned oppression or hegemony as barriers to a democratic utopia, a topic I take up in Chapter 7.

5.1 What Makes Reflection "Critical"?

Just as not all disorientation is constructive disorientation, not all reflection is *critical* reflection, as adult educator Jack Mezirow (1998) pointed out: "Reflection does not necessarily imply making an *assessment* of what is being reflected upon, a distinction that differentiates it from critical reflection … critical self-reflection involves critique of a premise upon which [one] has defined a problem" (p. 186, emphasis added). One may respond to mild disorientation with a strictly technical – and appropriate – response, such as making adjustments to a staff development program based on negative feedback from participants, or reflecting on a meeting and deciding that much of the agenda could have been conducted by email. These are examples of what Argyris and Schön (1978) have called "single-loop learning," making changes within a given framework of values and beliefs. Double-loop learning, on the other hand, requires that the assumptions behind the framework be cross-examined. For the examples just posed, a double-loop tack would lead one to ask such questions as, "why do we think we need a staff development program in the first place?" Or, "given that much of our business can be transacted electronically, what are the useful purposes of meeting face to face?" Critical reflection is not necessarily a more intense or probing form of reflection, but is more difficult, as it requires that we identify assumptions that we hold dear and put them to the test (Brookfield, 2009).

These kinds of assumptions belong to what Mezirow (2000) referred to as "meaning perspectives": "The structure of assumptions and expectations through which we filter sense impressions … [A meaning perspective] selectively shapes and delimits perception, cognition, feelings, and disposition by predisposing our intentions, expectations, and purposes. It provides the context for making meaning within which we choose what and how a sensory experience is to be construed and/or appropriated" (p. 16). Meaning perspectives (or "mental models," as Senge [2006] and others refer to them) may be conscious or subconscious, intentional or unintentional, idiosyncratic or culturally assimilated. These meaning schemes, consisting of clusters of beliefs and values, all have emotional origins and therefore can be extremely resistant to change, making true critical reflection hard and even painful.

Mezirow (2000) maintained that critical reflection is the most important element in transformative learning, and there is some empirical evidence to back this up (cf. Brock, 2010).

For all that has been written about critical reflection and its importance to deep learning, writers on the topic are relatively silent about how precisely the process is supposed to work. Some help comes from philosopher Jürgen Habermas (1984), who proposed that critical reflection must begin by gaining distance from the present, what he termed "distantiation." Put plainly, one must make a conscious choice to step back from the moment in order to, appropriating Ron Heifetz' metaphor (Heifetz et al., 2009) get "off the dance floor" and onto "the balcony" to understand the system of swirling dancers below. Ironically, perhaps, one must be mindful *of that moment* in order to know when to do this. We must learn to listen to our body's signals and to discern what to notice, to develop the habit of "mindful learning" discussed in Chapter 3, an implicit awareness of and openness to new perspectives. This is what Mezirow (2000) refers to as developing a more "dependable" meaning perspective, one that "is more inclusive, differentiating, permeable (open to other viewpoints), critically reflective of assumptions, emotionally capable of change, and integrative of experience" (p. 19).

Thus, the first step is developing mindfulness of the sort discussed in Chapter 3: cultivating a habit of mind that recognizes and then responds to the signals that distantiation might be in order. *These signals might not be initially disorienting.* In contrast to what Mezirow implies, deep learning is not just a reaction to felt disorientation, but a practiced habit that can also *produce* disorientation. Consider the simple example above about staff development programs. Certainly, the easier form of reflection would be to look to participant feedback and to reflect on that feedback as guidance for program improvement – an example of single-loop learning. A more critically reflective posture would be to go deeper, looking for more subtle clues. Consider the following responses to a typical end-of-workshop survey, asking what kept the experience from being more useful:

> The case studies handed out didn't reflect what really goes on in my organization.

It's too bad that top administrators couldn't be here, because they need this training more than we do.

I hope that some of the ideas we came up with will result in real change, but I have my doubts.

A "single-loop," technical response to each of the above might look something like this:

Make the case studies more realistic; maybe use more real-life examples.

Make an effort to include more "brass" next time.

Be sure to incorporate time at the end for more detailed action plans.

A "double-loop," more critically reflective response would be something like this: Workshop organizers would look to these comments and others and identify underlying themes that might signal the need for more adaptive learning, by definition more difficult and risky than technical solutions, and ask: What is the subtext behind these comments? What are the implicit messages, if any? What do they possibly reveal about a gap between strongly held values and the experienced reality (the definition of an "adaptive challenge") (Heifetz, 1994)? What might the adaptive challenge be, and how might we name it? Collective meaning-making, by naming and acting upon the adaptive challenge requires attention to both relational learning and political learning, subjects of the next two chapters in this book.

For now, I want to emphasize just how difficult true critical reflection can be, especially given the seductive appeal of technical rationality. Mezirow (1998) argued that critical reflection is a matter of "principled thinking": "impartial, consistent, and non-arbitrary" according to "universal constructs of reason" (p. 186). Unfortunately, using one's own powers of reason in this way works only when evaluating other people's assumptions. In *The Enigma of Reason*, Mercier and Sperber (2017) make the persuasive case that reasoning evolved in humans to justify one's own beliefs and to criticize others'. What people find difficult, they write, is "not looking for counterevidence or counterarguments in general, but only when what is being challenged is their own opinion" (p. 218). Thus, critical reflection is a lot easier when thinking through assumptions – about staff development programs, for instance – when they are someone *else's* and not your own pet theories. In Mezirow's terms, it is the difference between "objective reframing," critical reflection on the assumptions of others, and "subjective reframing," critical reflection on one's own assumptions (Mezirow, 2000).

Here is the essence of the difficulty. Letting go of a cherished belief results in a sense of loss of agency and efficacy and a feeling of regret, all of which can lead to lowered motivation to learn, increased cynicism, and even a dystopian view of human existence. Small wonder that cognitive biases, when challenged by others, become stronger; that conspiracy theories are so hard to dislodge; that superstitions are so hard to overcome! The way through the stress of critical reflection lies in having an alternative set of beliefs to turn to, what Mezirow (1998) calls "assimilative learning." Back in Chapter 1, I wrote about how difficult it was – and to some extent still is – for me to let go of the assumption that minds are changed by logic and evidence. I could not have coped with the new (for me) knowledge that empirical evidence does not *ipso facto* change people's minds without having an alternative available in the form of a set of *new* beliefs about how minds can in fact be changed – namely through the positive power of emotion, personal agency, curiosity, and social norms, all of which I explore later in this chapter and those following.

5.2 Critical Reflection and Mindful Learning

I introduced the notion of mindful learning in Chapter 3, as the habit of mind that consciously and routinely challenges existing assumptions. It is the sort of critical reflection that stems, not from an overt emotional disturbance, but rather from a cognitive reminder that the premises upon which we decide and act are always subject to question. This is the essence of reflexivity, which "brings the unconscious, taken-for-granted, habitual ways of thinking and reasoning to the surface for ideology critique and reconstruction in such a manner that the cognitive processes and self-formative processes merge" (Steet, 1992, quoted in Kucukaydin & Cranton, 2012, p. 52). While reflexivity and critical reflection are often used interchangeably, I view the former as a habit of mind, a core element in mindful learning, while the latter is the act itself. Reflexivity leads to more and deeper critical reflection. Reflexivity is especially important as a counterweight to what Stephen Brookfield (2009) calls "hegemonic assumptions," that is, our deeply ingrained presumptions about existing power relationships in society. He writes that this form of critical reflection "calls into question the power relationships that allow, or promote, one set of practices considered to be technically effective. [Critical reflection] assumes that the minutiae of practice have embedded within them the struggles between unequal interests and groups that exist in the wider world" (p. 126). One long-standing hegemonic assumption is that women are paid less than men for the same work because men are the more important "breadwinners," and thus will have a greater commitment to the workplace. Society demands different sex roles, and that's "just how things are." Another is the view that persons with physical disabilities are deficient and deserving of our charity, not as people with other qualities to offer. I will have more to say about reflection on hegemonic assumptions, a cornerstone of the intellectual tradition of critical theory, in Chapter 7. In essence, critical theory

> is grounded in three core assumptions regarding the way the world is organized: (1) that apparently open, Western democracies are actually highly unequal societies in which economic inequity, racism, and class discrimination are empirical realities; (2) that the way this state of affairs is reproduced as seeming to be normal, natural, and inevitable (thereby heading off potential challenges to the system) is through the dissemination of dominant ideology; and (3) that critical theory attempts to understand this state of affairs as a prelude to changing it. (Brookfield, 2009, pp. 126–127)

I quote Brookfield extensively here to make the point that hegemonic assumptions are experienced as just how things are, and thus external challenges to them are rather easily dismissed as the extremist views of those who do not know how to live in the "real world." As French philosopher Pierre Bourdieu (1977) put it, a hegemonic precept is one that "goes without saying because it comes without saying" (p. 167). It takes disorientation through other means, either unconsciously, as through the arts, or more overtly, as through political action, both of which are subjects of later chapters. The point is that mindfulness, and mindful learning, can forestall the immediate defensiveness created by perceived threats to one's entrenched worldview.

Critical reflection through mindful learning makes one attentive to potential disorientation, which becomes "constructive" when the criteria given in Chapter 4 – namely an environment conducive to adaptive learning and the conditions required for intrinsic motivation to learn – are met.

Consider the following scenario (inspired, as they say in the movies, by real events). An iconic civil rights organization in the United States, founded in the 1950s to combat segregation laws, has found itself in the post-civil rights era of the early twenty-first century. Legal barriers have long since come down. The new president of a regional chapter is anxious to revisit its mission, believing that it is time to direct attention to the more insidious forms of racism. He points to growing economic inequality, worse for African Americans, and laws passed by several Southern states that make it more difficult for people of color to vote. He schedules a "mission retreat" with senior staff and board members. He wants to use this time to create a sense of constructive disorientation in the group. He knows that the organization faces an adaptive challenge and thinks that he can make the case for it by inviting participants to critically examine the organization's existential purpose. But what then? he wonders. What if I present an alternative vision and the group doesn't go for it? He realizes that he needs more than the clichéd "buy-in." He needs for the group to engage in the kind of critical reflection that reflects a genuine commitment to reframing how the organization sees itself. He needs to ensure that participants have real voice, that they do not feel co-opted by the president's agenda. He needs to ensure the growth of social capital, the conscious experience of shared values and purposes. And finally, he must be able to communicate that the group's deliberations will lead to positive change. Using the terms of this book, the president will first stimulate disorientation with the message that chapter membership is drying up, as are financial contributions. He will then work to cultivate a spirit of *adaptive learning*, respect participants' *autonomy*, build upon the group's *relatedness*, and ensure a collective sense of *efficacy* about the impact of the retreat on work going forward.

None of the above is possible without authentic critical reflection, which is not just going through the motions as a cognitive exercise, but giving the process emotional energy as well. To underscore a point from the previous chapter: forces for stability can be extremely difficult to overcome. My Antioch colleague Donna Ladkin (2015) has written about what she calls "organizational mind*less*ness," the tendency to rely on old categories, act on "autopilot," and minimize attention to new information. The key to overcoming organizational mindlessness lies, I think, in Lynn Davies' (2015) notion of "educative turbulence": gently "nudging" a system into creative activity.

Here is the end of the above scenario: the retreat did not accomplish what the president had hoped. Participation by board members, while not overtly resistant, was at best desultory. They simply had no energy to do the hard work of real change. In retrospect, the president acknowledged that the disorientation was not enough for the group to experience an adaptive challenge. He also realized that he needed to do two things before scheduling another retreat: first, to repopulate the board with people having fresh ideas and a greater willingness to challenge orthodoxy; and second, to identify points of energy for change in the organization, those people and groups in favor of building a new order, and to encourage them, sponsor them, and connect them. He needed to give these sources of creative energy the space to undertake some revisioning, make sure that these thought experiments are tested through critical reflection on the organization's core values, and are tested further with the organization's key constituencies.

5.3 Critical Reflection and the Development of Expertise

Critical reflection is not limited to the transformation of mental models or meaning perspectives. Critical reflection is also important to developing expertise – learning carpentry, for example, or tennis, or a foreign language. One does not become more proficient in these things by simply acquiring new information. One has to also work with that new information, practice applying it, and reflect on the outcome of the practicing.

The development of expertise has been the subject of an enormous amount of research and theorizing ever since Donald Schön published his seminal book *The Reflective Practitioner* (1983). How is it that experts become experts? It is not, as we have seen, simply because they have learned and retained a vast storehouse of knowledge. Still, this was the assumption behind most organization development programs prior to the mid-1980s. As Fenwick (2008) notes:

> Before about 1985, workplace learning was characterized primarily as acquisition; individuals were believed to acquire and store new concepts and skills and behaviors as if knowledge were a package that didn't change in the transfer from its source to the learner's head. Learning workers were understood to be acquiring intellectual capital, increasing the organization's resources, and returning its investment on training. (p. 19)

In other words, those designing workplace learning programs bought into the specious assumptions of "institutional learning" (Vaill, 1996) – that learning has solely instrumental purposes, that those in authority know best what ought to be learned, and that a well-defined subject matter is "out there" to be absorbed by the learner.

Schön's point, first described in 1978 when he and Chris Argyris wrote about the "learning organization" (1978), is that expertise is developed by reflecting on practice – by surfacing, reflecting on, and problematizing what is encountered in the day-to-day, taking a conscious and mindful approach to what otherwise would be incidental learning. Reflection on practice depends however on the developmental stage of the learner. Consider Figure 5.1.

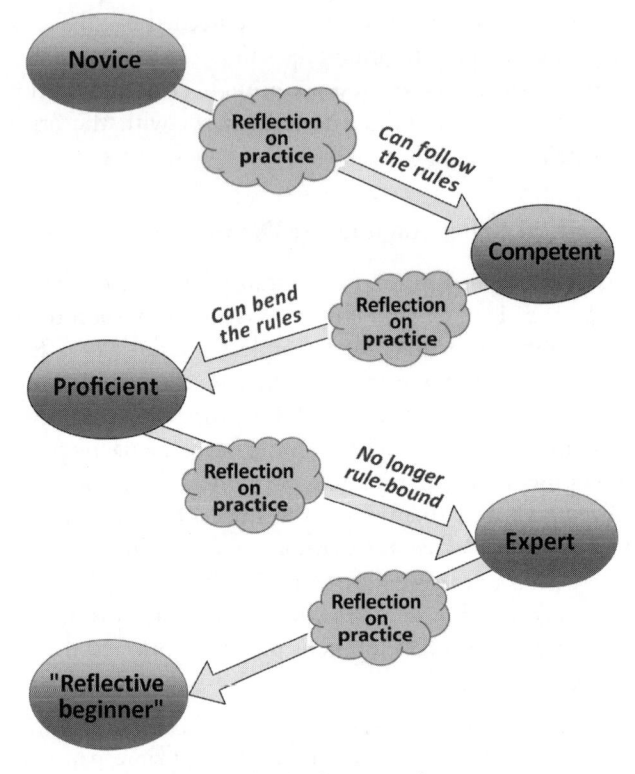

Figure 5.1 The development of expertise

Those who study the development of expertise typically characterize it as movement sequentially through various stages (cf. Anderson & Keltner, 2002; Grow, 1991). One begins in a particular knowledge domain as a novice, bringing to it only limited information and undeveloped knowledge perspectives. Once s/he has developed enough working knowledge to know what the "rules" are s/he moves to a level of minimal "competence." With practice the rules become integrated, automatic, and unconscious, and the individual rises to a level of "proficient." Finally, with a lot more practice, the practitioner has such a good sense of patterns and relationships that s/he is able to discern when the rules no longer apply, that more creative approaches are needed to deal with complexity, and thus becomes an "expert." If I want to learn how to bake, for example, I first need to become familiar with the tools and ingredients, and then how to follow a recipe. I then have the competence to make biscuits, as long as

5.3 Critical Reflection and Expertise

I follow the rules. After a while I become proficient enough with the recipe that I learn how to substitute ingredients, such as whole milk and vinegar for buttermilk. Finally, I have enough expertise to make biscuits strictly by "feel" without worrying about the recipe at all, and explore various ways of improving texture and flavor. (My mother was famous for her pie crusts but could never really explain why they turned out so well; her expertise was based entirely on what I describe below as "tacit knowledge.")

There is a certain order and logic to this. The problem is that the model falls apart without reflection on practice, at every stage. The "old school" approach to teaching beginners has been to assume that they first need to absorb a lot of information. The traditional model of medical school education has been infamous for this approach: before giving students any real clinical exposure they need to spend their first two years in school learning the "basic sciences," namely anatomy, physiology, biochemistry, and so on. Only then, the reasoning has been, could they learn how to care for actual patients. This is not, however, how budding professionals (or anyone else) learns most effectively – as anyone who has been through the medical school grind will tell you – and so in the last years of the twentieth century medical schools (and other professional schools) began to explore other approaches, such as problem-based learning (discussed in Chapter 4), which situates needed learning in practical problems posed to the learner (Curry & Wergin, 1993). Here is where Schön's thinking, based on systematic observation of clinical settings such as an architecture studio, has had such a profound effect.

Thus, the development of expertise does not take place in a linear way, depending on how much information the learner is able to absorb, store, and categorize. Instead, the path to expertise is through reflection, even at the novice level. Begin with some rudimentary tools; practice; reflect and problematize (e.g., "what made the biscuit batter so sticky?"); internalize new practices, and so on, through the stages. At the expert level, learning is no longer simply instrumental. Reflection on practice becomes a habit of mind. Experts, unless they become complacent in their expertise, learn what to notice, what to problematize, and when to examine their assumptions. They become mindful learners – and in a paradoxical way become what Vaill called "reflective beginners" (1996), never assuming that they have all the answers, that they always have something to learn.

There is an important caveat to all of this. Empirical evidence suggests that experience *alone* does not lead to reflective practice of the sort described above. "Experienced" is not the same as "expert." For example, Natalie Ferry and Jovita Ross-Gordon (1998) found evidence of reflection on practice in both novice and experienced practitioners. They write: "It appears that experience alone does not generate the emergence of reflection-in-action. Rather, how one uses experience may be the more crucial element to understanding why some individuals use reflection to grow in their professional learning" (p. 111). Thus, reflection on practice as a habit of mind seems to depend more on one's *propensity* to reflect (Roessger, 2014).

If true, then the development of *mindful learning* becomes all the more important. At the highest level of expertise development, "know-how" becomes mindful. Part of that mindfulness is raising consciousness about what has become tacit. As I pointed out earlier, much intuitive learning is helpful, even essential, to our understanding of the world. But some is not. Intuitive theories, left unexamined, can lead to a host of cognitive traps, persisting beliefs, and immunity to change. Mindful learning works to deliberately create constructive disorientation and to follow it. The disorientation does not have to be experienced as a jolt, as a "whoa!" moment, a disorienting dilemma. It can be an almost indistinguishable signal that something warrants our attention. One of the simplest and most powerful definitions of *consciousness* was offered by neuroscientist Antonio Damasio (1999), calling it "an organism's awareness of its own self and surroundings" (p. 4). In the context of deep learning, mindful learning is a particular form of consciousness, the awareness that in any given moment our "self" has something useful and important to learn, *especially* when that something might conflict with our current notions of how things are.

To summarize, deep learning is wholly dependent on critical reflection, whether that learning results in transforming one's mental models, or deepening one's expertise through instrumental learning. At the highest levels of expertise, learning becomes transformative as well.

Here, then, are the first core components of what I am calling the "deep learning mindset" (Figure 5.2), with more to be added to blank spaces in later chapters.

So far, we have seen that constructive disorientation can stem from two sources: one might experience a disorienting dilemma – an external stimulus – or routine mindfulness that stays alert for signals requiring conscious attention. Both external and internal sources of constructive disorientation engage critical reflection. Sometimes critical reflection will lead directly to transformation of meaning schemes; sometimes it will lead to instrumental learning in the form of expertise development. At the highest levels of expertise the learning becomes transformative, as one's key assumptions about what to do and when to do it are constantly in play.

5.3 Critical Reflection and Expertise

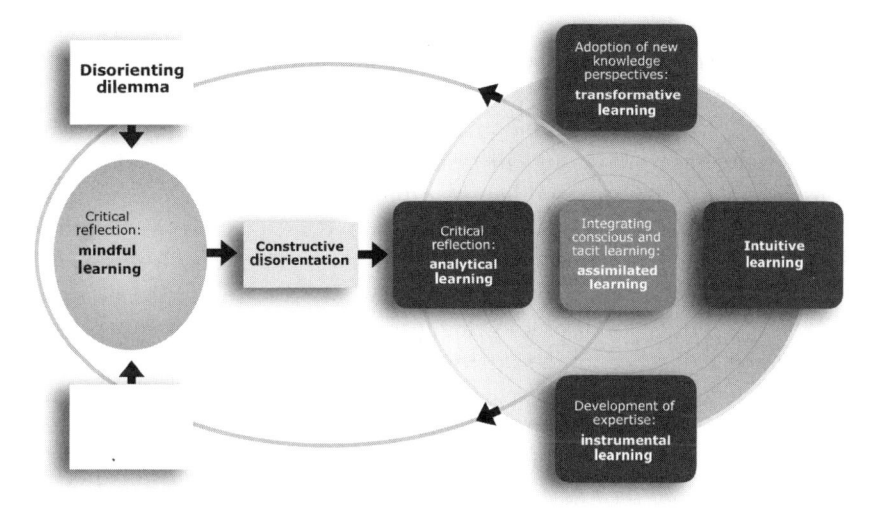

Figure 5.2 The deep learning mindset

The transformation of cognitive schema then becomes part of how the individual sees the world and his/her role in it, subject to further mindful learning.

An element of Figure 5.2 that I have not described yet is *intuitive learning*. Intuitive learning is the unintentional, even incidental learning that takes place below our conscious awareness. Transforming one's knowledge perspectives is not always a product of critical reflection. Sometimes transformation occurs on an intuitive, mindless basis, as when people resettle in foreign countries and gradually assimilate new habits of thought and living without being aware of it (Taylor, 1994).

Tacit knowledge, a term coined by Michael Polanyi (1966), is one of the most intriguing and least understood facets of human learning. It is the knowing we cannot express in words. Here is a quick thought experiment: Imagine trying to explain how we are able to immediately recognize an acquaintance in a crowd of people. You cannot say, "Well, first I look at the hair, and if that reminds me of someone then I examine the facial features, and put those qualities together, then try to guess the age." Of course not. You just *know*, at a glance, that this is your neighbor Janice from down the street. Here is another thought experiment. Imagine that you are riding a bicycle and all of a sudden you hit a patch of loose gravel and your bike begins to tip to your left. Which way do you turn the front wheel? Many would say "to the right," reasoning that you need to counteract the direction of the fall. But you would be wrong. You would never do this in practice, knowing in the moment that doing so would only accelerate the spill. You would know instinctively to turn the front wheel to the left. This is an example of *embodied knowing*, or simply, learning through the body. All of our early learning as humans is embodied: babies learn through sensations, toddlers by exploring through touch (Lawrence, 2012). Embodied knowledge precedes overt consciousness: a sensation leads to a constructed emotion, which leads in turn to one being conscious of, for example, fear. Embodied learning is what Aristotle referred to as the second of his three kinds of knowing, namely *techne*, or "know-how," and is the essence of reflection on experience.

Intuitive learning is often referred to as "incidental learning." As adult educator Victoria Marsick has noted, "When people learn incidentally, their learning may be taken for granted, tacit, or unconscious. However, *a passing insight can then be probed and intentionally explored*. Examples are the hidden agenda of an organization's culture or a teacher's class, learning from mistakes, or the unsystematic process of trial and error" (Marsick & Watkins, 2001, p. 26, emphasis added). Note the allusion to intuitive learning as an opportunity for critical reflection. The power of intuitive or incidental learning is hard to overstate. Research on continuing professional education programs has demonstrated that while people may be motivated to attend a conference or workshop to learn things from expert presenters, the more powerful learning moments occur in "hallway conversations" with colleagues, where participants compare notes, in an unplanned way, on how recommended practices might work – or not – in their own professional settings.

Back in the 1980s I directed a project sponsored by the American College of Cardiology where we investigated the degree to which attendance at its "Heart House" programs changed practice behavior. We found evidence of this "hallway conversation" phenomenon: when asked how, if at all, their practice had changed, and what most affected this change, cardiologists pointed to these very encounters (Wergin, Mazmanian, Miller, Papp., & Williams, 1988). (Reported changes in practice were backed up by random audits of patient charts.) Note how closely this finding parallels the research on transformative learning: knowledge perspectives are transformed only when new ideas are tried on in the presence of others.

The fact that learning grows out of spontaneous everyday encounters vastly more often than in formal educational settings has enormous implications for deep learning. Because intuitive learning is largely unconscious, unless it is deliberately surfaced and inspected it is subject to all of

5.3 Critical Reflection and Expertise

the cognitive biases I described in Part I of this book. Intuitive learning can be especially limiting when it takes place within hegemonic boundaries and assumptions. Women in highly patriarchal cultures may grow up with the intuitive belief that having little control over their own lives is "just the way things are." Helping oppressed people surface and question these beliefs, to discover their own power and agency, is the purpose of so-called "radical" education methods proposed by Paulo Freire and Augusto Boal, among others, and I take up the relevance of these methods to deep learning in Chapters 7 and 8.

To summarize, the core of a deep learning mindset consists of mindfulness, constructive disorientation, critical reflection, and transformative learning. The latter may be the direct result of critical reflection, the development of deep expertise, or reflection on intuitive learning. Because intuitive learning by definition occurs at an unconscious level, reflection on it plays a major role in mindful learning.

I will be adding other components to the deep learning mindset, one chapter at a time, beginning with a topic I have already introduced, namely the importance of *learning in the presence of others*.

CHAPTER 6

The Importance of Others

> Great minds discuss ideas; average minds discuss events; small minds discuss people.
>
> Eleanor Roosevelt

If constructive disorientation is the spark for deep learning, and critical reflection is the engine, then social discourse is the fuel.

The importance of learning with others may be the most common thread throughout all of the research and theorizing about human learning. To review:

- John Dewey wrote that all learning is a function of both continuity and interaction with one's environment. While human nature grows from within it must be completed through relationships.
- Transformative learning theory holds that transformation is most likely to occur, and is most powerful, when disorientation is followed by dialogue with one or more other people.
- Disorientation *not* in the presence of others can make existing beliefs even more powerful and resistant to change.
- One's identity (or concept of "self") is a major factor in motivation to learn and is always socially negotiated.
- Deep relationships are an important, even necessary part of self-actualization.
- "Relatedness," the feeling of connection with significant others in one's life, is one of the three pillars of self-determination theory.
- Development occurs as a function of periodically renegotiating the interaction between connection and independence.
- Relational affirmation is a key pathway to one's "best self."
- Adaptive learning in organizations requires a communal understanding of the adaptive challenge and how that challenge will be addressed.

- In both problem-based learning and action learning, the learning occurs in groups, with group members responsible for stimulating, informing, and challenging each other.
- Reflection on practice is most powerful when done with other practitioners.

Humans have evolved to be "communal animals," as Aristotle put it, and the primary purpose of learning is for social consumption, as an adaptation to the social niche humans have built for ourselves. There is little doubt that deep learning is facilitated in the right interactive setting. Other people perform several functions for us: they test our conscious reasoning; they model alternative perspectives; they provide richer opportunities for experiential learning; and they create accountability, the expectation that we will be called upon to justify our beliefs, feelings, or actions to others.

Despite the empirical evidence, a cultural norm lingers in Western cultures, perpetuated by our schooling system, that real learning is done alone, through individual immersion in a subject matter. Part of this may be due to a Western fixation on individual achievement, on "rugged individualism." Consider the following passage from Ralph Waldo Emerson's classic essay on "Self Reliance" ([1841] 2013):

> What I must do is all that concerns me, not what the people think. This rule, equally arduous in actual and in intellectual life, may serve for the whole distinction between greatness and meanness. It is the harder, because you will always find those who think they know what is your duty better than you know it. It is easy in the world to live after the world's opinion; it is easy in solitude to live after our own; but the great man is he who in the midst of the crowd keeps with perfect sweetness the independence of solitude. (p. 26)

In praise of self-reliance, Emerson constructs a dichotomy: one must be ruled either by the self or by the crowd. Conforming to social expectation is weakness; being true to self is strength. Narcissistic and authoritarian leaders would read this passage and find support for their worldviews, as would, paradoxically, their admirers who, unaware that they are being manipulated, act as if these leaders' views are their own.

Emerson's view that people must be either self-reliant or conformist is a false dichotomy. Learning to live effectively in the world requires learning not only how to live with others, but also how to *learn in the presence of others*.

Previous chapters have also, however, alluded to the dangers of deep learning in groups, traps that can inhibit deep learning or prevent it entirely. Of these, three are most serious.

First is the lack of diversity of beliefs in the group. When people are with others having like-minded beliefs, norms for acceptable deviations from these beliefs are narrow and impermeable, and those who stray beyond their confines will feel social pressure to conform. Cults are an extreme illustration of this, where individual identities are so enmeshed with group culture that fear of ostracism, or worse, becomes all-powerful.

Second and related is organizational "groupthink," the failure of group members to criticize each others' suggestions and consider alternatives. A particularly egregious example is how some of the "best and brightest" minds in America utterly failed to question the dubious assumptions leading to military intervention and escalation in Vietnam (Halberstam, 1972). Groupthink is the principal reason why brainstorming can be so inefficient and inadequate. Fear of embarrassing oneself by appearing to be an outlier can inhibit creative thinking; and brainstorming privileges those with dominant, extraverted personalities. (Various nominal group techniques such as Delphi can mitigate these deficiencies.)

Third, addressed more fully in the next chapter, is the lack of attention, conscious or not, to power differentials and hegemonic differences. With the exception of "radical" educators such as Paulo Freire (1970) and Stephen Brookfield (2009), adult educators and learning theorists in general have ignored or skipped over the degree to which unequal access to financial, social, or cultural capital affects opportunities to learn deeply.

In this chapter I explore how the lessons learned about social discourse might help facilitate deep learning. The evidence points to four key facilitators, and I will address each one in turn:

- Empathy: not only the ability to put oneself in another's shoes but also to understand the social context behind the other's beliefs.
- Social capital: social ties among individuals and the trust that arises from these ties.
- Participatory forms of engagement and learning.
- Minimal power differentials and shared responsibility.

6.1 Empathy

Empathy is quite simply the vicarious experience of someone else's experience, both cognitively and emotionally. One can be empathic without necessarily endorsing another person's point of view, or even caring about how that person feels. Empathy is not *compassion*, sympathy for another person's loss, for example. It is no comfort to someone who has lost a child to be told by someone who has not, "I know how you must feel."

Empathy is also not the same as *identification* with someone else, as psychologist Carl Rogers noted: "The state of empathy, or being empathic, is to perceive the internal frame of another with accuracy and with the emotional components and meanings which pertain thereto as if one were the person but without ever losing the 'as if' condition" (Rogers, 1959, quoted in Jarvis, 2012, p. 744). When presented with someone having a worldview significantly different from our own, our intuitive response is to generate reasons why the other's point of view is wrong. Empathizing with difference creates disorientation, and it can take a real effort to make that disorientation constructive. One of the best examples of this was when Anwar Sadat, as part of his historic visit to Israel in 1977, visited Yad Vashem, the Holocaust museum. His visit had a profound effect on all concerned, a show of empathy to the highest degree (Koven, 1977).[1] But given the political polarization that exists in most of the world today, the challenges to empathy are strong and, unfortunately, getting stronger.

The picture however might not be quite so bleak. In an informative TED talk, social psychologist Robb Willer (2016) describes an experiment in which he and his colleagues asked a group of people to read one of three essays on the environment, the first a standard plea for environmental protection espousing predominately liberal values (e.g., "It is essential that we take steps now to prevent further destruction from being done to our Earth"), one that tapped into mostly conservative values such as the importance of purity (e.g., "Reducing pollution can help us preserve what is pure and beautiful about the places we live"), and one on a neutral topic. When surveyed later for their environmental attitudes, those who had identified as "liberal" were strongly pro-environment no matter which essay they read. But those who identified as "conservative" were more likely to endorse pro-environmental policies if they had read the essay focusing on conservative values. The lesson, according to Willer, is that if we intend to persuade another to adopt our point of view, we need first to understand the other person's moral values and frame our message accordingly. "Empathy and respect," he emphasized, "empathy and respect" (minute 9:1).

The path to helping someone else learn deeply, in other words, is to find that space where constructive disorientation might exist, a place where one might be able to entertain an initially disorienting idea without forcing oneself or others to compromise deeply held beliefs and moral values (at least initially). Empathy is the medium for finding that space.

Thus, developing empathy has more than just pragmatic value; it also leads to deep learning itself. Developing one's sense of self requires an understanding of *others'* perspectives and trying these perspectives on for size. In Chapter 3, I wrote about "knowing thyself first" as the first key to deep learning. I did *not* write about "being *true to thyself* first!" In their theory of authentic embodied leadership, Donna Ladkin and Steven Taylor (Ladkin & Taylor, 2010) reference a study of emerging leaders enacting provisional leadership "selves," in which those who looked to emulate senior leaders (what Albert Bandura (1977) calls "observational learning") were more successful than those who took a "being true to oneself" strategy. The latter group, by choosing to rely on behaviors that were already part of their repertoire, missed opportunities to stretch and grow and, paradoxically, to become more "authentic" leaders.

While the literature on the relationship between empathy and learning is extensive,[2] the concept itself is not well understood. As psychologist Hank Davis (2002) observes, only partially tongue-in-cheek: "It's not hard to sing the praises of empathy, whatever it is. You don't need an iron-clad definition to appreciate empathy. We pretty much agree that the word denotes a good thing: empathy is the stuff of group cohesion, and may be the reason we attract, or are attracted to, one person over another" (p. 32). However, as Davis also points out, empathy is not *necessarily* "a good thing": it can lead to both affinity and deception. In their own perverse way, sociopaths are highly empathic. But despite the slippery connotations of the term, this much is agreed-upon in the literature: empathy is observed in all social animals, not just humans (Preston & de Waal, 2002); it is a learned social response in humans, not innate, and must be cognitively regulated to avoid emotional burnout (Bandura, 2002); it strengthens social bonds by providing emotional connection and strengthening group solidarity (Anderson & Keltner, 2002); and it tends to increase with age and cognitive development (Hoffman, 2001; Uzefovsky & Knafo-Noam, 2017). Evidence also suggests that the degree of perceived similarity between someone and another person or group affects the strength of the emotional response; thus, the greater the identification with another, the greater the empathy; the greater one's perception of the other as "the Other," the lower the empathy (Preston & de Waal, 2002).

An extreme example of this is what Lasana Harris and Susan Fiske (2011) call "dehumanized perception," the failure to "spontaneously consider the mind of another person" (p. 175). They show that while humans normally activate an empathic neural network when thinking about other people, parts of this network typically fail to engage when considering groups like drug addicts and homeless people, while areas of the brain associated with disgust are activated instead. If one begins to consider certain groups of people as undeserving of empathy they then become something less than

6.1 Empathy

human. Thus, when a politician associates migrants with "murderers and rapists," an entire class of people becomes dehumanized. From there it is not much of a stretch to see how these psychological mechanisms can lead to "ethnic cleansing" and other atrocities against humanity.

Thankfully, studies of children, adolescents, families, college students, teachers, counselors, and offenders, among others, indicate that not only is empathy a function of social learning, it can also be *taught* (cf. Bayne & Jangha, 2016; Daly & Suggs, 2010; Giordano, Stare, & Clarke, 2015; Pederson, 2010; Roseman, Ritchie, & Laux, 2009; Swick, 2005; Thompson & Gullone, 2003; Wilson, 2011). The evidence suggests that empathy conducive to deep learning can be facilitated by:

- *Identifying and taking the trouble to understand, without judgment, the values, attitudes, and beliefs of others.* Values and attitudes, especially, are deep-seated and highly resistant to change. Deep learning is extraordinarily difficult when these are threatened. This has been demonstrated with research going back as far as the late 1950s, with Sherif and Hovland's (1961) classic studies of communication and attitude change. Based on extensive research, the authors developed the concepts of "latitude of acceptance" and "latitude of rejection" as predictors of whether a stimulus, such as someone else's opinion, would be assimilated or rejected. One's latitude of acceptance for discordant information on a given topic lies just beyond one's current belief, but not *too* far beyond it, which is one's latitude of rejection. The key to attitude change, therefore, is locating the other person's latitude of acceptance as the field of play, so to speak. This can be done informally through observation or conversation, or more formally through surveys, interviews, or focus groups.
- *Looking to noncognitive means, such as the arts.* In Chapter 8, I address in detail the role of the written, visual, and performing arts in deep learning. For now, I will suggest that the arts can be a tool to develop empathy as a precursor to deep learning. Christine Jarvis (2012) has a lovely explanation of how reading fiction can do this, namely through its "capacity to promote an involuntary empathy that can help adult learners develop deeper understandings of difference and of excluded groups" (p. 743).
- *Continuously monitoring others' perspectives and feelings.* In his book *Enhancing Adult Motivation to Learn*, Ray Wlodkowski (2008) makes the important point that with so much learning – deliberate or incidental – taking place today at a distance through electronic media, understanding others' perspectives and feelings has become more challenging. We make

assumptions based upon small bits of information and can miss the essence. Or as Saint-Exupéry noted, "What is essential is invisible to the eye" (quoted in Wlodkowski, 2008, p. 66). In his book, Wlodkowski wrote that listening for understanding is the single most important skill necessary for empathy, and I completely agree. Recall that in the TED talk referred to earlier, Willer (2016) emphasized two words, *empathy* and *respect*. One of the cardinal principles in interviewing, I have learned, is to demonstrate that while you care about the speaker you do not care about what the speaker says. In practice this is impossible, of course: you *do* care about what someone says. You react instinctively to values, attitudes, and beliefs opposed to your own. But this is why empathy is a learned skill, and takes practice, best rehearsed in nonstressful situations.

- Wlodkowski (2008) sums up the importance of empathy this way: "Empathy is not simply an altruistic notion. It's a dynamic process, involving people's ability to express their thoughts and feelings to each other in ways that often change the relationship and, most important, continue the relationship" (p. 68).

6.2 Social Capital

Capital at one time was a strictly economic term, denoting the financial, physical, and human resources needed for an organization to carry out its work. The term "social capital" is a product of the last quarter-century, meaning "the social ties among individuals and the norms of reciprocity and trustworthiness that arise from those ties" (Haidt, 2012, pp. 338–339). Like "empathy," it is hard to imagine social capital being anything other than a good thing; but also like empathy, whether social capital is "good" or not depends on the purposes to which it is put. For example, tightly knit neighborhoods or communities need to worry much less about security; and organizations with high social capital need to rely less on regulation and bureaucracy. Extremist political groups, on the other hand, also have high social capital due to their homogenous views, but use it for the purpose of stigmatizing "the Other."

How, then, might social capital be used in the service of deep learning? Mercier and Sperber (2017) provide some answers. To recapitulate points already made: human reason is powerful but flawed. We are able to generate powerful reasons to support our existing views and equally powerful reasons to criticize the views of others. We find it much more difficult to reason *against* our existing views and *in support of* opposing ones. Now if this were always true, finding common ground would be impossible – but

6.2 Social Capital

of course negotiating agreement from initial disagreement happens all the time. And here Mercier and Sperber posit something that on the surface seems counterintuitive: that these self-serving reasoning processes have evolved *for specific social purposes*. They write:

> People are biased to find reasons that support their point of view because this is how they can justify their actions and convince others to share their beliefs. You cannot justify yourself by presenting reasons that undermine your justification. You cannot convince others to change their minds by giving them arguments for the view you want them to abandon or against the view you want them to adopt. (p. 331)

This is where social capital comes in: learning in groups is most beneficial when group members have different ideas but a common goal. Under these conditions the more that group members trust each other, that is, have developed social capital, the more likely it is that they will share their interests, lower their emotional defenses, engage in honest debate, and learn from one another.[3] In contrast, the lack of conflicting ideas in a group can lead to kind of social capital that polarizes attitudes (Haidt, 2012), and the absence of a common goal can exacerbate individual differences.

Therefore, social capital that leads to deep learning is facilitated when groups:

- *Have a "common bond or sense of a shared fate"* (Haidt, 2012, p. 105). I have borrowed this expression from Jonathan Haidt because it is particularly apt in this context. Having a communal sense of purpose is what leads to a common learning goal. Under these conditions group members are more likely to leave their egos at the door and find community (or *relatedness*, in self-determination theory terms) (Ryan & Deci, 2017). As Mercier and Sperber (2017) put it, "To the extent that members of a group share their interests, they can trust one another, and people who trust one another have a very reduced use or no use at all for justifications and arguments … Group discussion is typically beneficial when participants have different ideas and a common goal" (p. 334).
- *Have ideological and intellectual diversity.* Note the qualifiers "ideological and intellectual": greater diversity *of any kind* does not necessarily lead to greater social capital. The opposite, in fact, can be true. Sociologist Robert Putnam (2007), of *Bowling Alone* fame (2000), has presented some distressing data collected from communities large and small, all over the world, demonstrating an inverse relationship between the ethnic diversity of a community and the level of its social capital: that is, the greater the diversity, the lower the level of trust. What makes his

research particularly disquieting is that this relationship holds up when controlling for every conceivable intervening demographic variable. Worse, not only is trust between groups ("bridging") lower with greater diversity but trust *within* groups ("bonding") is lower as well. The result is greater social isolation, what Putnam calls "hunkering down."

Given that openness to broad and often disorienting diversity of views is the very stuff that makes constructive disorientation possible, how can this apparent paradox be resolved? First, we need to be careful not to extrapolate Putnam's findings unduly. His unit of analysis was whole communities and the focus was on ethnic diversity only, so generalizing to smaller social groups and other forms of diversity is shaky, at best. Still, Putnam's data should raise important cautions about creating social capital in the service of deep learning. For reasons that have been well explored by others, ethnicity is a different kind of difference and presents different kinds of challenges to group identity. These are challenges that can be overcome but cannot simply be brushed aside with naïve assumptions about the power of simple contact with difference. In our social lives, "trust has to be earned and remains limited and fragile" (Mercier & Sperber, 2017, p. 334).

- *Are open to the contributions of members.* Being open to the contributions of others refers to a willingness to suspend one's own beliefs and assumptions to make room for other voices. The guiding principle here is that everyone has something important to contribute, and one's own assumptions must be open to challenge, as difficult as this might be to do. Being open to others' contributions recalls Dewey's ([1938] 1997) point about the importance of dialogue with others as a weapon against "mis-education," and Mezirow's (2000) point that openness to others' perspectives is the key to resolution of disorienting dilemmas. "Openness" is not necessarily a passive quality, as those facilitating social capital will sometimes have to intervene to ensure that all voices are heard, or to take a stand against group consensus that is emerging too quickly (Preskill & Brookfield, 2009). Still, "when the overriding concern of people who disagree is to get things right, argumentation should not only make them change their mind, it should make them change their mind for the best" (Mercier & Sperber, 2017, p. 307).

- *Expect to be accountable to others.* As with group diversity, the role of accountability is complex. Psychologist Philip Tetlock, an expert on the subject, defines accountability in its simplest form as "pressure to justify one's views to another" (Lerner & Tetlock, 2003, p. 432). Tetlock's research indicates that "when people know in advance that they'll have to explain themselves, they think more systematically and self-critically" (Haidt, 2012, p. 88). Without group norms that hold people accountable to others, however, trust falls apart and the group is drained of its social capital. We all remember the infamous "group projects" from our college days, with the inevitable slackers who refused to pull their own weight – and how the work then fell to more conscientious students who made sure that at least their *individual* efforts would be recognized. But here is where the role of accountability becomes more complex: According to Tetlock's research, accountability only leads to an increase in social capital when the group knows in advance that it will be accountable to an external audience (a) whose views are unknown, (b) who is believed to be interested in accuracy, (c) who appears to be well-informed, and (d) who has a legitimate reason for asking for justification (Lerner & Tetlock, 2003). Consistent with Mercier and Sperber's (2017) research, at other times accountability pressures only encourage arguments aimed at persuasion.

The importance of social capital as a resource for deep learning is cross-cultural and cross-sector, noted not only in North America, Western Europe, and Australia, but also in Asia and Africa (cf. Moody, 2019; Okeke, 2018; Wang et al., 2019).

6.3 Participatory Forms of Engagement and Learning

In the last chapter I wrote about the power of informal and intuitive learning, learning that happens in the moment, often unconsciously. It is becoming increasingly clear that this learning is more powerful in settings that are more inclusive and democratic, and have more social diversity (Yorks, 2005). Current leadership theories are certainly moving in this direction. James McGregor Burns (1978), in his seminal work more than 40 years ago, wrote that leadership is both a relational and a collective process. Burns' book was one of the first to describe the shift from a "command and control" vision of leadership to one that is more inclusive and participatory. In his discussion of "transformative leadership," Burns suggested that by focusing on shared goals and values, leaders and followers would raise one another to higher levels of motivation and morality and thus engage in a conscious transformation process. As is true of many seminal ideas, Burns' notions of transformative leadership have often been hijacked by organizational leaders and used in ways he never intended, namely to attempt to "transform" the organization in a mostly unilateral fashion.

Still, Burns' work has been followed by many others'[4] who have called for a shift in perspective about leadership: from hierarchical to lateral, from command-and-control to participatory, from heroic to team-oriented, and from mechanistic to organic.

Despite these trends, organizations continue to pose significant barriers to deep learning. Taking time to build lateral, participatory, team-oriented, organic networks runs counter to traditional Western values of production and efficiency. The question is: Beyond developing empathy and social capital, how can one create this sort of social space, what Bill Torbert (2004) calls "liberating structures," which encourage forms of social interaction that lead to deep learning? How might this generative social space support cycles of action and reflection, where participants are free to reflect critically on their knowledge perspectives, listen to the diverse perspectives of others, follow the disorientation, and try new knowledge perspectives on for size?

There are two completely different, but potentially complementary, ways to do this, one through intervention, the other through cultivation.

6.3.1 Social Learning Through Action Learning

The most common form of creating social learning through intervention is action learning, discussed in Chapter 4. To recap, action learning brings together a group to address "wicked problems" (as originally conceived by Rittel and Webber (2017) in the early 1970s to describe issues riddled with difficulties and complexities), of the sort that Heifetz (1994) refers to as "adaptive challenges." A cross-functional group with minimal background knowledge comes together to ask fresh questions about the problem, questions that those in the middle of it might not think to ask. This group, or "set," takes on the role of Vaill's "reflective beginner" (1996), collecting needed information, challenging assumptions – including those about what the problem is – and engaging in collaborative learning, resulting presumably in creative approaches to the problem. Action learning has been used most extensively in the United Kingdom, particularly in the National Health Service, but variations of it have been implemented all over the world.[5]

Adult educator Lyle Yorks (2005) has provided a particularly illuminating case study of the benefits and challenges of action learning, which he calls a "collaborative action inquiry." Undertaken by the US Department of Veterans Affairs (VA), a diverse group of practitioners, professionals, and staff at all levels, came together with an interdisciplinary group of

6.3 Participatory Forms of Engagement and Learning

academics to address issues of workplace stress and aggression. In addition to coming up with workable strategies to address these issues, explicit attention was given to the learning process, specifically how to create the social space that would allow this diverse and often skeptical mix of people to learn together. Several key insights relevant to participant engagement and deep learning emerged from this case study, consistent with the empirical research on the effectiveness of action learning in other contexts:

1. *The diversity of knowledge perspectives brought to a group-learning project brings forth both positive and negative energy, leading to a tension that must be managed carefully.* The more varied these perspectives are, the potentially richer and deeper the learning will be. However, organizational, disciplinary, and personal differences can threaten this learning if the experience of having a shared goal is lost. As Yorks (2005) observed:

    > Holding the inquiry together at its core is the growing realization that generating meaningful actionable knowledge requires learning from each other in a way that synergistically creates knowledge and meaning, transcending the additive combination of contributions from the various distinct areas of practice. Learning, as the key to realizing the shared goal of making the VA a better place to work, is the countervailing force holding the project together. (pp. 1229–1230)

2. *One cannot assume that discussion will lead naturally to dialogue.* Conversations will be marked initially by advocacy of participants' own points of view. This was clear in the case study. Early team meetings were characterized by "tense negotiations" about such issues as data validity, project control, time and place, and role separation.

    > Underlying these tensions were more fundamental issues of purpose and visions of what would constitute a successful project, diverse motivations for participating, and the confrontation between deeply held worldviews about what constitutes meaningful knowledge, how it can be generated, and what would be required to have it taken seriously by various audiences both within the organization and among broader publics. (pp. 1232–1233)

As Michael Newman (2014) has noted, conventional discussion is a "sharing of monologues," moving from statement to statement, locking us into the present, and discouraging speculation. Dialogue, on the other hand, is "a form of collective, and generative inquiry," where "an individual's point of view is valuable if it extends the group's understanding of the object of thought, which is not the view of any one person" (p. 349).

3. *Because of Points 1 and 2 above, participants will first need to learn how to learn together.* Recognizing this, Yorks (2005) and his colleagues sought to introduce several "learning practices" into the project such as reflection and dialogue, the "learning window," the "ladder of inference," and various methods for "harvesting the learning." The learning window, for example,

> is a metaphor that asks participants to carefully differentiate between "what they know they know" (with reference to their data for making this claim and obtaining consensual validation of this claim from others), "what they think they know" (and how they can test these inferences through actions and data), and, based on actions, data, and reflection, "what they know they don't know" (and need to learn effectively to address the issue). (pp. 1230–1231)[6]

4. *Successful group learning is marked by a qualitative shift in the nature of the conversation, a signal that true dialogue is taking place.* Yorks' study participants described this as a "threshold," a "sense among team members of inhabiting collaborative space … a liberating structure that is both productive and educative" (p. 1232), "where the learning practices had become tacit and part of their natural way of working together" (p. 1234). One cannot expect however that participants will all walk together through some kind of transformative portal, never to regress to their pre-collaborative states. Instead, the group learning space is fragile, "simultaneously stressful and energizing," and "subject to disruption by strong personalities and situational forces" (p. 1234). This point reinforces my earlier one about the nature of trust in social groups, hard to develop and easily lost.

6.3.2 Social Learning Through Communities of Practice

"Communities of practice," a term popularized by learning theorist Etienne Wenger (1998), are, most simply, groups of people who "spontaneously select themselves to develop capabilities and to build and exchange knowledge" (Manuti, Impedovo, & de Palma, 2017, p. 219). Thus, whereas variants of action learning are interventionist, and based on "outside-in" approaches, communities of practice are groups formed naturally, unconstrained by organizational or functional boundaries, purely on the basis of common professional interests. Learning occurs from the "inside-out," in the form of "mutual engagement, a sense of joint enterprise, and a shared repertoire of communal resources" (Manuti et al., 2017, p. 219). Thus, in contrast to an action learning team, group norms are not imposed or

6.3 Participatory Forms of Engagement and Learning

prescribed, but rather are based on relationships inside the community formed around a practice. As Wenger (2000) notes, communities of practice have been part of human civilization for hundreds, even thousands of years, in various forms, such as guilds of potters, masons, carpenters, and others. Today these communities take the form of informal networks – online groups of scientists discussing latest development in particle physics, for example. More to the purposes of this book, communities of practice exist as elements of "social learning systems," which Wenger defines this way:

> Knowing is a matter of displaying competences defined in social communities. The picture is more complex and dynamic than that, however. Our experience of life and the social standards of competence of our communities are not necessarily, or even usually, congruent. We each experience knowing in our own ways. Socially defined competence is always in interplay with our experience. It is in this interplay that learning takes place. (Wenger, 2000, p. 226)

John Dewey would be nodding in agreement, were he alive today.

Within social communities is where we become competent, following the process of expertise development, as discussed in Chapter 5. But the *boundaries* of these social communities, where competence interacts with experience, are where we experience constructive disorientation, and, thus, where we learn deeply.

Recall my earlier discussion of the importance of social capital as a key facilitator to learning with others. Communities of practice are fueled and held together by social capital, and thus can serve to both encourage and inhibit deep learning. "Communities of practice cannot be romanticized," Wenger (2000) writes. "They are born of learning, but they can also learn not to learn. They are cradles of the human spirit, but can also be its cages" (p. 230). Three elements of a community of practice are key to maintaining its vitality as a social learning system:

1. *Enterprise: the level of learning energy.* How much initiative does the community take in keeping learning at the center of its enterprise?
2. *Mutuality: the depth of social capital.* How deep is the sense of community generated by mutual engagement over time?
3. *Repertoire: the degree of self-awareness.* How self-conscious is the community about the repertoire it is developing and its effects on its practice? (Wenger, 2000)

Communities of practice, because they coexist within and across formal organizational structures, have sometimes been viewed as an irritant to organizational purposes. In colleges and universities, for example, faculty communities of practice routinely chafe at the latest administrative initiative, and university leaders routinely cite "faculty resistance" as a thorn in their sides. Organizational leaders would do well to take Wenger's advice to heart: "[They] need to learn to foster and participate in social learning systems, both inside and outside organizational boundaries. Social learning systems are not defined by, congruent with, or cleanly encompassed in organizations. Organizations can take part in them; they can foster them; they can leverage them; but they cannot fully own or control them" (Wenger, 2000, p. 243).

6.4 Minimal Power Differentials

With this fourth and final key facilitator of learning in groups I introduce a topic so important – the politics of learning – that I devote an entire chapter to it, to follow. One of the findings of the case study described in the preceding section was the struggle among participants to make sure that previous roles demarking organizational or professional hierarchies were left at the door of the meeting room, giving an equal voice to everyone. Just as deep learning requires overcoming the impulse to rely on intuitive theories and to defend entrenched beliefs, it also requires the ability to overcome hegemonic assumptions, including expectations of deference to authority, whether conscious or unconscious.

As I have noted previously, hegemonic assumptions are typically deep-seated and highly resistant to change. Just as simple exposure to diversity does not guarantee an increase in social capital, gaining a seat at the table does not guarantee a reduction in power differential. Two of my doctoral students have extensive experience working to empower urban African American communities, one in Richmond, Virginia and one in Miami, Florida. Both have shared the same story with me: initial access to an essentially White power structure was through community representation on a citywide commission or board. These new Black members felt silenced and intimidated, while existing members could not understand why they didn't speak up. Both groups were trapped by hegemonic assumptions: the Black community representatives by internalized oppression leading to a habit of deference to White power structures and the lack of tools that would help them negotiate what to them was a foreign culture; the existing White members by the false assumption that the new members would know what to do and how to act. Each of these groups would have benefitted by the "learning practices" described in the case study above.

A principal reason why diversity efforts have such a spotty record is the insufficient attention paid to the stubbornness of hegemonic assumptions. Establishing a chief diversity officer or a center for multicultural affairs will not do it. Neither will diversifying the ranks of professional staff, although that is an important first step. Neither will so-called "diversity audits" of organizational policies and practices, as necessary as these may be. There are no quick fixes here. What is needed are more safe spaces for engaging in sustained dialogue – not a single conversation or one-off professional development programs, but space for "thoughtfully listening, expressing compassion, and engaging in a long-term relationship with people who are disenchanted, yet committed to seeing change" (Gigliotti, Dwyer, & Ruiz-Mesa, 2018).

There is a role here for critical theory, the notion that power relationships are endemic and self-reinforcing, and that systemic corrective action is necessary. According to critical theory, including a more diverse array of voices in an organization may simply reinforce existing forms of domination (Alvesson & Spicer, 2014), exemplified by the two personal experiences I described above. Addressing the power imbalance requires affirming participants' voices by explicitly surfacing power relations, and focusing on participants' potential in the organization (Chandler & Kirsch, 2018). But even this may not be enough: if institutional structures and norms remain the same then any change may be merely cosmetic.

I should admit at this point that while I admire the perspective critical theory has brought to the study of social and organizational change, I am more pragmatist than ideologue. I am more attracted to approaches that say, in effect, "Yes, we know that power inequalities will hinder our ability to learn from one another … so let's develop strategies that not only recognize this problem but strive to mitigate it."

Strategies designed to mitigate power differentials will take different forms, depending on the context and purpose of the intended learning. Interventionist approaches of the action learning variety must meet hegemonic assumptions head-on, while the cultivation of social learning systems such as communities of practice calls for more subtle approaches, embedded in reflection on practice.

Regarding the former, management scholar Russ Vince (2004) has noted that while action learning groups are often "safe havens for individuals to reflect on projects and problems," their own isolation makes them "disconnected from action related to questioning established assumptions and the politics and power relations through which such assumptions were enacted" (p. 74). Unless these hegemonic assumptions are addressed through destabilization of contradictory power relations (Vince, 2012), true organizational learning is unlikely. Vince's point is of critical importance. Work of any learning group that seeks to catalyze larger organizational change must recognize that such change will inevitably involve shifting power relationships, and that these do not occur easily or without conflict.

A form of action learning called *critical* action learning addresses this challenge squarely by making conscious those power relations that have previously been unconscious and thus unavailable to notice. As Vince (Vince, Abbey, & Langenham, 2018) put it, "[whereas] action learning encourages people to tackle important organizational or social challenges and learn from their attempts to improve things, critical action learning additionally connects with the emotions and power relations that both *promote and prevent* people's attempts to learn and improve things" (p. 86, emphasis added). An action learning set is the place to surface unconscious power relationships: As participants are put into a destabilizing political environment, where their usual ways of working are no longer tacit or intuitive, the resulting discomfort and "social friction" (Warwick, McCray, & Board, 2017) provides an opportunity to create constructive disorientation. Note how such a setting can, with some work, meet all of the criteria necessary for disorientation to be constructive: first, the action learning set is given a problem that requires not a technical solution but adaptive learning; second, members of the set experience the three elements necessary for intrinsic motivation, namely autonomy, efficacy, and relatedness. Members will feel autonomous motivation if the presenting problem sparks their curiosity and working on it is consistent with their internalized organizational values. They will feel efficacious if they have reason to believe that their work will have a positive impact. And they will have a sense of relatedness if they feel a connection to others in their set and feel that they have a significant role to play. This last criterion may be the most difficult one to meet, as it requires developing the necessary social capital. Recall the four necessary requirements for social capital: a common bond, intellectual and ideological diversity, openness to contributions of others, and presumed accountability. The third of these, openness to others' contributions, is the one most vulnerable to existing power differentials, and this is where skills of the group facilitator become most critical, making sure that all voices are heard and contributions noted.

In sum, an action learning set, or something like it, can be a safe space to explore new ideas and try out new identities while also bounding that space with organizational norms, expectations, and accountabilities. The combination of an adaptive problem with the right kind of motivation creates constructive disorientation, as long as previously unconscious power relationships are uncovered and dealt with. Critical reflection on these and other assumptions can lead to the adoption of new knowledge perspectives and development of new expertise.

Dealing with power dynamics in communities of practice is a bit of a different story. The power differentials are of two kinds here: within the community and at its boundaries with other communities. Within-community politics are typically matters of expert versus nonexpert power, as novices in the practice attempt to develop competence to equal that of the masters. These novices of course also enter the community with fresh ideas, thus setting up conflict with the presumed holders of the expertise. But if there is an acknowledgment of this tension, and clear recognition in the group of the contribution by both old and new members, the potential exists for those with greater expertise to, in effect, provide the sort of Vygotskian scaffolding that will help those with less expertise develop their own professional identities (Pemberton, Mavin, & Stalker, 2017).

The challenge of minimizing power differentials in communities of practice takes on a different form at the boundaries of these practices, where opportunities exist for learning with *other* communities. The opportunity for transformative learning is greater at the intersections of professional communities than within them; but whether these engagements turn out well or badly depends on how power relationships are negotiated. A good example of this is a study reporting on how different medical specialties in Norway needed to come together to learn the technique of laparoscopy (or "keyhole surgery"), a procedure that requires a significantly different skillset of the general surgeon (Mørk, Hoholm, Ellingsen, Edwin, & Aanestad, 2010). One of their main findings was that "in such a transition process mastery changes from being based mainly on past merits, to being based increasingly on the ability to continuously learn new practices, mobilize arguments and build networks" (p. 576). Echoing Vaill's (1996) point that true experts have to see themselves as "reflective beginners," Mørk and his colleagues (2010) write that "in a very basic sense everyone was reduced to apprentice status because they all had to explore and learn what the new practice could come to be. In innovation processes, knowledge and practice need to be constantly explored, tested and negotiated" (p. 589).

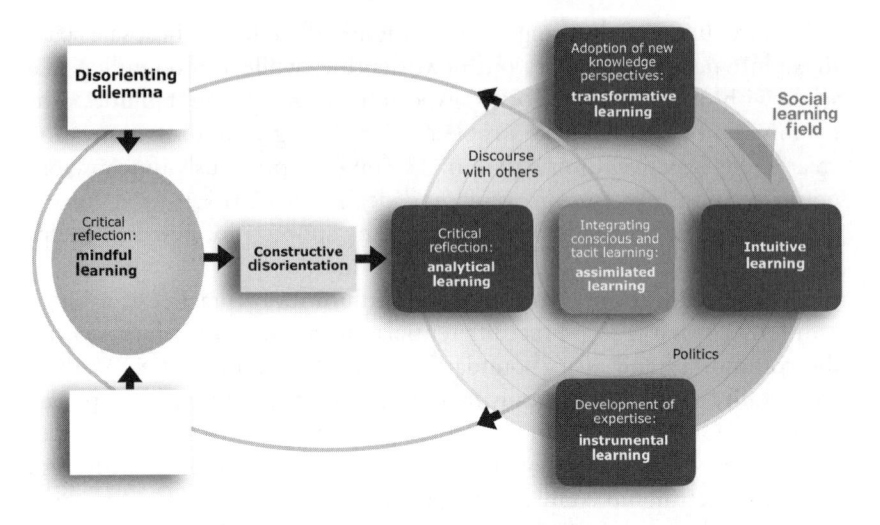

Figure 6.1 The deep learning mindset, including the social learning field

6.5 Summary

In this chapter I have tried to make the case for the critical importance of social interaction to deep learning. While acknowledging the dangers of social and professional groups as potential barriers to deep learning, stemming from the lack of diversity in the group, "groupthink," and failure to acknowledge hegemonic differences, I also presented four ways in which deep learning can be facilitated: by promoting empathy, developing social capital, encouraging participatory forms of engagement, and minimizing (or directly confronting) differentials of power. I have focused on social learning in smaller, bounded groups. But what about the larger and far more complex social system of an organization or an entire society? How does the politics of learning work at the macro level?

In the addition to the model of a deep learning mindset I now add the field in which social learning occurs, composed of both group discourse and politics (see Figure 6.1), the subject of the next chapter.

Notes

1 My thanks to Norman Dale for this reference.
2 Cf. Preston & de Waal (2002).

3 Mercier and Sperber (2017) provide a comprehensive review of this research in chapter 15 of their book.
4 Notably, the work of Ron Heifetz, already cited extensively in this book.
5 Evidence for this can be found by browsing through the journal *Action Learning: Theory and Practice*.
6 Yorks cites as the source of the learning window T. A. Stewart's *Intellectual Capital: The New Wealth of Organizations* (1997). I am probably not the only one who, reading this passage, was reminded of former US Secretary of State Donald Rumsfeld's notorious distinction between "known knowns," "known unknowns," and "unknown unknowns."

CHAPTER 7

The Influence of Politics on Deep Learning

Conflicts are the midwife of consciousness.

Paulo Freire

If constructive disorientation is the spark for deep learning, critical reflection the engine, and social discourse the fuel, then politics is the lubricant. Just as the lack of motor oil will freeze up an engine, the lack of conscious attention to political dynamics will freeze up the space for deep learning. How does small-scale learning lead, or not, to organizational learning? Politics. How do innovative, potentially disruptive, ideas become adopted, or not, by the larger organization? Politics.

It is astonishing to me how, until very recently, politics and learning, especially at the organizational level, were rarely discussed together. Peter Senge (2006) in his book on organizational learning barely mentions "politics" at all; and as recently as 2003, in an otherwise excellent manual on action learning, the authors advise against group members dealing with "politically sensitive" issues (Dilworth & Willis, 2003). Popular books on leadership and organizational change, on the other hand, take politics very seriously – Ron Heifetz and his colleagues, for example, devote an entire chapter to it (Heifetz et al., 2009), as does Oxford's recent handbook on leadership and organizations (Day, 2014). In this chapter I want to bring the neglected relationship between politics and learning front and center.

In Chapter 6, I introduced politics at a micro level, by writing about the need to deal with power differences in learning groups. In this chapter I look at the role of politics in learning with a much broader sweep. I begin with a brief review of how the avoidance and dismissal of conflicting views has soiled civic discourse, and how some of the barriers to deep learning discussed in Chapter 1 can explain this. I then revisit the topic of transformative learning, and extend its focus beyond personal growth and development to how it can be a means to transform organizations and the larger society. I then return to John Dewey's thoughts on learning and democracy, and reimagine his thinking as it might apply to the world we live in today. Finally, I bring everything back around, from society at large to people and organizations, and consider how making explicit the power of politics can enhance the potential of deep learning.

First I should be clear about what exactly I mean by "politics." As the reader may have inferred from my use of the term in the previous chapter, I do not mean the general definition of politics (*politicá*) used by the ancient Greeks, that is how communities go about making decisions for their members. My use of the term is in a narrower and more academic sense, denoting how that process actually works: Politics is group conflict over limited resources, whether real or perceived, leading to the use and manipulation of power.[1]

Societies, just like people, can't have everything. Some resources are clearly finite, such as natural resources and various forms of capital. Others, such as the flow of information, can be *made* scarce by those who have an interest in protecting them. The real or perceived scarcity of resources sets up competition among those persons or groups who have an interest in getting more of these resources, and conflict is resolved by wielding various forms of power, whether coercive or more subtly through social norms. Any action is political, therefore, when it threatens to disturb the current balance of power. Democratic elections are, obviously, highly political; but so are virtually all organizational decisions that involve distribution of resources or benefits.

Consider for a moment, then, how deep learning can be a political act.

Deep learning changes one's perspective on how the world works and, by extension, how one should be in the world. This shift in perspective, brought about by resolving constructive disorientation in the presence of others, will include insights about needed changes from the status quo, which, when acted upon, will create disturbance in prevailing power relationships. Imagine this scenario:

> A young woman has been raised in a male-dominated culture where women are treated largely as chattel and sending them to school beyond the early grades is frowned upon. Her father has moved to another country and has come to realize that he wants a better life for his daughter. He sends for her, enrolls her in school, and supports her education. The young woman grows to appreciate the impacts of oppression in her native country, and vows to work to change the system.

Granted, this is a particularly dramatic example, but it is also a true story, a single instance of how educational resources are routinely withheld from women as a way of maintaining power over them. It is not difficult to think of other, more quotidian examples, such as those cited in the last chapter of workgroups that, having discovered strategies to approach complex problems, only find implementation blocked by the powers that be. Whenever new knowledge threatens to disturb the existing political equilibrium, learning becomes a political act.

7.1 Politics, Social Discourse, and Deep Learning

Recall from Figure 1.1 in Chapter 1 the multiple ways in which sources of intuitive beliefs lead to myside bias, belief persistence, and attitude polarization. Four of these cognitive traps are especially pernicious in politics, large and small.

First is what Brafman and Brafman (2008) call "diagnosis bias," a blindness to all evidence that that contradicts initial assessment of a situation. A clear example is the stubborn insistence by the Bush administration in 2003 that Iraq possessed "weapons of mass destruction" as a pretext for invasion, in the face of clear evidence to the contrary. Diagnosis bias is a form of confirmation/myside bias, filtering out any information that is inconsistent with preexisting belief.

Second and third are these twin fears: *loss aversion*, the tendency to go to extreme lengths to avoid possible losses (Kahneman, 2011), and *exposure anxiety*, "a belief that failure to act in a manner perceived as firm will result in the weakening of one's position" (Shore, 2008, p. 221). In her classic book *The March of Folly*, historian Barbara Tuchman (1984) chronicles how governments since ancient times have so often acted in ways contrary to their self-interest, due to the "impotence of reason in the face of greed, selfish ambition, and cowardice" (quoted from dust jacket). (It seems almost gratuitous to note that Tuchman's book can be read profitably today.) While these monumental blunders, from Troy to Vietnam, are indeed full of greed, ambition, and cowardice, a more psychological perspective reveals plenty of evidence as well of loss aversion and exposure anxiety. President Lyndon Johnson fell prey to both of these cognitive traps when he capitulated to fear of loss by continuing to escalate the war in Vietnam, even though he had said this early on: "I don't think it's worth fighting for and I don't think we can get out" (quoted in Brafman & Brafman, 2008, p. 37). Political leaders, and humans in general, hate to look weak and will go to great lengths to save face, digging themselves into deeper and deeper holes in the process. Psychologist Daniel Kahneman put it this way: "To withdraw now is to accept a sure loss, and that option is deeply unattractive. The option of hanging on will therefore be relatively attractive, even if the chances of success are small and the cost of delaying failure is high" (Kahneman & Renshon, 2007, p. 38). These three irrational forces function as psychological defense mechanisms, protecting the individual from potential embarrassment. They interact with the fourth irrational force, *reductive thinking*, which oversimplifies complex situations into "mental sound bites" (Shore, 2008, p. 211). As I noted in Chapter 1, humans are constitutionally uncomfortable with ambiguity and will avoid it whenever possible. Clever politicians know this instinctively and use it to their advantage in speeches, TV ads, and Twitter and Facebook postings.

Consider for a moment how the term "diversity" has, due to reductive thinking, become laden with political connotations on college campuses and organizations in general. As I explained in Chapter 6, group diversity *may or may not* lead to deep learning and yet, depending on one's political leanings, diversity is either a means to social justice, important enough to justify speech codes and "centers for diversity excellence," or a tool to muzzle conservative voices and create cultures of victimization.[2] An avoidance of reductive thinking would lead to a more difficult but accurate appraisal: that group diversity is absolutely necessary for meaningful learning, but simple contact with difference is not enough and can make people even more tribal. Colleges therefore need to create more spaces for honest conversations and multiple points of view, rather than assume that problems caused by encounters with the "Other" require more administrators and regulations.

Thus, irrational forces work to inhibit deep learning in institutions and organizations, not just in the larger body politic. Recall from the discussion of constructive disorientation in Chapter 4 that more-than-optimal levels of anxiety will inhibit deep learning or prevent it entirely. Diagnosis bias, loss aversion, and exposure anxiety are all evidence of someone having dug in their heels, and at that point dislodging beliefs that have these strong emotional ties will be extremely difficult. The trick, therefore, is to keep these defenses from kicking in in the first place, by keeping the learning challenge at manageable levels.

Here is what makes doing this a political activity. First and most obviously, we must recognize how psychological defense mechanisms can and are being used for political purposes. Combining diagnosis bias, loss aversion and exposure anxiety with reductive thinking is a toxic mix. Second, deep learning is fundamentally social; learning in the presence of others requires creating an atmosphere of trust, or social capital. The greater the social capital, the greater the potential for *political* capital, that is, the degree of influence one has over others. Political capital is a scarce resource and must be spent wisely. I will come back to some ideas about how to do this later in the chapter.

7.2 Deep Learning as Political Consciousness

In an earlier chapter I wrote about the "rationalist delusion," a product of the worship of reason in Western philosophy. If reasoning is our most noble attribute, the logic goes, then by extension those who reason best should have the most power (Haidt, 2012). This notion, however, was debunked centuries ago by Aristotle:

> Now if arguments were in themselves good enough to make men good, they would justly ... have won very great rewards ... But as things are ... they are not able to encourage the many to nobility and goodness ... What argument would remold such people? It is hard, if not impossible, to remove by argument the traits that have long since been incorporated in the character. (Aristotle, *Nicomeachean Ethics*, 1179, quoted in Sloman & Fernbach, 2017, p. 77)

Opening a space for deep learning thus requires more than logical reasoning, as I've argued throughout this book. Some disturbance is necessary, and often this disturbance must take the form of political action. Several influential thinkers from the late twentieth century held this view, including emancipatory educator Paulo Freire (Brazil), "folk school" founder Myles Horton (United States), and philosopher Michael Foucault (France). I will profile each of them in turn and discuss how their ideas might be applied to creating a space for deep learning.

Paulo Freire is widely regarded as the founder of "critical pedagogy." He believed that formal education serves to replicate the dominant culture, where it is taken for granted that, because educators have all the relevant knowledge, their role is to bestow that knowledge on people who know nothing (Freire, 1970). By promulgating the dominant narrative, education is an insidious force that keeps oppressed people unaware of their own oppression. Children grow up to believe that this is just how things are supposed to be. Freire's central idea is "conscientization," a process by which people are made more aware of their oppression and its sources, thus providing a counter-narrative that will empower transformation of society, vs. adaptation to the status quo. "No pedagogy [that] is truly liberating can remain distant from the oppressed by treating them as unfortunates and by presenting for their emulation models from among the oppressors," he wrote. "The oppressed must be their own example in the struggle for their

7.2 Deep Learning as Political Consciousness

redemption" (Freire, 1970, p. 5). Conscientization presupposes a group dialogue characterized by perceived equality and mutual trust and respect among participants, and is achieved through *praxis*, which for Freire is critical reflection on one's own condition, comparing that condition with alternatives, and then acting on the new awareness and using it to transform oppressive structures. "People have the right to know better than they already know," he said. "Knowing better means precisely going beyond the *common sense* in order to begin to discover the *reason* for the facts" (Horton & Freire, 1990, p. 157, emphasis in original). Because action changes reality, it is therefore itself subject to further critical reflection. In this sense Freire's thinking is much in line with empirical research on critical reflection and experiential learning.

Myles Horton founded Highlander Folk School (now the Highlander Research and Education Center) in the mountains of eastern Tennessee in 1932. Unlike Freire, who left behind a large body of scholarly writing, Horton's written record is sparse, consisting mostly of stories and anecdotes. He preferred to work outside the formal "schooling system," as he called it. But the two men had much in common. Like Freire, Horton rejected the notion that education could be politically neutral, maintaining that "neutrality is just being what the system asks us to be … you've got to take sides" (Horton & Freire, 1990, p. 102). Also like Freire, Horton faced violent opposition to his work, much of it directed to him personally, especially during the McCarthy era of the 1950s and the civil rights movement of the 1960s. Both men grew up in the poorest regions of their countries, where their childhood experiences shaped both their political philosophies and their approaches to education. Both also devoted their careers to using education as a tool to fight oppression. Freire took a post-Marxist approach, convinced that the very structures of society needed to be changed: "It is possible to convert individuals of the ruling class, but never the ruling class as a class" (Horton & Freire, 1990, p. 190). Horton was more like John Dewey, believing that social structures could be changed from within, through creation of a society that lived up to its democratic ideals.

More to the purpose of this book, both Horton and Freire believed that change, driven by effective political organizing, must begin with the wisdom of the people, and then stretching this wisdom with new information. For Freire this was accomplished through *praxis*; for Horton it was by asking questions:

> I use questions [in my work with people] more than anything else … I don't think of a question as intervening because [people] don't realize that the

> reason you asked that question is because you know something. What you know is the body of the material that you're trying to get people to consider, but instead of giving a lecture on it, you ask a question enlightened by that. Instead of you getting on a pinnacle you put them on a pinnacle. (Horton & Freire, 1990, p. 146)

Horton also realized the difficulty in knowing just how far to stretch people's thinking: that is, finding the delicate balance between bringing out the knowledge of the people and going beyond that knowledge. "This is a problem that has always bothered me, [namely] how far you could go in stretching people's experience without breaking the thread" (p. 154).

Thus, both Freire's and Horton's views on, respectively, critical reflection and (what I call) constructive disorientation are consistent with current research on adult learning. Especially noteworthy is that these views came about through direct experience and reflection on that experience, rather than theory. In Freire's case reflection led to theorizing, while for Horton it led to more informed educational practice.

Philosopher Michel Foucault wrote about many things in his foreshortened but brilliant and influential career, but what he is probably best known for is his analysis of power-knowledge with its implications for how individuals must struggle against the many, concealed ways in which dominant organizational knowledge controls them. He wrote about both institutional power and the (often unconscious) power we give others. Like Freire, Foucault believed that people learn to obey authority through the knowledge it sanctions (and does not), and thus young people must develop a consciousness about power/knowledge connections. As one of the early postmodern theorists, Foucault rejected the notion that power is always institutional and hierarchical and vested in formal structures. Instead, power is decentralized and pluralistic, and therefore can be a force for both repression *and* emancipation – in the latter sense by people realizing that they do not have to let themselves be defined by the formal structures around them: "What makes power hold good, what makes it accepted, is simply the fact that it doesn't only weigh on us as a force that says no, but that it traverses and produces things, it induces pleasure, forms knowledge, produces discourse" (Foucault, 1980, p. 119).

Foucault had similar postmodern thoughts about the nature of "truth," which for him was seldom if ever absolute:

> Truth isn't the reward of free spirits, the child of protracted solitude, nor the privilege of those who have succeeded in liberating themselves. Truth is a thing of this world ... and it induces regular effects of power. Each society has its regime of truth, its "general politics" of truth: that is, the

7.2 Deep Learning as Political Consciousness

types of discourse which it accepts and makes function as true … [Thus,] by truth I do not mean the "ensemble of truths which are to be discovered and accepted," but rather the ensemble of rules according to which the true and the false are separated and the specific effects of power attached to the true. (pp. 131–132)

In other words, Foucault dismissed positivist notions that hard objective facts are "out there" waiting to be discovered. Societies construct rules on what is to be considered "true" and what is not.

And finally, Foucault believed that "it is impossible for power to be exercised without knowledge; it is impossible for knowledge not to engender power" (p. 52). He was also quick to point out that we can also let bodies of knowledge *define us*, particularly in the human sciences, which on the surface may seem to be sources of objective truth but in fact dictate how we should think of ourselves and what we should do.

Foucault developed his ideas by taking the thought of ancient philosophers and applying them to modern problems as he saw them, rather than looking to modern science. As such, the value of his thinking for understanding and encouraging deep learning lies in the questions he invites us to ask – fresh questions about some of the most basic assumptions we use to rule our lives. How can we use the power within us, not just to resist oppression and better position ourselves, but also to produce consequential knowledge – knowledge that carries its own power – and a healthier discourse? How might we accept and deal with multiple, even conflicting, "truths"? How do we avoid becoming imprisoned by the elaborate and highly developed knowledge structures that we have built for ourselves?

So how do the ideas of these three intellects, from different cultures and life perspectives (Foucault, unlike Freire and Horton, grew up in a comfortable middle-class environment), come together to help us understand how to use politics in the service of deep learning, to go beyond the individual to broader and deeper organizational learning?

First, learning is itself political, because what is important to learn has been determined through political means – not just in the most obvious sense, such as local school boards deciding what students should read and not read, but much more subtly as well.

Second is the importance of disruption as a means for creating space for critical reflection on assumptions. The disruption must be intentional, and calibrated.

Third is the need to challenge existing truths, understanding that these truths may be so embedded in one's life perspective as to be unconscious, even unquestioned.

Fourth is the understanding that one of these existing truths for nearly everyone is an entire set of assumptions about power: who has it and what can be done with it. A key challenge to these assumptions must be that "empowerment" is not something that must be won but is there already.

And fifth is the message that enlightenment is not enough. Enlightenment must lead to action, and action has consequences, good and bad, which must be reflected upon if further learning is to occur.

7.3 Recasting Dewey

Elsewhere in this book I have discussed John Dewey's ideas as they relate to human learning: in short, his belief that learning is achieved by reflecting critically on one's experience, in the presence of others having divergent views. Dewey believed that both children and adults learn most effectively and most deeply this way – and as we have seen, Dewey's thinking has been backed up by decades of empirical research. Dewey wrote about "education" in the traditional sense – formal education – but always in the context of education as a way of life, as a cornerstone of democracy. Democracy will survive and flourish, he believed, only when citizens develop inquiry into their experience as a habit of mind and free themselves from what he called "dogmatic thinking" (Dewey, 1981). Here is his oft-quoted definition of democracy:

> Since a democratic society repudiates the principle of external authority, it must find a substitute in voluntary disposition and interest; these can be created only by education. A democracy is more than a form of government; it is primarily a mode of associated living, of conjoint, communicated experience. The extension in space of the number of individuals who participate in an interest so that each has to refer his own action to that of others, and to consider the action of others to give point and direction to his own, is equivalent to the breaking down of those barriers of class, race, and national territory which [have] kept [people] from perceiving the full import of their activity. (p. 87)

To say that these words, composed more than a century ago, have resonance today is a vast understatement. Let us take a moment to unpack this passage. Democratic societies do not obey any external authority, including, presumably, religion. Democracies do not exist as faraway government institutions, but rather in the daily business of life. Successful democracies require that people learn to understand their own beliefs and actions, to reflect nondefensively on these in the presence of others having different beliefs and experiences, and to use this "conjoint, communicated experience" to develop new understandings in the pursuit of the common good.

This last part of the definition is what gives learning such political heft. Dewey has been criticized by many for being naïve about the realities of political power; and while it is true that he viewed democracy as social rather than political in nature, he was not at all indifferent to power (Stark, 2014), as is evident by the many political causes he engaged in over the years. He was idealistic, yes, believing that proper education of individuals would lead to social improvement, the primary aim of a true democracy. But he also knew that the active engagement of a reflective citizenry is a constant challenge, one undertaken in the face of the forces of dogmatism. This is why he saw democracy as always unfinished, always as a process of understanding, through inquiry into collective experience. He had strong opinions on the perils of not doing so, as the following passage illustrates:

> There must be a large variety of shared understandings and experiences. Otherwise, the influences which educate some into masters, educate others into slaves. And the experience of each party loses in meaning, when the free interchange of varying modes of life experience is arrested. A separation into a privileged and subject-class prevents social endosmosis.[3] The evils thereby affecting the superior class are less material and less perceptible, but equally real. Their culture tends to be sterile, to be turned back to feed on itself; their art becomes a showy display and artificial; their wealth luxurious; their knowledge over-specialized; their manners fastidious rather than humane. (Dewey, 1981, p. 90)

Because Dewey saw education as the fundamental method leading to social progress and reform, he, like Freire and Horton, viewed education as a political act. Dewey mainly wrote about individuals and their place in the larger society, not about the power of reflective dialogue as a force for change in organizations; but I believe that a close reading of his work reveals five insights useful for understanding the politics of deep learning.

First is *the importance and power of inquiry as a way of life*, not just for the individual but for society as whole. Dewey often wrote about finding truth through "scientific inquiry," but not in the narrow, positivist way of determining objective "facts," as many of his critics have claimed, but rather, as the ultimate pragmatist he was, by using inquiry to uncover working explanations for the problems at hand, always subject to challenge, further reflection, and revision. Learning, therefore, is always about the process, not about the result (Stitzlein, 2014). Thus, perhaps counterintuitively, Dewey presaged critical theorists, believing, like Foucault, that all truth is contextual.

Second and relatedly, this process of *inquiry must be ongoing, resulting in new discoveries and rediscoveries, new organizations and reorganizations.* Neglecting this, the community will regress into what Dewey (1981) called "bourgeois democracy," a quasi-democracy where power rests in the hands of others. The takeaway here is that the mindful, continuous practice of Deweyan inquiry in an organization will inhibit the growth of a stifling bureaucracy.

Third, Dewey, as have so many others since, recognized *the importance of disturbance*, referring to these occasions as "openings for inquiry." A challenge to one's beliefs, he wrote, creates "a state of perplexity, hesitation, doubt" which in turn becomes the stimulus for critically reflective thought (Dewey, 1910, quoted in Stark, 2014, p. 93). This is why group diversity is so important (given the cautions noted in Chapter 6).

Fourth, Dewey (1933) was insistent on *the need for "open-mindedness" during inquiry*. He did not mean that one should simply resist rigidity in thinking; rather, "it is something more active and positive than these words suggest. It is very different [from] empty-mindedness … [It stems from] alert curiosity and spontaneous outreaching for the new" (p. 30). As I've indicated in previous chapters, open-mindedness is most likely when individuals and groups are in a state of constructive disorientation.

And fifth, Dewey insisted that group inquiry must *rely on honest dialogue*. He understood that the purpose of true democratic inquiry is not to eliminate conflict but to use it in a dialectical fashion to reach workable solutions for the community (Stark, 2014). By "dialectic" he meant neither formal debate nor consensus-building, but rather achieving agreement through *maieutic discussion* – that is, by asking a series of questions in a Socratic fashion, intended to surface participants' latent ideas into consciousness. With the proper facilitation, this model has the potential to be a uniquely powerful way of building respect and understanding (that is, social capital) among participants (Stark, 2014).

Gregory Fernando Pappas encapsulates the urgency of attending to Dewey's philosophy of learning and democracy today:

> Of all the problems of democracy, the one that strikes me as most urgent today is simply that democracy is not experienced as a task or problem. This happens when it is taken for granted, or worse, when many people have no ideal or sense of how things could be better. Without awareness that there is a crisis of democracy, there is not the felt, problematic situation that can lead to inquiry about how to ameliorate present conditions. (Pappas, 2008, quoted in Stitzlein, 2014, p. 61)

It might seem strange to think about John Dewey's notions about democracy within the confines of an organization: organizations are, obviously, not democracies. And I am not arguing here that they should be. The reason I have chosen to profile Dewey in this way (as I have Freire, Horton, and Foucault before him) is to suggest that *because* the very nature of organizations is to protect order and stability and avoid disruption (Uhl-Bien, 2018), the keys to deep learning that I have discussed until now – knowing oneself, creating space for constructive disorientation, engaging in critical reflection, and doing this in a diverse social space – can *all* be in place and deep learning still may not occur without political consciousness.

In this chapter I have profiled four men, all White males, albeit from different countries and with different worldviews; while true, both Freire and Horton well understood the forces of oppression and experienced it, and Horton himself was a mentor to Rosa Parks, an icon of the US civil rights movement, during her days at Highlander.

The issue is not simply one of giving a nod to other voices. That is not good enough. Adult education programs, even those designed to decrease inequalities, may instead have the opposite effect, namely one of "cumulative disadvantage" (Kilpi-Jakonen, Vono de Vilhena, & Blossfel, 2015). A key target of the Europe 2020 agenda of the European Commission has been to significantly increase participation rates in adult education, a worthy goal, but only if participation leads to the desired outcomes. In a study encompassing 13 countries, Kilpi-Jakonen and her colleagues (2015) explored the patterns of participation in adult learning activities and the consequences of this participation on career trajectories. While they noted substantial cross-national differences, they found that overall, "higher participation rates do not necessarily lead to lower social/educational inequalities in participation," that "those already better off in society are better able to access adult learning and tend to see greater benefits in career progress," and "therefore, additional efforts should be made to make adult learning more accessible to underrepresented groups, in particular those disadvantaged educationally and on the labour market" (p. 543). In short, inequalities in access lead to inequalities in learning.

The problem of social inequality and how to address it is huge – and well beyond the scope of this book. I hope however that the points raised in this chapter will stimulate more reflection on how learning, both individually and in organizations, has inescapable political overtones.

As I have done in previous chapters, I end this one with some thoughts on how explicit attention to political dynamics can make deep learning more likely, namely to: (1) identify existing systems of power relationships;

(2) surface unconscious assumptions about how learning is advantaged and disadvantaged by these relationships; (3) cultivate *parrèsia*, or the art of speaking truth to power; and (4) develop forms of procedural justice.

1. *Identifying existing systems of power relationships*, as fundamental as this is, may not be obvious when thinking about one's own learning or about how to create space for deep learning in others. Following Foucault's lead, we must ask some very basic questions right out of the gate: In what ways are the highly developed knowledge structures that we and others have developed over the years products of politically and culturally sanctioned "truths"? How do we recognize the ways in which accepted "truths" privilege some and disadvantage others? How is differential power related to differential access to learning in an organization? How can we help others recognize the power within themselves to engage the work required for deep learning?

2. *Surfacing unconscious assumptions*, as I've argued throughout this book, is a precondition to learning, an acceptance that something important is to be learned. Paradoxically perhaps, the more expert one becomes in a certain field the more likely one will become blind to the effects of existing power relationships (Warwick et al., 2017). Teams of people in organizations have ways of being and working that to them are unconscious and "natural" – what French sociologist Pierre Bourdieu (1977) called *habitus*. One's *habitus* should be understood as a predisposition to act, or sensitivity to ways of being, rather than the more common understanding of "habit" as an inclination to repeat identical acts. This distinction is key, because unlike the intractability of deep-seated beliefs, *habitus* is malleable, and under the right conditions – those of constructive disorientation – reflecting on the "figurations of power one is part of" (Warwick et al., 2017, p. 108), and how these configurations have privileged some forms of knowledge over others, can be powerful stimuli for deep learning.

3. In his discussion of when and how to speak truth to power, Foucault (2008) used the term *parrèsia*, an ancient Greek term for free-spokenness, to describe "a disciple's obligation to tell the master the truth of himself" (p. 47). Defining "truth" was always problematic for Foucault, because as I have noted he did not believe in truth in an absolute sense, but rather that what is "true" becomes accepted by "general politics" (his term) and human discourse. Those who speak their own truths emphasize their freedom as individuals. *Parrèsia*, therefore, is a particular way of telling the truth – it is not demonstration,

persuasion, teaching or debating. Rather, *parrèsia* is "situated in what binds the speaker to the fact that what he says is the truth, and to the consequences which follow from the fact that he has told the truth" (p. 56).[4] Accordingly, one must believe that speaking truth in the face of power will not be a futile exercise, but will contribute instead to human discourse. Those who wish to enhance deep learning in an organization will develop the social capital to potentially shift power relationships, allowing truth-telling that has lower social and political risk.

4. Brafman and Brafman (2008) use the term *procedural justice* to refer to humans' expectation to be treated fairly. They review empirical evidence that one's sense of justice is determined more by the process than the outcome, as counterintuitive as that may seem! Judging the fairness of the deal one gets in buying a car is determined as much or more by how the customer is treated than by the deal itself. Convicted felons' judgments of the fairness of their treatment by the courts is related more to the length of time their lawyers spent with them than on the length of their sentences (Casper et al., 2008, referenced in Brafman & Brafman, 2008). This notion of procedural justice means that when engaging in *parrèsia*, discourse will be facilitated when the emphasis is less on arguing the merits of the truths at hand, and more on talking through how these truths have been arrived at and communicating what in that organizational or cultural context is considered to be the "fair" way to proceed.

Attention to politics is essential to deep learning. Does this mean that deep learning is always political? No. Deep learning can be achieved in numerous ways, but always through mindful, critical reflection on experience. When the outcome of this reflection threatens to disturb the political equilibrium, deep learning becomes a political act.

There is one other way to disturb the personal and political equilibrium, and that is through the arts, the subject of the next chapter.

Notes

1 I picked up this definition many years ago and have long since forgotten its source.
2 As an example of the latter, see Will (2018).
3 Defined in the Merriam-Webster Dictionary as "passage of a substance through a membrane from a region of lower to a region of higher concentration."
4 Defining "truth" was always problematic for Foucault; as a postmodernist he did not believe in truth in an absolute sense, but rather that what is "true" becomes accepted by "general politics" (his term) and human discourse.

CHAPTER 8

Constructive Disorientation Through the Arts

The role of art is not only to show how the world is, but also why it is thus and how it can be transformed.

Augusto Boal

On a crisp afternoon in mid-October, my wife and I are sitting on a hillside in Richmond, VA, along with several thousand other music fans waiting for a performance by Mavis Staples, legendary gospel and rhythm and blues singer. She is one of the headliners of an annual folk music festival here that draws nearly a quarter of a million people to listen to music ranging from classic American folk to Afro-Pop. It is 2018, during one of the most divisive and polarizing eras in American history, and less than a month before the mid-term elections. Walking into the festival we were greeted by campaign signs and people handing out political literature. People were wearing hats and buttons touting this or that candidate. But now I look around and notice the diversity of people sitting together: millennials with baby boomers, blacks with whites, multiple generations of families, some with kids in strollers. Some people are standing, but those sitting behind them don't seem to mind. A burly guy accidentally steps on my hand and apologizes. An elderly woman puts her hand on my shoulder to steady herself as she moves through the crowd. Ms. Staples begins her performance. A couple about my age sings and claps along. Three women of different ethnicities dance in front of us, all moving to the music in their own way. A group of twenty-somethings to our left, looking studiously cool, stop talking and listen. To our right two toddlers play on a blanket spread out in the grass, taking in the joy of the moment. This, I think, is what the arts are for.

This vignette is an example of one of the core functions of art in society: to bring diverse groups of people together into a shared experience, creating empathy and openness to new perspectives of viewing the world. Earlier in this book I have often alluded to the importance, indeed the necessity of emotion in deep learning, in the form of a disturbance *experienced* as a disturbance. In this chapter I explore the role of the arts as catalyst for that disturbance, one of the most useful ways of creating space for constructive disorientation and, hence, deep learning.

I begin, yet again, with John Dewey. While deservedly his reputation rests largely on his pragmatist philosophy and his views on the function of education in a democracy, Dewey also had a lot to say about the role of the arts as an integral part of the human experience. Dewey was interested in aesthetics his entire life, but it was not until the early 1920s that he developed a series of lectures that served as the basis for his masterpiece, *Art as Experience* (1934),[1] inspired by his friendship with renowned art collector Albert Barnes. Remarkably, Dewey did not approach the subject with the pragmatist philosophy he had already developed so well: indeed, he conceded that pragmatism has little to say about it. Instead, we have this three-word title, signifying that art both stems from experience and is experience itself. When we think of art, Dewey wrote, we tend to think of art *objects*; but the real art is the experience of making or encountering the object. Thus, a true work of art is a refined and intensified form of experience. Dewey biographer Jay Martin (2002) captures the essence this way: "Art is not 'about' experience; it is not an 'imitation' of an action; it is not a 'reproduction' of history; it is not a 'spiritual' experience; it is not a 'description' of experience; and it is not – as in the concept of 'art for art's sake' – a substitution for experience. Rather it is a quality that permeates experience" (pp. 404–405). Art, in short, is the consummation of experience and what gives it meaning. I had an aesthetic experience at the music festival even before the music started. Art permeates everyday life and is not just the province of "artists." Dewey (1934) cites as one of many examples:

> [T]he zest of the spectator in poking the wood burning on the hearth and in watching the darting flames and crumbling coals ... If questioned as to the reason for [his] action ... would say he did it to make the fire burn better; but he is none the less fascinated by the colorful drama of change enacted before his eyes and imaginatively partakes in it. He does not remain a cold spectator. (p. 5)

Recall that Dewey – as have numerous scholars of learning since – considered all meaningful learning to be based on experience. The life of an organism is a series of transactions between it and its environment, marked by periods of both equilibrium and disequilibrium, and "the moment of passage from disturbance into harmony" is when growth occurs. Here is the connection between *art as experience* and the phenomenon of deep learning, best expressed by Dewey (1934) himself:

> The rhythm of loss of integration with environment and recovery of union not only persists in man [*sic*] but becomes conscious with him; its conditions are material out of which he forms purposes. Emotion is the conscious sign of a break, actual or impending. The discord is the occasion that induces reflection. Desire for restoration of the union converts mere emotion into interest in objects as conditions of realization of harmony. With the realization, material of reflection is incorporated into objects as their meaning. *Since the artist cares in a peculiar way for the phase of experience in which union is achieved, he does not shun moments of resistance and tension. He rather cultivates them, not for their own sake but because of their potentialities, bringing to living consciousness an experience that is unified and total.* (p. 15, emphasis added)

Dewey's ideas about the power of aesthetic experience have found expression in some recent research on the aesthetic responses of communities to three school shootings in North America (Maarhuis & Rud, 2017). Integrating Dewey's writings on *art as experience* with his philosophy on the role of education in democracy, Maarhuis and Rud use a Deweyan lens to examine how communal works of art serve not only to help communities heal after school shootings but also to reestablish shattered social bonds. They write:

> Responsive works of art, while prompting inner reflection, beckon the viewer to bear witness, to relate, and to learn through associated living. This process of relational reconstruction is not simple problem-solving or individual behavioral change. It is a generative aesthetic understanding and purposeful interpretation by the community and individuals about how to relate, adapt, and return to *communal* associated living. (p. 238, emphasis added)

So how did the communities where these abhorrent acts of violence took place do this? Despite the differences in settings (high school, junior high school, and elementary school), community, and magnitude of the violence and its impact, the authors found several common themes spread across multiple art forms. They found aesthetic responses and "artful conduct" in each case, taking place in seven stages: (1) previous practice of "associated living"; (2) the experience of a disruptive event (the shooting), creating the potential for (3) a motivated aesthetic response, leading to (4) engagement in transactional aesthetic projects,[2] in turn leading to (5) movement toward consummation and reconstruction, which (6) allows for reclamation, restoration, and representation; and to complete the loop (7) return to stability in associated living. In each of these communities where violence shattered their relational bonds, works of art were able to "create an open and accessible milieu, where it [was] safe to explore consummation and reconstruction toward alternative perspectives, outcomes, and possibility of changing one's frame of reference and future actions" (p. 254).

Maarhuis and Rud not only tell a story about the arts as a path to community healing, they also tell a story about deep learning. Art allowed the survivors, families of victims, and the entire community to make meaning out of a senseless, violent event.

Deweyan scholar Maxine Greene (2005) has reflected on how inevitable moments of crisis can spark aesthetic experience and new spaces of creative imagination. It is an opportunity, she writes, to "act on what we imagine, what we believe ought at last to be … to move towards possibilities, to live and teach in a world of incompleteness, of what we all are but are not yet" (p. 80).

Author and scholar Ellen Dissanayake has a different take on the role of the arts in society. She has focused her work on the anthropology of art, and argues that the arts have biological and evolutionary origins, helping humans create cultures that span generations. She writes that arts "throughout most of human existence encapsulated and transmitted group meanings that further confirmed individual feelings of belonging, meaning, and competence, and united individuals into like-minded, like-hearted groups" (Dissanayake, 2000, p. 168). Today, she argues, we live in environments very different from our ancestors, and so have moved away from the arts as core expressions of human concern; instead, they have been dismissed by Western society as either "deviant and dangerous" or "superfluous and elite." As I will show later in this chapter, art that is "deviant and dangerous" has in fact served a useful purpose in creating constructive disorientation. Dissanayake makes a much better case that we dismiss the arts as "superfluous and elite" at our peril: If we are biologically predisposed to engage in the arts then they are even more important in our fast-paced, technologically driven, information-saturated lives.

"Superfluous and elite" would never describe the life and work of dancer and choreographer Martha Graham, who revolutionized modern dance by moving away from an "ornamental manipulation of the limbs" that characterized classical ballet to work that was "initiated form the center of the body … firmly grounded and connected, barefoot, to the floor" (Lee, 1998, p. 433). Graham's genius was seeing dance as a means of using body movement to express deep human emotion, and the tension between "unruly passion and the constraints of duty" (p. 434).

The arts contribute to what Dirkx (2008) has called "mytho-poetic" knowing, those forces within the emotional, affective, and spiritual dimension of our lives. Most of the scholars of transformative learning I have cited so far in this book have viewed transformative learning as primarily a rational process that depends upon conscious, critical reflection on experience. The arts release a different, extra-rational kind of energy and have a different kind of transformative power, as demonstrated by the artful healing example above. A growing number of scholars of adult learning have recognized their potential (Cranton & Taylor, 2012). Jacqueline Davis-Manigaulte and her colleagues (Davis-Manigaulte, Yorks, & Kasl, 2006) have pulled together several case studies showing how these ways of knowing are both different from and complement more traditional theories of adult learning that privilege rational or analytical knowing. Their analysis revealed that artistic engagement accomplishes several purposes: it helps learners be attentive to their learning by getting them out of their usual perceptual field and into a more open emotional space; it creates an empathic environment in which difficult issues can be explored in a supportive context; it creates a pathway to surfacing unconscious knowing; and it codifies new insights through story and metaphor.

Thus, by serving as the bridge between mere sensation and true experience, by engaging all of our senses, by cultivating moments of tension, and by challenging us to expand our perceptions and rearrange our meaning schemes, art,[3] by either creating or making meaning of a disturbance, can be a source of constructive disorientation.

So how, exactly, does this work? Constructive disorientation through art can occur through both *encounter* and *artistic expression*.

Constructive disorientation through artistic encounter can occur through various forms of media: movies, TV, literature, social media, theater, musical performance and street art. As Batson and Ahmad (2009) point out in their review of research on the power of empathy to improve intergroup relations, exposure to counter-stereotypes of "the Other" through these media has a much higher potential of creating empathy and thus, attitude change. They write:

> There is clear evidence that media material can lead one to imagine how the protagonist is thinking and feeling and, at times, to imagine one's own thoughts and feelings in the protagonist's situation as a stepping-stone, leading to feelings of empathic concern even for members of stigmatized out-groups … There is also clear evidence that people react to what they know to be fictional characters in much the same way, and perhaps even more strongly, as they react to real people in similar situations … There is evidence that positive media exposure to individual members of an out-group can lead to more positive attitudes toward the out-group as a whole. (pp. 169–170)

Examples of the power of these media are everywhere: movies like *BlacKkKlansman* (Spike Lee); TV series like *Roots*; documentaries like *I Am Not Your Negro* (James Baldwin); plays like *Six Degrees of Separation*. In each case the viewer is invited, at very low risk, to live vicariously within the life of another and to imagine what that life is like. This potential for empathic connection is what gives the arts their emotional wallop, far more powerfully than rational argument could do. In the best of cases, the creative artist is able to find a point of optimal tension – the point that lands within the viewer's "latitude of acceptance" (Sherif & Hovland, 1961).[4] I began this chapter with a vignette about a Mavis Staples concert. One of the songs she sang was "Down in Mississippi":

> As far back as I can remember
> I either had a plow or hoe
> One of those 'ole nine foot sacs
> Standing at the old turn row
>
> Down in Mississippi
> Down in Mississippi
> Down in Mississippi where I was born
> Down in Mississippi where I come from
>
> They had a hunting season on the rabbit
> If you shoot 'em you went to jail
> Season was always open on me
> Nobody needed no band
>
> Down in Mississippi
> Down in Mississippi
> Down in Mississippi where I was born
> Down in Mississippi where I come from
> Down in Mississippi[5]

Notice how the song begins as a bit of nostalgia but then creates disturbance – *Season was always open on me*. The abruptness of this line takes the listener from images of hard-scrabble country life to those of the Jim Crow South. Artists are able to "work with the tension of innovation and tradition – as well as other tensions, such as randomness and rigidity, and the impulses of the individual and the imperatives of collectives – to construct forms that enliven but do not overwhelm the perceptual capacities of their audiences" (Bang, 2016, pp. 369–370). This point is key: artists are able to create a direct pathway from lived experience to constructive disorientation.

A particularly stunning example of this is Picasso's painting *Guernica*. It is almost impossible to view this iconic work impassively. Here is what Picasso himself said:

> What do you think an artist is? An imbecile who has only eyes, if he is a painter, or ears if he is a musician, or a lyre in every chamber of his heart if he is a poet, or even, if he is a boxer, just his muscles? Far from it. At the same time, he is also a political being, constantly aware of the heartbreaking, passionate, or delightful things that happen in a world, shaping himself completely in their image. How could it be possible to feel no interest in other people, and with a cool indifference to detach yourself from the very life which they bring to you so abundantly. No, painting is not done to decorate apartments. It is an instrument of war. (Quoted in Eliot, Silverman, & Bowman, 2016, p. vi.)

Constructive disorientation through artistic expression occurs as one engages in "expressive ways of knowing," meaning "those forms of expression that engage a learner's imaginal and intuitive processes" (Yorks & Kasl, 2002, p. 47). April Bang (2016) has written a splendid review of research on how artistic expression can facilitate transformative learning. "Whether or not people entering [an] artistic activity are already intrinsically motivated to cooperate," she writes, "they are nonetheless learning how to cooperate, or improving their capacity to do so through the endeavor. In addition to the learning or honing of skills for cooperation, the artistic experience itself engages the mind, body, and spirit in ways that could bring transformation" (p. 358).

Lyle Yorks and Elizabeth Kasl (2006) show how rational ("propositional") and extra-rational ("experiential") knowing complement each other: propositional knowing is expressed through intellectual statements, experiential knowing through emotions. As we have seen, emotion is key to both critical reflection in individuals, and empathic connection and critical discourse in groups – and thus the complementarity.

Yorks and Kasl (2006) write that artistic engagement can help people

> bring into awareness tacit and subconscious forms of knowing, making them accessible for critical reflection. Transformative learning is social as well. Expressive ways of knowing provide pathways among individuals by giving individuals more ready access to the experiential knowing of the other, thus bringing learners into an empathic connection for learning-within-relationship. The pathway between critical discourse and the field of empathic connection deepens a group's capacity to engage one another's worldviews at profound levels of mutual respect, trust, and authentic understanding. (p. 61)

Thus, as with engagement through encounter, engagement through expression relies on the power of empathy. Recall from previous chapters that diversity is a necessary condition for deep learning in groups; but diversity can also lead to polarization if not handled well. The arts can help stave off this danger by creating an "empathic field" that "provides a supportive context within which difficult issues can be pursued without rupturing the relationship" (Yorks & Kasl, 2006, p. 61). Art carries "the potential for making conflict rooted in diversity more constructive for learning" as well as "the power to make psychological and societal boundaries more porous" (Hayes & Yorks, 2007, p. 92).

So to summarize: having an aesthetic experience is an extra-rational way of knowing, which can challenge us to rearrange how we see the world. This disturbance, if cultivated, can lead to constructive disorientation, helped along by engaging in low-risk engagement with others in ways that broaden our empathic field. Doing so weakens ethnic and other hegemonic boundaries and hence increases the potential for critical reflection on experience and deep learning – and also the potential for political change. In a 2016 op-ed piece for the *New York Times*, columnist David Brooks noted how Frederick Douglass, the most photographed American of the nineteenth century, used his portraits – as a serious and dignified African American – to deliberately challenge the image White Americans had of Black people. "He was using art to *reteach people how to see*," he wrote. "This is where artists make their mark, by implanting pictures in the underwater processing that is upstream from conscious cognition. Those pictures assign weights and values to what the eyes take in," and therefore, instead of involving themselves directly in political life, artists' "*real* power lies in the ability to recode the mental maps that people project into the world" (Brooks, 2016, emphasis added).

In 2017 my collaborator (and former student) Susie Erenrich and I published an edited book titled, *Grassroots Leadership and the Arts for Social Change* (Erenrich & Wergin, 2017). The chapters in this book, covering music, theater, photo-journalism, street art, film-making, dance, and museums, provide compelling evidence of the power of the arts to provoke; to create disquiet; and ultimately to inspire learning and change. Below I provide thumbnail sketches of five of these chapters, all of which exemplify how the arts can lead to deep learning:

Banksy the "trickster." The trickster artist, Banksy, already notorious for tweaking the stuffy arts establishment, became infamous in October 2018 for the intentional shredding of his work "Girl With a Balloon" immediately after its sale at auction for $1.4 million. (Just watching the astonished and bemused expressions of those in the high-brow audience is a special treat.[6]) Banksy represents what Jarc and Garwood (2017) call the "benevolent subversion" of street artists and tricksters. They write,

> The archtypical artist as trickster infuses society with a much-needed subversive viewpoint. Without this kind of what we call *cultural vaccination*, communities face stagnation, stasis, and a decline into cultural entropy. By injecting a small dose of disorder into the system, [subversive artists] encourage the community to recognize a threat to its well-being and hopefully coalesce around it to find a solution. (p. 98)

Banksy began his career as a "bomber," that is, someone who paints graffiti in public spaces. He has remained anonymous for more than 20 years, gradually evolving from spray painting to a more sophisticated practice of stenciling messages onto public spaces, and he has done this all over the world as a form of social commentary. Some of his work, such as the "Girl with a Balloon" stunt is intended to poke fun at social pretense. Other work has a more serious social purpose. A prime example is a series of paintings in 2005 on the concrete dividing wall along the West Bank, depicting a girl floating with a handful of balloons next to a boy with a ladder. Artists like Banksy challenge "the very nature of [an oppressive] system in order to shine a light on the plight of those for whom the system does not work" (p. 103).

Benevolent subversion through art creates disorientation. When done skillfully it can turn the revulsion and contempt we might feel when encountering urban graffiti – interpreting it as simply in-your-face vandalism – into, instead, an invitation to "question how we define terms like good, evil, normal, weird, decent, or fair" (p. 106).

French photographer JR creates disorientation in an entirely different way. Like Banksy, JR began his career as a graffiti artist, but his life changed forever when he picked up an old camera that had been abandoned on a Paris subway and realized the power of photographs to bring people together, to create emotional connections between the center and the margins of society. "[By] using visual arts as a way to communicate solidarity and unification," Anu Mitra (2017) writes, "JR forces people to reframe the parameters of social interrogation and explore alternative ways in which to make things happen" (p. 112). JR thus seeks to break down stereotypes: "To change the way you see things is already to change things themselves," he is quoted as saying (p. 117).

How does he do this? In conflict-ridden communities all over the world, "A community issue is identified, solutions are jointly studied and enacted;

art pieces are produced that become the conjoint work of community and artist; and ongoing reflection on outcomes becomes the focal point that leads the social conversation to another, more relevant place" (p. 115). In one of his most famous projects, the *Face2Face* series in the Middle East, JR placed photos of Arab and Jewish faces together on the Separation Wall along the West Bank, identical sets on each side. JR explained his purpose:

> Passers-by were invited to guess who was the Israeli and who was the Palestinian – often they could not tell them apart. By participating, everyone was showing support to a two-state solution in which Israel and Palestine could live peacefully within safe and internationally recognized borders … The project showed that what we call "possible" can change; this artistic action, which experts had thought impossible, proved that limits can move. (Quoted in Mitra, 2017, p. 116)

Both Banksy and JR use their art to provoke: Banksy, by pointing out hypocrisy and pretense; JR, by using his photographs of everyday people to create connection and solidarity. Their purpose however is the same, namely to use their art in public space to unsettle, to create disorientation, to reframe perceptions, and to broaden the possibilities for the kind of deep learning that can lead to social change.

Intercultural choreographic practice in Palestine. The arts are a gateway to embodied learning, that is, learning that is not just intellectual but physical, social, spiritual, and emotional as well – and what could be a more obvious example than dance? Nicholas Rowe and coauthors Noora Baker and Ata Khatab (Rowe, Baker, & Khatab, 2017) describe how choreography can create a space that bridges cultural divides. "Dance," they write, "embodies the diverse sociopolitical contexts in which it is created, amplifying a community's ideals, norms, and distinctions" (p. 282). Thus,

> An intercultural dance forum is a *political laboratory*. It allows participants to physically realize relevant new ideas and envisage diverse potential futures. Through creative dance activities with an *Other*, the diverse pasts, presents, and futures of those participating in the experience can be deconstructed and reimagined. When managed equitably, these forums can inform political and cultural directions across the globe. When inequitable, however, intercultural exchanges can simply extend the oppression of one cultural group over another. (p. 282, emphasis in original)

The authors all participated in the El-Funoun Popular Dance Troupe, a nongovernmental arts organization in Palestine, engaging intercultural activities with artists from around the world. The work of El-Funoun rests on three fundamentals: the collective generation of ideas, a consensus on how these ideas are to be represented in a joint composition, and a presentation through dance that has broad social significance. A particularly striking example of how this works was a project called *The Shape of Water* (not to be confused with the movie of the same name), a collaboration of seven artists, from Palestine, Greece, and Brazil, exploring the cultural perspectives of "occupation and territory." The rehearsal and performance took place in an abandoned factory near the segregation wall in the West Bank:

> We spent ten intensive days working with dust, broken glass, and holes in the structure of the building; the segregation wall in front of us and an Israeli army jeep watching us like a hawk. During this period we explored the concept of an active audience, and experimented with objects, light, and sound to create different images, actions, and stories ... Spending eight hours a day in one space, eating, drinking, speaking, and working physically together allowed us to bond, break down, and understand our differences; to become one group, working toward one goal. (p. 290)

Note how this vignette illustrates the ways in which the development of social capital can lead to deep learning, as I discussed in Chapter 6: the group has a common bond and sense of shared fate; it has a norm of equality and openness to the diverse contributions of its members; and it has a shared sense of both individual and mutual accountability. The authors acknowledge that this was not easy to do, that ownership of ideas was not easy to give up. However, "this ownership turned into sharing slowly and with each of the artists trusting in the process and *being curious* about what will develop ... For the most part, we put our frustration to work, to create and to question. It was food for the mind working with interesting artists" (p. 290)

Using the language of this book, I would suggest that these artists were able to combine creative conflict with curiosity to produce constructive disorientation and deep learning, both for themselves and for their eventual audience. During the performance the audience was led through a "ghost factory" and invited to consider that just as "people bring life to places, so through their absence are they helping [to] kill these places?" (p. 291).

These three examples of how the separation wall became the object of activist art shows how art can create three kinds of energy: though provocation (Banksy), imagining (JR), and performance (El Founoun).

ACT UP, organized by AIDS activists in New York City in the late 1980s and 1990s, showed how works of art can move audiences in ways that arguing and brow-beating could never do. David Edelman (Edelman,

2017), an actor and leader in the gay rights movement and participant in the early attempts to raise awareness about AIDS, writes:

> The history of America's early response to AIDS was largely written by the collective anger of a large community of gay artists who were both victims of the disease and leaders of the movement to fight back. They found their "ordinary" artistic careers recast in an unexpected and unasked for direction and changed the world's response to AIDS. It's a story of compassion and heartbreak, of raising fists and raising funds, and waking the public health establishment and the legislators who provided the funding. (p. 174)

It is also a story about the arts and deep learning – and the limits of persuasion through logical argument. One of the leaders was Larry Kramer, Oscar-nominated director, who founded the Gay Men's Health Crisis (GMHC). The early efforts of this group were feeble; and frustrated by the lack of attention this new crisis was getting from the health authorities and the gay community, Kramer published an incendiary manifesto in 1983 railing against public indifference – and promptly left the country. By the mid-1980s more collective action began taking hold, with movie icon Elizabeth Taylor providing a public voice and Broadway performers collecting money from their audiences. Kramer returned from his self-imposed exile and produced a largely autobiographical play titled *The Normal Heart*, which opened at the Public Theater in New York in April 1985 and ran for nine months. Kramer and other artists had realized that "they could do as much, if not more, to raise consciousness of AIDS through their creative work than through polemics alone" (p. 181). Still not satisfied with the public response, Kramer helped form the street group ACT UP (AIDS Coalition to Unleash Power), described in its charter as a coalition of "diverse individuals united in anger and committed to direct action" (p. 183). Edelman describes the "direct action" this way:

> Their modus operandi was disruption, at once colorful and confrontational, and police arrests were not only common but desired. From its founding in 1987 through the early 2000s, the group would be recognized worldwide for its particular brand of civil disobedience with branches in cities around the globe. ACT UP forced the U.S. public health service and the pharmaceutical industry to speed up the funding, testing, and approval of new drug therapies, it helped secure the passage of the Ryan White Comprehensive AIDS Resources Emergency Act, of other federal laws and regulations designed to protect the civil rights of persons with AIDS, and it ensured that PWAs [persons with AIDS] were at the table. (pp. 183–184)

Noteworthy for the purposes of this book, Edelman's history of the artists' activism is in roughly three stages: logical arguments about why "something must be done"; having artists use their public exposure to stimulate awareness and support for their cause; and using cacophonous street performances to disturb the status quo, demonstrate strength, and mobilize political action. It is an almost-perfect marriage of art and politics, which together have been able to surface both rational and extrarational consciousness, to create space for reframing dialogues, and to lead to deep learning.

Theatre of the Oppressed was developed by Brazilian Augusto Boal in the late 1960s as an activist response to an oppressive military dictatorship. His work has since become renowned and copied all over the world as an example of how the arts can create hope and energy for social change. Unlike the other artists profiled here, Boal's intent was less to unsettle and more to spark a vision of how life could be different. "When conflict and oppression seem overwhelming," practitioner Mecca Burns and her colleagues write, "drama can offer a sliver of hope, a playful way in, a pathway of incremental steps. Theatre bridges the actual with the possible, letting people imagine how tensions and circumstances could be transformed" (Burns, Beti, & Okuto, 2017). Theatre of the Oppressed (ToP) is participatory theater and it takes several forms, all of which invite participants to imagine and embody this "bridging" between the actual and the ideal. One of these variations is called Image Theatre, where participants are invited to create a series of frozen poses, beginning with a representation of the current repressive state, then an image of a potential ideal state, then a series of intermediate, incremental steps connecting the two. Perhaps the most famous version of ToP is the Forum, in which a play is presented that has an oppressive ending, but is then presented again, this time with the audience encouraged to step in, take over one or more of the characters, and change the storyline for the better. ToP is often adapted to the culture and political issues of the community. In Kenya, it took the form of "Weaving the Rainbow," bringing together members of a community terrorized by militia groups with former members of these groups. "The objective was peace and healing through participatory theatre, which offered an interactive forum for creative and redemptive dialogue. Both victims and perpetrators shared painful memories, using theatre techniques to move toward reconciliation in the region" (p. 197).

Theatre of the Oppressed is designed to raise awareness of oppression and to stimulate positive energy for change, and is modeled on Paulo Freire's (1970) ideas about conscientization. It is an intensely political process, and like the other arts-as-activism work profiled here, meant to disturb the social status quo. As Boal (2006) himself put it, "Theater is the beginning of a necessary social transformation and not a moment of equilibrium and repose" (p. 6).

8.1 Art and Politics

Each of the above profiles is an example of the intersection of the arts and politics – using the arts as a way to stimulate the need for change in power relationships in society. This chapter has shown how the arts can contribute to political change by honing in on, and disturbing, emotional equilibrium. They do this by inviting us to get out of our perceptual fields for a moment – to appreciate the world differently, empathize with others' life experience, and through either encounter or expression, to create new visions of how life should be lived. Recall from the previous chapter the four ways in which political dynamics can contribute to deep learning; here is how these are furthered with aesthetics, using examples from the profiles:

1. *Identifying existing systems of power relationships.* The arts have the power to challenge long-standing "truths" about privilege, more through invitation than exhortation. With the "benevolent subversion" of depicting two children at the Separation Wall, their innocence in the face of ugliness, Banksy invites us to confront the Wall as a symbol of oppression.
2. *Surfacing unconscious assumptions.* The arts also have the power to bring to our consciousness the mental models we have that stand in the way of our learning. With his juxtaposition of Arab and Israeli faces on the Separation Wall, JR forces us to acknowledge and confront the stereotypes we have of "the Other." The El-Funoun Popular Dance Troupe dismantled cultural stereotypes as well, doing the hard work of taking diverse cultural traditions and creating something new and powerful through performance.
3. *Cultivating the art of speaking truth to power.* The arts can speak truth to power without engaging in overt persuasion or debate; and as the organizers of ACT UP learned, skillful grassroots organizing followed by artistic expression can develop the political capital necessary to get the attention and eventual action of the powers that be.
4. *Developing forms of procedural justice.* The arts can invite us into a space where we experience, not just the outcomes of systematic discrimination but also the processes that bring these outcomes about. One of the great virtues of Theatre of the Oppressed is how it invites participants

Figure 8.1 World War II poster
Source: Image courtesy of PublicDomainPictures, Pixabay.

not only to experience the pain of everyday unfairness but also to create scenarios for how life might be different.

I should pause here in my praise of aesthetic experience to acknowledge that the power of art in politics can cut both ways. Art can disturb the emotional equilibrium so as to create empathy for the other; it can also have the opposite effect, rallying a community around a cause, in both positive and negative ways. Consider the US war poster in Figure 8.1, depicting the iconic figure "Rosie the Riveter." This is a positive image that promotes pride and seeks to inspire patriotism. Other war posters were designed to inspire hated and xenophobia. One of the milder versions of these depicts Uncle Sam rolling up his sleeves after the surrender of the Axis Powers, saying, "OK Jap, you're next!"

Perhaps more than any other artist in recent memory, Leni Riefenstahl is an example of how artistic talent can be used in the service of demagoguery. A gifted German cinematographer, Riefenstahl directed the notorious Nazi film *Triumph of the Will*. As reviewer David Davis (2003) noted, "Alternating between stark close-ups and panoramic shots, Riefenstahl glorified Hitler's orations and his sycophantic audience of brown-shirt-clad storm troopers. Indeed, 'Triumph' presented Nazism in all of its horrific intensity, earning Riefenstahl the nickname 'Hitler's filmmaker.'" The film became a demagogic instrument for an evil cause, even though Reifenstahl always insisted that it was nothing more than a straightforward documentary.

So, when is art a stimulus for deep learning and when is it a propaganda tool? The answer lies in how the emotional response is constructed by the viewer. Does the art provide comfort, a sense of belonging and community, and reinforce existing values? Or does it create disquiet, inviting one to question these values? Consider the "Rosie" poster (Figure 8.1) for a moment. It could do both, depending on the viewer. To women called out of their homes to work in the factories, it could have a galvanizing effect; to men used to seeing women in stereotypical gender roles, it could lead to constructive disorientation.

8.2 Aesthetics as a Pathway to Deep Learning

When it comes to deep learning, art is not – to use several food metaphors – just a condiment, a spice, an icing on the cake. The arts can be an independent, if complementary, pathway to constructive disorientation and deep learning. Let me return to the criteria for constructive disorientation I laid out in Chapter 4. Recall that in order to achieve a state of constructive disorientation one must be confronted with an experience that creates a disturbance, and is *perceived* as a disturbance. If one makes meaning of that disturbance in a way that s/he feels encouraged to follow it and not ignore it or escape from it, then the disorientation is potentially constructive. The potential is most likely to lead to a positive outcome when the following apply:

A situation requiring adaptive learning, defined as a gap between the values people stand for and the reality that they face, coupled with an awareness that existing perspectives will not lead to a resolution. Given what we know about the insidious influence of cognitive bias, leaving one's own comfort zone and coming to this awareness can be very difficult. Artists make raising consciousness easier by inviting people to give license to their creative imagination, at low personal risk.

The presence of intrinsic motivation, a combination of autonomy, efficacy, and relatedness. We humans are hard-wired to be intensely curious about and to have control over our internal and external worlds. We will respond to adaptive learning challenges when, and only when, we are intrinsically motivated. The arts are capable of stimulating all three aspects of intrinsic

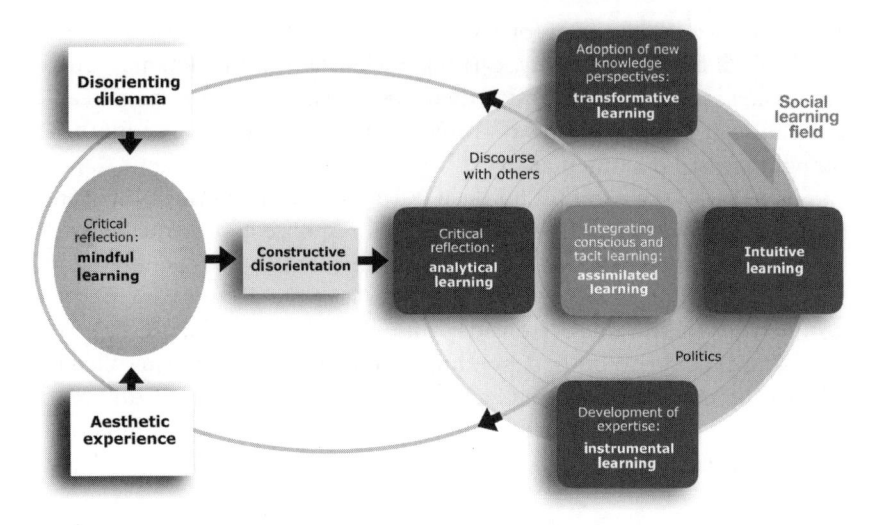

Figure 8.2 The deep learning mindset with aesthetic experience added

motivation (autonomy, efficacy, and relatedness). By inviting others into a different cognitive and emotional space, artists create an atmosphere of encouragement, often subliminally. "Here," they say, "experience this with me" – and whether the experience is through encounter or expression, those invited have autonomous choices. Because artistic experience invites a vision of how things could be different – the essence of conscientization (Freire, 1970) – one is empowered to imagine how things *could* be different and thus experience efficacy. Finally, the empathic field created through artistic expression surmounts cultural boundaries and promotes belonging, connection, and community.

In Chapter 5 I introduced the diagram of the *deep learning mindset* (Figure 5.2). I suggested that constructive disorientation could come from both disorienting dilemmas (experiences that do not make sense to us and are not resolvable without some change in our views of the world) and mindful learning (the integration of conscious, instrumental learning with intuitive and embodied learning). In Chapter 6 I added the social learning field (Figure 6.1), showing how deep learning is enriched through discourse with others and the wise use of politics. Given the importance of aesthetic experience to deep learning, another element to the model must now be added (see Figure 8.2).

Aesthetic experience, as we've seen, can *by itself* lead to constructive disorientation, as when we enter an empathic field through someone else's lived experience. Or it can produce a disorienting dilemma, as when a particularly provocative piece of street art knocks us off balance and challenges our assumptions and sense of what is right or true. Art can shake our world up, sometimes violently; and art can help put it back together. Aesthetic experience can also enrich mindful learning, as we begin to appreciate John Dewey's point that art, and potentially aesthetic experience, is all around us, every day.

Notes

1 Dewey dedicated the book to his friend Barnes.
2 In the Deweyan sense, learning as transaction between a person and his/her environment.
3 Defined broadly as any form of creative expression, including visual, literary, movement, and theatrical arts.
4 Sherif and Hovland (1961) anticipated the power of the media to effect attitude change more than a half-century ago.
5 Words and music by J. B. Lenoir. Copyright 2007 Arc Music Corp. All rights administered by BMG Rights Management (US) LLC. All rights reserved. Used by permission. Reprinted by permission of Hal Leonard LLC.
6 "Banksy Shredding the 'Girl With a Balloon' Video," hypebeast.com, retrieved October 21, 2018.

CHAPTER 9

The Art of Maintaining Essential Tensions

The words of truth are always paradoxical.

Lao Tzu

Throughout this book I have alluded to the importance of tension for deep learning. Recall that John Dewey (1934) wrote about an interruption in homeostasis as the basis of individual growth, Lev Vygotsky (1978) stressed the importance of creating "zones of proximal development," and Mihalyi Csikszentmihalyi (1990) described flow states, optimal for learning, as the tension between challenge and competence. Peter Senge (2006) and Ron Heifetz (2009) emphasize the importance of "creative tension" and a "productive zone of disorientation," respectively, for organizational growth. Underlying all of these are what I call "essential tensions." Tension is a requisite outcome of our innate curiosity to know our world, and maintaining this essential tension is an art.

An art? How so? Consider what artists do: they "work with the tension of innovation and tradition – as well as other tensions, such as randomness and rigidity, and the impulses of the individual and the imperatives of collectives – to construct forms that enliven but do not overwhelm the perceptual capacities of their audiences" (Cohen, 2006, p. 72). It is not much of a stretch to imagine how this works in contexts outside the arts. For example, those who are good at managing conflict may look to create an "optimal tension," which Coleman and Deutsch (2014) define as

> a state in which there is not too little tension regarding the problem being faced in a conflict (where the disputants are not sufficiently motivated to deal with the issues and conflict remains unresolved) or too much tension (which can lead to conflict avoidance because it is so threatening, or conflict escalation as the tension limits one to an oversimplified black-and-white perception of the issues). (p. 485)

Managing tension is more than just a highly developed skill; it also requires a certain kind of artistry in the form of having just the right combination of intuition and mindfulness *in the moment* in order to maintain the tension at an optimal level.

In this chapter I suggest that creating the conditions for constructive disorientation and deep learning require the intentional management of certain essential tensions – tensions that cannot easily be resolved, and in fact should not be. These tensions are in the form of paradoxes, those conflicting values and purposes we need to hold onto without choosing among them. A good example is Csikszentmihalyi's (1970) depiction of flow as the optimal tension between two competing human needs, namely for challenge and support. We need both but they conflict. We need challenge in order to grow; but a challenge is by definition something that is beyond our current competence. Managing this essential tension means being able to hold these values in optimal balance. When they are out of balance no meaningful learning occurs: too much challenge creates debilitating anxiety and too little challenge leads to boredom and distraction.

The artful balancing of challenge and support is essential to deep learning; but as I pointed out in Chapter 4, it is not sufficient. A mindful orientation to deep learning requires attention to other essential tensions, not just the balance of challenge and support. I explore some of these below.

9.1 Intuition and Deliberation

Intuition and deliberation[1] is Daniel Kahneman's (2011) distinction between "thinking fast" and "thinking slow." We have evolved as humans the ability to make quick, intuitive responses to stimuli. A physician usually knows what is likely wrong with a patient after a quick examination; a motorist hits the brakes when another car squeezes in front of him on a crowded freeway; a worried spouse knows when something is bothering her partner. Intuitive responses are key to survival and thriving. But as we have seen, an overreliance on intuition, the easy, fast-thinking response to a stimulus, can fall prey to a host of cognitive biases. Mindful learning of the sort I discussed in Chapter 3 can help us recognize those occasions when our intuition is likely to lead us astray, and allow deliberation, in the form of critical reflection on experience, to kick in. For example, skillful clinicians teach their medical students, mostly through modeling, how to employ handy heuristics to cut through all of the diagnostic possibilities; but they *also* emphasize how to be alert to so-called "zebras" – those rare outliers that can fool the unsuspecting novice into thinking that they are looking at "horses."[2] Motorists are angry about being cut off on the highway but mostly resist the temptation to retaliate. Worried spouses may have some intuitive theories about their partners' distress, but talk with them about it before jumping to conclusions. Mindful learning manages the tension between intuition and deliberation by accepting intuition as containing useful clues to the appropriate response, but also realizing that intuitive behavior is always a function of previous experience, which, therefore, may or may not be useful in the present moment.

> *The center and the edge: curiosity and reflection; risk and consolidation; discovery and conservation; disruption and order; interaction and continuity; complexity and coherence; differentiation and integration; boundaries and communities.*

These eight tensions all relate to the same general paradox: how do we deal with two opposing forces, one pushing us to the edge, the other bringing us back? We are innately curious beings, but reflection on experience is what gives meaning to that experience. Critical reflection puts our worldviews at risk, so we need to pull back and consolidate new knowledge perspectives with the old. We are driven to discover, but we also must conserve our resources, responding to what Csikszentmihalyi (1997) calls the "effort imperative." Disruption in our perceptual space is necessary for constructive disorientation, but we must do something with that disruption to return to homeostasis. We need to be able to recognize and appreciate the infinite complexity of our world, but to survive, both physically and emotionally, we have to make meaning of that complexity. These tensions between centrifugal and centripetal forces – going to the margins and coming back to the center – are key to our understanding and management of constructive disorientation.

Whereas complexity/coherence is an essential tension at an individual level, differentiation/integration is an essential tension at the organizational level. My colleague Laurien Alexandre and I recently published a book chapter entitled, "Differentiation and Integration: Managing the Paradox in Doctoral Education" (Wergin & Alexandre, 2016). In it we cite a seminal article written by Lawrence and Lorsch more than 50 years ago (1967), in which the authors wrote about how to deal with the differentiation/integration paradox. Working from the principle that effective performance of an organization depends on its ability to interact with, and adapt to, a changing environment, the authors found that high-performing organizations were able to optimize two seemingly antagonistic pulls, segmentation (differentiation) and unity of effort (integration).

Such organizations were able to do this by employing several "integrative devices," including:

1. An intentional balancing of interests that allowed for an "interpersonal orientation."
2. A focus on professional expertise rather than blind adherence to hierarchical authority.
3. A concern with organizational performance rather than just individual achievement.
4. Perceived "high influence" throughout the organization rather than a concentration of power at the top.
5. Influence and decision-making centered at the "requisite level."
6. Modes of conflict resolution that recognize conflict among units as normal, even critical for organizational health and growth.

Note the resonance of these "integrative devices" with many of the themes touched upon in this book, especially those having to do with creating an adaptive challenge, facilitating social discourse, and paying explicit attention to politics.

In his work on social learning systems and communities of practice, Etienne Wenger writes about the tension between communities and their boundaries. "Deep expertise," he writes, "depends on a convergence between experience and competence, but innovative learning requires their divergence. In either case, you need strong competences to anchor the process. But these competences also need to interact. The learning and innovation potential of a social learning system lies in its configuration of strong core practices and active boundary processes" (Wenger, 2000, p. 234). According to Wenger, achieving a generative tension between the two requires that four conditions be met: "some intersection of interest," "open engagement with real differences as well as common ground," "commitment to suspend judgment," and ways to find a common discourse "so that experience and competence actually interact" (p. 233). Note the convergence here between Wenger's principles and the keys to deep learning through discourse that I discussed in Chapter 6.

Philosopher Robert Nisbet (1983) argues that great periods of achievement in history feature forces in tension with one another, such as new ideas pitched against settled wisdom, leading to what he calls "the blaze of creativity." This is a classic *dialectic process* – thesis tussling with antithesis, resulting in synthesis – which then becomes a more complex thesis. The synthesis is a victory for neither conventional thinking nor new ideas but an integration of the two, a reinvention of the old that incorporates the new. Here is an everyday example. My wife often chides me for complaining about things I cannot control, such as the weather. I realize that she is right, of course, but I still do not enjoy cold, wet, and gloomy days. However, I make the best of it in cold weather by sitting in front of the fire sipping a nice winter cocktail. My complaining is the thesis; my wife's response is the antithesis; and my adaptation is the synthesis.

9.2 The Self and the Other: Independence and Connection and Community

Managing these tensions is fundamental to our development as adults. Recall that psychologist Robert Kegan (1982) sees development as a dynamic struggle between independence and connection – between the need for autonomy and the need for acceptance by important others. These are always in conflict and in a state of "fundamental alteration," first one becoming dominant and then the other. As they shift back and forth, independence and connection become integrated into an increasingly complex self, again a dialectic process.

The second essential tension in this group – diversity/community – relates to both individuals and organizations. As instinctively communal animals, humans seek community with others, safe spaces where they feel accepted and nurtured and understood. But communities can become insular, a possibility more insidious in an age of social media and cable news. Taken to an extreme, identification with particular communities becomes a petri dish for cognitive bias, breeding tribalism and xenophobia. Disorientation requires challenges to one's worldview, and this cannot happen in an echo chamber. Simply injecting diversity into a community will not by itself reform meaning-making, and can even backfire, as we have seen countless times, sadly, with efforts to racially integrate schools and other social institutions. This is why community and diversity exist in a state of tension: Social capital in groups is enhanced by having a diversity of perspectives, but only when the "empathic field" (Yorks & Kasl, 2006) is broad enough to admit them. One of the ways to open up this empathic field, as I indicated in the last chapter, is through the use of artistic engagement. The art of managing this tension is the ability to engage in discourse in ways that produce constructive disorientation: using difference to spark curiosity without leaning too far toward total identification with another person or group, at one extreme, or finding no common ground, at the other.

9.3 Dialectical Thinking

As I have implied above, the way to manage essential tensions is through dialectical thinking. The word "dialectic" stems from the compound Greek word *dialektikos*, meaning discourse or discussion (Grossman, 2018). Philosophers through the ages have extolled the virtues of dialectical thinking. Probably the most famous of these is Socrates, the archetypal questioner who, by asking questions of others, then exposed contradictions in their answers. He does this not to demonstrate his own wisdom, which he professes not to have, but to show the wisdom in *not* knowing. "He seems to be the only one around who lacks epistemic self-reliance," writes Tommi Hanhijärvi (2015). "He is the only one who asks, while everyone else is just answering. Everyone else is preaching so much that they can't hear each other. Only Socrates listens. Herein is his wisdom" (p. 33). Note how Socrates seeks to induce constructive disorientation: by asking questions of people who then try to answer them, he uncovers their core beliefs; when these are exposed, he asks whether these beliefs should be true in all cases, using phrases like "what if?" or "what about?" The goal is to shed one's illusions, and only when this is done is someone capable of achieving noble goals. Note also the importance Socrates attaches to dialogue, not just as a means of expression, but, more importantly, in the power of dialogue as a means to self-revelation.

The classic Greek philosophers (Socrates, Plato, and Aristotle), and the more recent Western European ones, including Kant, Hegel, and Marx, all viewed dialectical thinking as primarily analytical, linear, and rational. For Socrates, the process leads to a freeing of the mind; for Kant, it leads to the ability to make ethical decisions; for Hegel, it consists of finding contradictions in the concrete examples of abstractions; and for Marx, the dialectic is all about uncovering the social contradictions between producers and holders of wealth. In each case, dialectical thought consists of a starting point (the thesis), which generates an opposing idea (the antithesis), leading to a compromise or resolution (the synthesis).[3] Classical East Asian philosophy (Confucianism, Taoism, Buddhism), has had a much different view of dialectical thinking, less dependent on rationality than on spiritual balance: change is cyclical rather than linear, contradiction is natural and inevitable rather than a state requiring resolution, and "all objects, people, systems, or ideas are invariably interconnected," rather than capable of analysis by themselves (Spencer-Rogers, Anderson, Ma-Kellams, Wang, & Peng, 2018, p. 3). For me, some of the best examples of East Asian philosophy reside in the teachings of Lao Tzu, author of the *Tao Te Ching* (or *Book of the Way*), written in the sixth century BC. The *Tao* is about the art of living, achieved by following a path of contentment and balance. Here is an example from the *Tao*, Chapter 2:

> When people see some things as beautiful, other things become ugly.
> When people see some things as good, other things become bad.
> Being and non-being create each other.
> Difficult and easy support each other.
> Long and short define each other.
> High and low depend on each other.
> Before and after follow each other.
> Therefore the Master acts without doing anything and teaches without saying anything.
> Things arise and she lets them come;
> Things disappear and she lets them go.
> She has but does not possess, acts but does not expect.
> When her work is done, she forgets it.
> That is why it lasts forever. (Lao Tzu, 1988, chapter 2)

In this chapter I am using dialectical thinking in the East Asian sense: that holding the essential tensions described above requires us to accept and be comfortable with contradictory ways of thinking and feeling without being compelled to resolve the contradictions.

One rather simple way to think about dialectical thinking is to imagine three cognitive conditions: *absolutist*, that reality is fixed and unchanging, including natural laws and human qualities (think: IQ tests and trait theories of leadership); *relativistic*, that everything is contextual, and that all knowledge is subjective; and *dialectic*, that both of these apparent polar opposites are true (Kramer & Melchoir, 1990). While acknowledging that phenomena are ever-changing and contradictory, the dialectic thinker also recognizes the need for sense-making and good judgment in zones of uncertainty.

This view of dialectical thinking resonates with much of what we know about the keys to deep learning, going all the way back to the early chapters of this book. Both absolutist and relativist ways of thinking keep us from engaging in the sort of critical reflection that leads to honest assessment of our beliefs and prejudices. Absolutist thinkers will resist challenges to what to them are obvious truths, reinforced by myside bias; relativist thinkers will shrug off diverse ways of thinking and knowing as, in the extreme, "alternative facts": you see it your way and I see it mine. Neither mindset will lead to constructive disorientation – unless the person is hit with a particularly unsettling disorienting dilemma. For example, an absolutist, dualistic thinker believes that homosexual behavior in any form is abhorrent and wrong – and then discovers that his beloved sister is gay. Or a relativist thinker is forced to make a painful and irrevocable moral judgment such as approving a "do not resuscitate order" for a mortally ill parent. The point is that both absolutist and relativistic thinking provide seemingly safe and complacent spaces, retarding the kind of constructive disorientation that can lead to deep learning.

Here is how dialectical thinking relates to managing essential tensions: "Dialectical thinking can be seen as the logic of paradox and the recognition that uncertainty and the limits of knowledge frame human existence and force resolution of seemingly irresolvable dilemmas" (Bassett, 2006, p. 299). Dialectical thinking, therefore, is two things at once: it recognizes the complexity of the world around us and, at the same time, acknowledges our lack of capacity as humans to understand that complexity.[4] Our developmental task is to achieve increasingly complex levels of synthesis, knowing that pure understanding will always be elusive.

Writings on dialectical thought can be maddeningly abstract, obscure, and (dare I say) contradictory, so I will try here to cut through the fog by suggesting how dialectical thinking can help us hold essential tensions and keep open the pathways to constructive disorientation and deep learning.

First, it is helpful to distinguish dialectical thinking from other forms of thought. As I noted earlier, it is seen by most modern scholars as a more advanced level of adult cognitive development. Classical cognitive development theory, stemming from Jean Piaget's seminal work (1954), holds that the apex of cognitive development is the so-called "formal operations" stage, where one learns to think in terms of abstract concepts and logic. This normally takes place in adolescence. After that, cognitive development is a matter of refining these skills. Hardly anyone in the world of developmental psychology holds to that view anymore; instead, the dominant belief is that adults develop various forms of "post-formal" thought (or the various forms of "post-conventional" thinking described in Chapter 3). For example, psychologist and psychotherapist Michael Basseches (2005) asserts that while "formal operational thinking as described by Piaget can be understood as efforts at comprehension that rely on the application of a model of a closed system of lawful relationships to the phenomenal world" (p. 51), formal logic is simply insufficient to address ill-defined, open-ended problems. Basseches' view is joined by many others,[5] all of whom assert that in order to succeed in both one's personal and professional life, other, higher-order mental capacities are needed, one of which is the ability to think dialectically. This view is supported by empirical research showing that dialectical thinking is linked to coping ability and reduction of anxiety in stressful situations (Cheng, 2009), the strengthening of intrinsic motivation (Li, Sheldon, & Liu, 2015), and, unsurprisingly, the ability to manage conflict (Bai, Harms, Han, & Cheng, 2015).

The penchant for thinking dialectically appears to be strongly correlated with age.[6] It is one of the few, if not only, cognitive skills that does not diminish noticeably in the sixties and seventies. As short-term memory and the ability to reason symbolically decline during these years, our ability to think in dialectic terms remains fairly constant, and for some, actually increases (Baltes & Staudinger, 2000).

Naturally, different scholars view dialectical thinking through varying lenses: some see it as the ability to deal with the complexities of modern life, one of the markers of wisdom; some as the ability to integrate formal learning with tacit knowledge; some as a constant struggle between disharmony and synchrony; some as the complex interplay between emotional and intellectual capacity. Further, some scholars view dialectical thinking as a higher developmental stage, while others see it as a parallel, complementary ability. All of these theoretical perspectives have empirical evidence to back them up, which to me only indicates that post-formal theorizing is itself in its adolescent stage of development.

Klaus Riegel (1973) was one of the first to propose a theoretical model of development in later life with dialecticism as its signature feature. Riegel's argument was that, whereas the tasks in early adulthood are largely matters of solving problems, as we get older we begin to understand that what may be experienced as a contradiction between, for example, intuitive and deliberate thinking, is completely natural, and one does not have to overrule the other. "The individual does not necessarily equilibrate these conflicts," he wrote, "but is ready to live with these contradictions; stronger yet, the individual accepts these contradictions as a basic property of thought and creativity" (p. 366). Gisela Labouvie-Vief (1990) calls this a tension between *logos* and *mythos*, ancient Greek terms for thinking that is, on the one hand, logical, rational, and analytic, versus thinking that stems from sensation, emotion, and imagination. She writes, "Logos thinking is aimed at the removal of variation, at stability and reliability. Mythos thinking, on the other hand, seizes the novel and leaps out of the constraints of analytical precision. It disturbs the control and stability that are logos' ideal, but it is also an important source of innovation and creativity" (p. 44).

Riegel (1976) makes an interesting connection between dialectical thinking and aesthetic activity:

> Development requires a delicate synchronization between progressions along different dimensions. In this sense a dialectical interpretation of human development is comparable to orchestral compositions. If there were only two instruments in an orchestra and if both were always playing in unison, they would merely increase the sound volume of the melody … Classical music allows the different instruments to vary the theme but retains synchrony through its emphasis on harmony. Modern music produces deviations through disharmonies but retains synchrony through rhythm and beat. Only random alignments create sounds that have neither temporal patterns nor synchronies. They represent music as inappropriately as a series of uncoordinated progressions would represent human development. (p. 69)

Classical music offers an even clearer example of the dialectic in the concerto. Contrary to common belief, a concerto is not about "harmony," even though the players are acting "in concert." Instead, the term *concerto* is Italian, probably a compound of two Latin words: *conserere* (to weave) and *certamen* (competition). Thus, in a concerto the soloist and the orchestra alternate between moments of independence, opposition, and cooperation – a classic dialectic.[7]

While Riegel saw dialectical thinking as a property of more complex cognitive development, Michael Basseches (1984) went further and suggested that dialectical thinking is itself a transformative process. Similar to Kegan's (1982) notion of development as a sort of spiral, alternating between focusing on the self and the nonself, Basseches views development as a series of transformations in habitual thinking. His 1984 book, *Dialectical Thinking and Adult Development*, contains some limited empirical support for his hierarchical model, placing dialectical thinking as a sign of development.[8] More recent research provides stronger evidence for this (Grossman, 2018). The problem is that, depending on the cultural context, dialectical thinking can develop independently of the ability to engage in formal logic. For example, people in East Asian cultures are more prone to use dialectical thinking, and at younger ages, than are Westerners (Kim & Markman, 2013). So, as Eeva Kallio (2011) writes, "If contradictory, open-system and ill-defined problem-based thinking is already possible in some forms in earlier development, why is it necessary to suppose it also to be the stage after formal operations? It seems more reasonable to assume two separate lines (causal and dialectical) of development parallel to each other" (p. 795).

Most scholars now also agree that, whether its development is hierarchical or parallel, dialectical thinking is required to deal with "the mental demands of modern life," as Kegan (1994) put it. By integrating theoretical knowledge with practical expertise, one is able to make judgments in complex, contradictory situations. The personal and professional demands of modern life inevitably create emotional distress, and, according to Labouvie-Vief (2003), the ability to tolerate this tension is a mark of the healthy psyche in adulthood. Doing so is made more difficult, she contends, by the Western culture's prizing of intellectual capacity at the expense of more "childlike" imagination and emotional expression. In a recent book Labouvie-Vief (2015) integrates her research with the neuroscience literature to show how managing the tension between cognitive and emotional development is the key to optimal functioning: how well we do this, she writes, depends on how well we are able to manage increasingly complex relationships with others.

An emerging consensus is thus taking shape: If adults are to deal successfully with disturbances to homeostasis and progress to a more autonomous self, they need to acquire the ability to reduce their reliance on socialized norms while not discarding them entirely. Recall that according to self-determination theory (Ryan & Deci, 2017), autonomy is more than simply the freedom to do whatever one wants, and relatedness is more than feeling accepted by others, but rather the sense also that one is contributing in unique ways to the greater good. This notion of one's self as part of a larger whole, unity within relationship, is very much in accord with East Asian dialectical thought, as well as with the Zulu notion of *Ubuntu* in South Africa, meaning that a person is a person through other people (Ifejika, 2006).

In summary, the dialectic view of adult development, beginning in the 1970s as developmental psychology's crazy uncle,[9] has matured considerably since then: dialectics is now a respected member of the family, full of creative ideas and interesting research. And more to the point of this book, understanding how adults learn to think this way is the key to appreciating the art and the power of maintaining life's essential tensions.

Just how to *develop* a dialectic cognitive style, however, is as yet unclear (Grossman, 2018), and more's the pity. If I have successfully made the case that deep learning is increasingly important – and increasingly difficult – in the modern world, then devising means of advancing it is increasingly urgent. Here is one of many possible illustrations. On the occasion of the death in late 2018 of conservative former US president George H. W. Bush, many American liberals were aghast that any of them would offer flattering comments meant to honor his memory. *New York Times* columnist Frank Bruni wrote that this demonstrates what he called "the transcendent curse

9.3 Dialectical Thinking

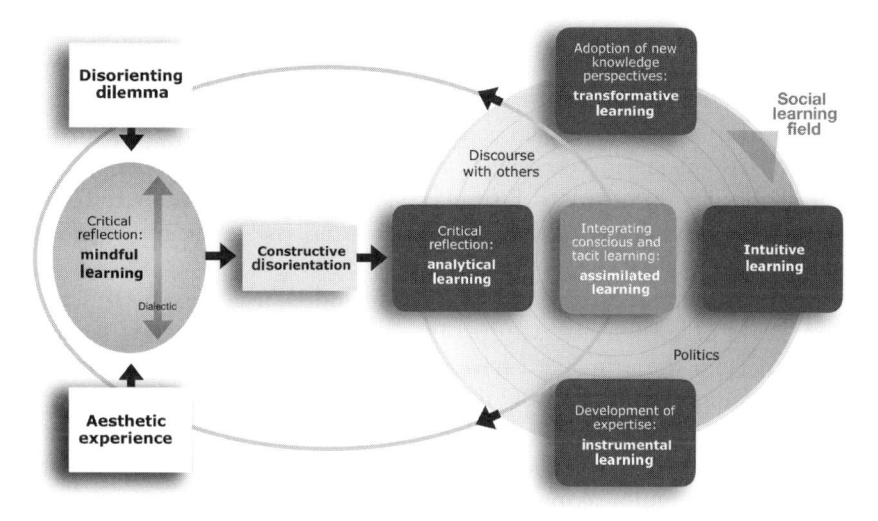

Figure 9.1 The deep learning mindset, complete

of these tribal times: Americans' diminishing ability to hold two thoughts at once" (Bruni, 2018). "Too many of us tend to interpret events, political figures and issues in all-or-nothing, allies-or-enemies, black-and-white terms, blind to shades of gray," he continued. "We like our villains without redemption and our heroes without blemish, and we frequently assign those roles in overly strict alignment with our ideology."

I am persuaded by the available research that developing both the ability and, more important, the *disposition* for dialectical thinking is a necessary condition for the sort of mindful learning that can lead to deep learning. Yes, learning that is transformative is possible through other means, such as experiencing a disorienting dilemma. But because dialectical thinking is neither natural nor inevitable,[10] deep learning *as a way of being* depends on the ability to manage essential tensions in dialectical terms as part of mindful learning.

The disposition to use dialectical thinking thus completes the model of the deep learning mindset (Figure 9.1).

9.3.1 Can One Develop Dialectic Thinking as a Disposition?

Clearly, given the relative scarcity of dialecticism as a state of mind in adults, we cannot count on gaining this ability simply as a function of age, or even as a function of one's experiences and environment, at least in Western cultures. Despite the now-abundant research and theorizing about the nature and value of dialectical thinking, there is an almost complete absence of literature on how this way of viewing the world can be helped to evolve. Michael Basseches (1984) pointed the way back in the early 1980s with an interview-based tool to measure cognitive complexity; but neither he nor others with similar theoretical views, have risen to the challenge of taking the next step, namely, using assessment for developmental purposes.

The lack of attention to a quality so useful, indeed necessary, for thriving in a world of complexity is surprising, to put it mildly. In this section I depart from the principle I have used throughout this book of basing every suggestion for enhancing deep learning on solid empirical research and theory, and go beyond research evidence to speculate on what a developmental model for dialectical thinking might look like. This discussion is based on groundbreaking work on cognitive complexity by my former student Iva Vurdejla (2011).

Vurdejla adapted Basseches' (1984) tools for measuring complex "thought forms" into a simpler (but still complicated!) interview protocol and scoring system, based on four major elements of dialectical thinking:

- *Context*: The ability to understand the structure of the current system or organization (the *thesis*).
- *Process:* The ability to recognize what is emerging in the system that is disturbing the context, including where the disturbance is coming from, and reframing interpretations of the past (the *antithesis*).
- *Relationships:* The ability to create space that will bring previously separate elements together, making synthesis possible.
- *Transformation:* The ability to orchestrate *synthesis* of the previous three elements into an organizational symmetry.

She used this new approach to assess the propensity for dialectic thinking in a group of leaders shepherding organizational change, and found that while all of them exhibited dialectical thinking, each had a distinct pattern of strong and weak elements. Simply sharing her findings with individual participants seemed itself to have a developmental impact, as they were able to see where they might take advantage of their strengths and shore up their weaknesses.

So how then might this process be helped along? Translating the above four elements into solid pedagogy is a work in progress, but developing and strengthening two distinct predispositions would be a good start. I explore these below.

9.3 Dialectical Thinking

First is *accepting the reality that learning itself is a paradox.* Learning is based on past experiences, which are used to direct future behavior; but the past can be a poor predictor of what is needed to cope with the future, and often gets in the way of that coping. It is not that we always have to "unlearn" mental models, as some would argue.[11] We do not delete our mental models but rather detach from them, modify and rearrange them, while at the same time guarding ourselves against letting new meanings take us away from the person we are and want to be (Grisold & Kaiser, 2017). Dialectic learners value their learning *and* understand the limits of projecting from the past into the future. Here is an example of this kind of nuanced thinking. Grisold and Kaiser (2017) make a useful distinction between a *goal* and an *intention*: "While a goal specifies a concrete end state, which is dependent on expectations and thus is hindering, we must have an *intention* to drop familiar and proven routines and practices and embrace states of disequilibrium ... An intention provides motivation to search and find *something* but it does not specify *what* this something is" (p. 46, emphasis in original). In other words, both people and organizations can be prisoners of stated goals if they do not realize how inadequate they can be as statements of the possible. Intentions, on the other hand, recognize the limitations of projecting from the past. A dialectic thinker and leader grasps this distinction, knowing that one can both understand the limits of planning and appreciate the potential of aspirations.

Understanding and appreciating the learning paradox can be taught. Abundant evidence exists that coaching and/or mindfulness training can help others become more critically reflective on experience; and here the focus would be on assisting others to reflect on the usefulness of past experience as a guide to future behavior. The simplest of questions can stimulate useful reflection on mindless routine: What am I doing? Why am I doing it that way?

But sometimes critical reflection will not be enough. Sometimes answering the "why am I doing it that way" question will lead to aspirations that, try as we might, we seem incapable of reaching. Kegan and Lahey's (2009) ideas on immunity to change (ITC) can help break the logjam. During my mid- to late career I did a lot of consulting with colleges and universities on how to encourage transformative change. In a typical workshop (say, with a group of academic departments) I would ask participants to generate two lists, one for the resources supporting quality work, the other for the *barriers* to quality work. I would then ask them to generate some ideas about how to reduce the strength of the barriers, based on the notion that progress is more likely to be helped along by weakening barriers than by strengthening supports. We would then discuss ways of evaluating the feasibility of their ideas and devising means of putting the most promising ones into practice. It was all very logical. The problem was that most often, nothing much changed after I left the campus. ITC helped me to understand why: deeply embedded and largely unconscious immunities to change in the form of what Kegan and Lahey call "competing commitments" got in the way of the best of intentions. For example, an organizational unit might have an honest and firm commitment to becoming more ethnically diverse. It develops and implements outreach strategies to attract more people of color to apply for available jobs – but still diversity does not improve. One reason could be that the unit might *also* have a commitment to hiring the "best qualified" person for the job. Because "best qualified" is often synonymous with "most privileged," the unit hires the White candidate because he or she has more impressive credentials – at least by the conventional meaning of "impressive," which is inextricably entangled with mainstream cultural attributes. (Similar scenarios might apply to units characterized by lack of gender diversity.)

In sum, the paradox of learning is this: while the sole purpose of learning is to help us use the past to help with the future, past experience may not be all that useful and may even be what John Dewey ([1938] 1997) called "mis-educative." Dialectical thinking helps us hold this paradox: it keeps us from projecting experience mindlessly into the future, at one extreme, or ignoring experience altogether, at the other. Critical reflection on experience is not a natural state for humans, but as I have shown throughout this book, it can be learned, and can prepare us for thinking dialectically.

Appreciating the learning paradox leads to the other key disposition critical to dialectical thinking: *knowing when it is needed*. A dialectical thinker recognizes the difference between *complicated problems* requiring only formal logic and technical solutions, and *complex situations* calling for adaptive learning and dialectical thinking. For example, landing men on the moon and bringing them home safely was an extraordinarily complicated problem, requiring equally extraordinary feats of engineering. But in April 1970 a complicated problem became a complex situation when an oxygen tank exploded during the Apollo 13 mission. Flight engineers had to devise a way to keep the crew alive and bring them back to earth with only makeshift materials and limited power, which thankfully they were able to do (Lovell & Kluger, 2006).

Dealing successfully with complex situations requires a deep understanding of one's current environment as a system of interrelationships, and the ability to discover the causes of recurrent patterns.

9.3 Dialectical Thinking

This is Brazilian philosopher Moacir Gadotti's (1996) first principle of dialectics, namely that everything is related, that everything has something to do with everything else. He writes: "For dialectics, nature is presented as a coherent whole in which objects and phenomena are related to each other, reciprocally conditioning each other. The dialectic method takes this reciprocal action into account and examines objects and phenomena in an attempt to understand them in a concrete totality" (p. 18). Doing this requires gaining some distance from the patterns, what Ron Heifetz calls "getting on the balcony" (Heifetz et al., 2009, p. 7). Otherwise, as Peter Senge (2006) notes, "structures of which we are unaware hold us prisoner" (p. 93). Gaining a systems perspective requires that while standing on the "balcony" we look at the reality below, first by identifying discrete events, then by recognizing patterns of behavior over time, and then by observing how these patterns form an underlying structure (Kreutzer, 1995). One of the barriers to deep learning is failing to go beyond the first step, reacting to individual events as if they had no relationship with each other, and resorting to short-term fixes. These may afford some immediate relief but will probably not resolve the underlying system problem. For example, taking cold medication might relieve the symptoms temporarily but will also disturb other systems in the body and will not cure the cold. An intensive fund-raising effort might temporarily prop up a nonprofit that suffers from a structural deficit, but might not address the more systemic problem of an obsolete mission and chronic neglect of stakeholders.

Getting a handle on the system and its patterns requires what has been called "systems sensing" (Ryan, 1995): that is, knowing which hunches and curiosities to follow. Learning how to become a better systems sensor calls for practice of two very different but complementary kinds of learning. The first is to engage in the kind of mindfulness I described in Chapter 3. Experts on mindfulness with diverse disciplinary backgrounds[12] agree on the importance of two positionalities of mindfulness practice, both of which take time and discipline:

- *orientation to the present moment*, aware of body sensations as clues about what is important to notice, and able to take in what is to be learned in that moment; and
- *attention*, whether implicitly or explicitly, to different contexts; sensitive to multiple perspectives; alert to distinction; and open to novelty.

A second and more immediately practical way to learn and practice systems thinking is to create a "causal loop diagram" (Kreutzer, 1995), a graphic that shows the interrelationships among the elements of a system, including how tinkering with the system will cause changes that loop back. My diagram of the deep learning mindset (Figure 9.1) is an example of such a causal loop: external and internal stimuli create disorientation that, if certain criteria are met, leads to critical reflection, when new learning is achieved and then assimilated, thereby creating new opportunities for mindful learning.

Not every problem requires dialectical thinking. How then can one use systems sensing to discriminate between complicated problems and complex situations? Between those calling for technical and those needing creative solutions? When presented with a problem our default response is to go to what has worked before, the tried and true. It is always more soothing to tell ourselves that the solution is already "out there" and we just have to find it. Accepting the possibility that we might have to question our assumptions and redefine the problem itself is much more difficult. It is not a matter of deciding rationally whether a situation calls for dialectic thinking, because our body knows this already. We have to recognize our sensing of a system disturbance when it occurs, and follow the disorientation the disturbance produces. Mindfulness makes otherwise-unconscious signals conscious, and systems-sensing tools can help us visualize them.

Both of the dispositions I have just described can be learned. They are not developed as a function of time or experience, and – unfortunately – are generally not taught in school. But if we are to develop dialectical thinking in adults, recognizing the paradox of learning and knowing when dialectical thinking is needed are, it seems to me, where we ought to begin.

Notes

1. This term appears in Sloman & Fernbach (2017).
2. Obviously, this metaphor works only for Western students, not those in Africa for whom encountering a zebra may not be considered a rare event.
3. Interestingly, dialectical thinking is almost entirely absent among Anglo-American philosophers, some of whom are its most vehement critics. John Dewey studied Hegelian philosophy as a young man but abandoned it as his pragmatist views began to take shape. See Martin (2002).
4. This position is expressed most eloquently in Immanuel Kant's *Critique of Pure Reason* (1998), in which he implies that our intellectual curiosity as humans will always outpace our ability to answer the essential questions of life, and thus each new generation has to confront the same moral dilemmas.
5. Cf. Baltes, Sternberg, Bassett, Labouvie-Vief, Kegan, Riegel.
6. This is true at least in Western cultures, where growth through childhood and adolescence is defined in terms of individualism. Research examined by

Grossman (2018), however, suggests that in East Asian cultures dialectical thinking emerges much earlier.
7 https://en.wikipedia.org/wiki/Concerto#Etymology. Many thanks to Norman Dale for the reference.
8 Basseches, 1984. By "limited" I mean that his research subjects were all students and faculty members at Swarthmore College.
9 Riegel's article even contains a "Manifesto for Dialectical Psychology," ending with the words, "Dialectical psychologists unite! You have nothing to lose but the respect of vulgar mechanists and pretentious mentalists; you will win a world, a changing world created by ever changing human beings" (p. 697).
10 Consistent research findings indicate that those who are predisposed to think dialectically are in the clear minority, even among mature adults.
11 See, for example, Scharmer (2018).
12 Three examples: learning scholar Helen Langer; organizational psychologist Bill Torbert; and mindfulness teacher Charles Tart.

CHAPTER 10

Cultivating a Deep Learning Mindset

> Anyone who has begun to think, places some portion of the world in jeopardy.
>
> John Dewey

I want to accomplish two things in this last chapter: to summarize and highlight the key themes from previous chapters; and then to shift in perspective and tone, from an academic argument for a deep learning mindset to a more pragmatic discussion of how to put its principles into everyday use.

10.1 The Deep Learning Mindset: A Recap

Deep learning is a disposition, a way to be in the world, one that is always on the lookout for challenges to our current way of thinking. These challenges do not stem from cognitive puzzles, but from physical sensations constructed as emotions. Some of these emotions are perceived as disorienting, and can stem from three sources. The first is an encounter that forces us to examine our assumptions about what is true or real, known as a disorienting dilemma. The second is a learned mindfulness that actively and regularly *seeks out* opportunities to question these assumptions. The more we are able to engage in dialectical forms of thinking – the ability to hold onto contradictions – the better we are able to deal with these first two forms of disturbance. The third source of disorientation is having an aesthetic experience, an invitation to step into someone else's lived experience, whether through an encounter with written, visual, or performing art, or through one's own artistic expression.

Not all disorientation leads to deep learning. In order for that to happen the disorientation has to be perceived as constructive, that is, it unsettles us and sparks our curiosity, both at once; and it does so in a way that we perceive an opportunity to change how we perceive the world, and for the better.

Whether constructive disorientation is perceived as constructive depends on several things. Do we find ourselves unable to deal with the disorientation using the cognitive tools we know and normally use? And, does the motivation for dealing with the situation come from within? That is, do we feel that we have real options, and are we confident that new learning will have a positive impact? When an optimal tension exists between the need to see things differently and the sense that we are willing and able to meet the challenge, we are in a state of constructive disorientation, a space that is necessary – if not sufficient – for deep learning to occur.

Constructive disorientation, then, sets the stage for honest, critical reflection on experience. This is rarely easy, as a host of cognitive and emotional traps exist to trip us up, all working to preserve or strengthen our current beliefs and meaning perspectives. Critical reflection, therefore, is a learned skill, requiring practice. Deep learning is wholly dependent on critical reflection, whether that reflection results in transforming one's mental models or deepening one's expertise. Deep learning can also result from intuitive learning, the largely unconscious, "embodied" learning, when that learning is made conscious and reflected upon. All of these sources of deep learning become assimilated into our ways of viewing the world, and therefore subject to further disturbance.

This deep learning field is enriched when we pay attention to two key phenomena.

The first is discourse with others. Deep learning is most powerful – and often necessary – in the presence of others who will help us see the world through other sets of eyes. Social learning can be either positive or negative. The early possibilities of online conversation have been corrupted, and deep learning now faces an even steeper path. Youngsters and people much older are burying their faces and brains in social media, selected by them and by the platforms to narrow the mind, to exclude any potentially disorienting information and perspectives. Groups that are too homogeneous, whether through demographics or ideology, can serve to reinforce one's existing beliefs, and therefore stifle deep learning. The markers of social discourse facilitating deep learning include: a sincere and sustained interest in others' beliefs, especially ones out of sync with our own views, adequate trust or social capital, a generative social space with authentic engagement, and minimal differences in power.

This latter quality, attending to the politics of learning, is the second enabler, one that is often ignored. Deep learning is a political act whenever it threatens to disturb the existing political equilibrium, and it thus requires political consciousness. Our societies determine what is important to learn, and deep learning requires that these be examined, reflected upon, and even intentionally disrupted in the service of the common good. Healthy democracies depend on a citizenry that recognizes existing systems of power relationships and endorses free inquiry into existing systems, including systems of power relationships that privilege some forms of knowing over others.

A deep learning mindset requires all of these elements working together as a system, as was shown in Figure 9.1.

10.2 Cultivating a Deep Learning Mindset

Embedded in each of the previous chapters are implications for how to enhance deep learning in oneself and others. I won't rehash all of these; instead I'll try to recast them into a set of working principles for everyday professional practice – and for living.

10.2.1 *Pay Attention*

In other words, be mindful of the present moment. You don't have to wait to be hit with a disorienting dilemma. Potentially constructive disorientations are all around us if we make the effort to notice them – that is, if we engage in mindfulness. Back in Chapter 3, I defined mindfulness as a state of heightened alertness, one that is conscious of body sensations, accepting these without judgment, and focused more on the present moment than ruminating about the past or worrying about the future. Mindfulness practice allows us to get inside and understand what Otto Scharmer calls our "blind spot," that unconscious inner space "from which we operate when we act, communicate, perceive, or think. We can see *what* we do (results). We can see *how* we do it (process). But we are usually not aware of the *who*: the inner place or source from which we operate" (p. 6, emphasis in original). Mindfulness allows us to step back from our conceptions of how the world is and to see how imprisoned we can be by them, to borrow Doris Lessing's phrase (Lessing, 1987). It allows us to realize, in Bob Kegan's terms (Kegan & Lahey, 2009), just how "subject" we are to these mental constructions and invites us to observe them at a distance, as "objects." It allows us the freedom of reflecting on why we are prone to think or act in a particular way. Am I discarding a perception that might disturb my sense of things? Am I putting an experience into an unexamined conceptual box? Am I finding comfort in confirming what I already thought was true?

A spirit of mindfulness accepts the tension between the need for mental models, which help us to cope with a complex environment, and the understanding of how the act of creating and using them interferes with true experience. Mental models freeze experience into categories into which future experience must conform. Mindfulness helps to defrost these categories and create a space for constructive disorientation that might not otherwise exist.

Mindfulness not only protects us from mindless complacency but also keeps us from being defined by what we perceive as our successes and failures. When one is being mindful, thoughts, for example, are experienced "as temporary phenomena without inherent worth or meaning, rather than necessarily accurate reflections of reality, health, adjustment, or worthiness" (Baer, 2003, quoted in Weick & Putnam, 2006, p. 279). Mindfulness is not about protecting our ego, and so in that sense it is the opposite of narcissism: everything is not always *about us*. Neither is mindfulness about self-improvement, as Amanda Sinclair (2016) reminds us; we don't practice it to change anything. We do it to open ourselves up to experiencing the present moment without automatically trying to put some meaning into that moment – that is, by treating every experience as a fresh experience, allowing us to see every encounter as an opportunity to be what Peter Vaill (1996) calls a "reflective beginner."

A full discussion of mindfulness practice is beyond the scope of this book, but excellent, readable sources are available. For the general reader my personal favorite is the classic *Living the Mindful Life*, by Charles Tart (2001). For the academically inclined I'd recommend an excellent scholarly review of the empirical evidence of the benefits of mindfulness practice, by Kirk Warren Brown and others (2007).

Mindfulness practice *in organizations* has not received nearly the attention it deserves. Leadership theorist and Antioch colleague Donna Ladkin (2015) has written about "organizational mind*less*ness," in which organizations rely on past categories and act on autopilot, minimizing attention to new information. Organizations, by their very design, avoid disruption, focusing instead on maximizing efficiency and productivity, both of which are threatened by the inevitable turbulence in their environment. Like individual people, organizations have to work to free themselves from the default setting of routine action.

Organizational psychologist Karl Weick has spent much of his career studying collective mindfulness and sense-making. In his research on so-called "high-reliability organizations" that are especially good at reading and responding to their environments, he uncovered several practices that he called "mindful organizing." He writes that these organizations do five things:

> [They] spend (a) more time examining failure as a window on the health of the system, (b) more time resisting the urge to simplify assumptions about the world; (c) more time observing operations and their effects, (d) more time developing resilience to manage unexpected events, and (e) more time locating local expertise and creating a climate of deference to these experts … Collectively these five processes focus attention on the discriminatory details that get lumped into categories. *It is that shift from perception to conception that threatens rich awareness of discriminatory detail.* (Weick & Sutcliffe, 2006, p. 516, emphasis added)

Just as personal mindfulness maintains a healthy tension between experience and meaning-making, organizational mindfulness does the same by making the effort to interrupt mindless routine, inviting disruption of that routine by questioning labeling and categorization. Just like people, organizations need concepts in order to cope; but they also need to recognize that the very act of conceptualizing interferes with experience.

A particularly dramatic case in point is the Challenger shuttle disaster in 1986. Failure to attend to what proved to be early warning signals of potentially catastrophic defects was attributed to what was termed "normalizing deviance," that is, treating anomalies or uncertainties as unexceptional deviations from acceptable norms, rather than as events that should have been singled out for special attention (Vaughn, 1996, cited in Weick & Sutcliffe, 2006).

Mindfulness keeps us alert to both what is going on around us and how we are choosing to interpret that experience. By forcing us to notice how quickly we put experience into unexamined conceptual boxes, we are invited to examine how and why we are doing that. This momentary space creates an opening for constructive disorientation.

10.2.2 *Confront Your Biases*

Challenging one's biases is hard work – difficult and uncomfortable and unnatural, but necessary. As useful and necessary as automatic responses may often be, they are also subject to a whole host of cognitive traps created by the very categories we use to navigate our world. As I noted above, mindfulness creates the potential for examining and reflecting critically on our assumptions about the world, to get out of our ruts and make a fresh appraisal, before a disorienting dilemma is thrust upon us. In a lovely TED talk, Verna Myers (2014) invites us to face our biases,

10.2 Cultivating a Deep Learning Mindset

and instead of denying them ("I'm not racist!"), walk *toward* them; and as difficult as this might be, approach the discomfort that doing so creates. What does this mean in practice? It means, first of all, that we acknowledge that everyone is biased, and that not all biases are bad. We have what Hans-Georg Gadamer (1989) calls both *enabling* and *disabling* bias. Enabling biases are those learned perspectives that have, through experience, given us tools to understand phenomena at a deeper level. For example, expert psychotherapists are able to spot the subtle messages their patients are giving them, and by reflecting them back, help to achieve personal insights. An experienced parent is able to know whether a child is crying from hunger or from pain. An experienced teacher is able to sense a learning opportunity in class, whether it's in the lesson plan or not. We need enabling biases, as long as we reflect critically on them, as true experts do. Failing to do this is what leads to disabling bias, the purest example of which is confirmation (or myside) bias, filtering incoming information so as to accept only that which is consistent with our current beliefs.

Unfortunately, we are all afflicted with myside bias. We can argue about its evolutionary purposes, but we can't argue about its negative effects on our personal growth, and on the health of our society. Myside bias contributes to and strengthens our current beliefs, making them both more rigid and less permeable. Moreover, we are now more vulnerable than ever to myside bias, given the one-sided messages on cable news and social media, enticing us to attach what we see and hear to a current belief system, giving us no incentive to think things over before the next wave hits.

The next step after acknowledging bias, therefore, is to take the time to cross-examine how we are treating new information – not just which conceptual box we're putting it into, but also the feeling that comes with it. Myside bias is always emotional, never dispassionate; if it were more detached, we wouldn't be so quick to find comfort in it. This is why myside bias is so pernicious: we fuse our beliefs with our identities, letting our perspectives about the world define who we are. We have to be able to step back and objectify our beliefs, holding them at arm's length, and giving ourselves permission to put them to the test. We have to be able to tell ourselves: "I may hold these beliefs, but they don't hold me." In her book on mindful leadership, Amanda Sinclair (2007) suggests that we reflect on our own thinking, which is often analytical, evaluative, judgmental, even ruminative or catastrophizing. When caught in these often-repetitive thoughts she advises that we ask ourselves two simple questions: "How am I thinking? And, why am I thinking that way?" To those I would add,

"What is causing me to *feel* that way?" Immunity to change theory (Kegan & Lahey, 2009) suggests that with especially deep-seated and emotionally charged beliefs, we challenge them in stages, one small step at a time. For example, some theologians hold that religiosity is strongest and healthiest when followers are encouraged to question rather than simply to accept what is told them as dogma (e.g., Meyers, 2009). Those who feel that their very souls are at stake, would be encouraged to take on small, relatively safe issues before moving on to more central ones.

The third step in confronting bias is to take Verna Myers' advice and walk toward it, knowing full well the discomfort this will cause and the challenges this will pose. Daniel Kahneman, authority on cognitive bias and a self-described pessimist, notes this near the end of his book *Thinking, Fast and Slow*: "The question that is most often asked about cognitive illusions is whether they can be overcome. The message ... is not encouraging" (Kahneman, 2011, p. 341). With respect, I don't agree. While it's true that humans will never rid themselves of myside bias and all its stealthy cousins, that doesn't mean that we are incapable of overcoming *specific* disabling biases, as uncomfortable as this may be. I noted in previous chapters that overcoming entrenched beliefs is very difficult to do alone: We need a force from the outside in the form of other people, who are more able to spot the flaws in our thinking than we are. Others, in particular those with diverse worldviews and most particularly those we see as "the Other," can nudge us out of our categorical thinking and give us an alternative.

10.2.3 *Engage the Tensions*

Constructive disorientation is always a balance of opposing forces or tensions. These are of three general types. One is the tension between fast intuition and slower deliberation; another is the tension between pushing to the edge while holding to the center; a third is the tension between the self and the other. We learn most deeply when these essential tensions, as I've called them, are held in an optimal balance, with the scales not tipping too far in either direction. While admittedly this notion is highly abstract, numerous examples of how it plays out are scattered throughout the book. Here are three more, one for each type:

Confronting bias is an example of the tension between intuition and deliberation. Intuition is a bias to think and respond quickly to a disturbance in our perceptual field. As I noted earlier, intuition is potentially an enabling bias, using what we have learned through our past experience to take on problems of the present, but only when it exists in tension with deliberation. Suppose that you are an official of a local school district, and you have been tasked by the superintendent with conducting an evaluation of a new program, an outreach initiative to parents. You know that this is the superintendent's pet project. You conduct the evaluation and put together a draft report indicating that the program has had only mixed success. Your intuition tells you that your boss won't be happy with anything but a glowing review, and you fear that your report will be whitewashed, or withheld completely. You could ignore this signal, reasoning that you will "just let the chips fall where they may"; or you could follow the disorientation and deliberate, with others, how to make the report palatable to the superintendent, without compromising the report's authenticity or your own integrity.

Here is an example of pushing to the edge while holding to the center. The governor and attorney general of your home state, both of whom you admire, become embroiled in controversies that have to do with racist behavior as young men.[1] It is revealed that in his college yearbook, the governor included a photo of a man in blackface (a caricature intended to mock African Americans) standing next to someone dressed in the robe and hood of the Ku Klux Klan. The attorney general later confesses that as a college student he once attended a costume party dressed as a rap singer, putting on a wig and darkening his skin. You are presented with a disorienting dilemma: how could these men have behaved in a manner so counter to the image you have of them? But instead of taking an absolutist position, that in the spirit of zero tolerance both officials should resign, you hold the contradiction, and reflect on how much or little we should count the misdeeds of youth and weigh these against more typical behavior of each man at maturity.

The essential tension between self and other is, to my mind, the central challenge of adulthood. We need to be both autonomous and connected. How we hold this tension will determine whether we develop or stagnate, flourish or languish. Suppose that you're a working mother, struggling to balance the demands of both job and family. You find your career fulfilling, and relish the sense of efficacy your work brings. But the culture scripting from your childhood creates a sense of guilt that you are not spending enough time at home with the kids. You could attempt to resolve this tension by simply working harder to fulfill both roles equally well; or you could decide to hold the tension and look for ways to restructure your life so as to integrate the competing roles more successfully. Now flip genders and suppose you're a man who has built a successful career, but as you approach your mid-fifties you begin to feel a different pull, wanting to connect more deeply with your family and close friends. You could try to resolve this tension by dismissing the regret, reasoning that this is the price of success, or you could hold the tension, take it seriously, and reflect on how you might better integrate the changing priorities in your life.

By holding essential tensions we give ourselves the space to acknowledge that contradictions are inevitable in life and that we should embrace them as opportunities for growth.

10.2.4 *Maintain a Humble Curiosity*

As I've noted several times in this book, we humans are hard-wired to be curious. Curiosity is one of the forces that pushes us to the edge of our comfort zone, and I cannot imagine deep learning without it. The best form of curiosity is fired by knowing that there is always more to learn, along with a certain comfort that you don't have to learn everything. As an educator I have always been frustrated with a schooling system that, intentionally or not, assumes that the most important learning is when we take in someone *else's* learning, not discovering things for ourselves. Of course, we have a lot to learn from the past; but a reliance on received wisdom can blind us to emerging possibilities.

Expressing a humble curiosity toward learning is to follow John Dewey's recommendation to live a life of inquiry. A contemporary expression of Dewey's advice is a recent book by Judi Marshall (2016), where she defines a life of inquiry – what she calls "first person action research" – as "a person cultivating an approach of inquiry to all they think, feel, and do, including being curious about their perspectives, assumptions, and behavior" (p. 7). Note how closely this resembles mindfulness, but mindfulness that is purposeful. A life of inquiry is much like action research at a personal level. As I described it in an earlier chapter, action research is a form of experiential learning. We perceive something that warrants exploration, a spot of disorientation in our perceptual field. We reflect critically on the disorientation, bring our current knowledge to bear on it, theorize about what might be going on, take action, and see what puzzles remain.

Doing so requires that we let go of the past, knowing that while the past has shaped the present, we need also to embrace emerging opportunities (Scharmer, 2018). Carol Dweck has written a hugely popular book on what she calls the "growth mindset" (2016). While those having a fixed mindset, she writes, look upon failure as a negative reflection on their self-worth, as proof of their inadequacy, those with a growth mindset view failure as an opportunity, a challenge to learn something new. In short, we need to fail in order to grow. Dweck's work recalls this aphorism from Sir Francis Bacon: "Truth emerges more readily from error than from confusion." Entrepreneur Leticia Gasca (2018) offers this caution, however: Don't fall for the trendy "fail fast" mantra: Failing fast and often, while accelerating learning and saving time, is not a good way to – in my terms – learn deeply. Instead, she advises, we should "fail mindfully": "aware of the impact, of the consequences of the failure, of the lessons learned. And [we should be] aware of the responsibility to share those learnings with the world."

Part of what contributes to a fixed mindset is "loss aversion," the tendency to be motivated more by fear of loss than by promise of gain. As I wrote in an earlier chapter, loss aversion is one of the most dangerous cognitive traps. It is, in the case of a compulsive gambler, literally throwing good money after bad: he is unable to cut his losses, walk away from the table, and ask himself what made him throw his money away. It is, in the case of a military intervention in another country that is not going well, vowing to stay the course "because we've invested so much already," rather than admitting the mistake and reflecting on what lessons are to be learned. We need to overcome loss aversion in our lives and be willing to take on reasonable risks. As immunity to change theory would suggest (Kegan & Lahey, 2009), we do this incrementally, in a series of small steps, and hold ourselves accountable, not for achieving success, but for learning from the experience.

Here is an example of what I mean, one from my own experience. A college professor wants to introduce more cooperative learning in his classes. He's seen the research showing that learning is more powerful and long lasting when students learn together. He worries, though: Will this look like I'm shirking my job? Isn't the job of a professor to "profess"? How will this affect my student ratings? He decides against a complete pedagogical overhaul, and plans instead to introduce cooperative learning activities a little at a time, and to carefully observe how they work. He knows in advance that because students are not used to active learning, there will be some grumbling, but he vows not to take the criticism as evidence of his inadequacy but rather as useful data. Sure enough, this first-person action research eventually pays off in the kind of student learning he has always hoped for.

A way to capitalize on this kind of research on practice is to engage in what has been called "prospective hindsight" (Meissner & Wulf, 2015), that is, imagining that an event has already occurred. I often used a form of prospective hindsight when designing program evaluation studies. I would ask prospective stakeholders, "What evidence do you think you will use to judge the worth of the program?" And then, I would take their responses as a guide to help decide what data to collect. A clever variation of this technique is to do what Gary Klein has called a "project premortem": "In a premortem, team members assume that the project they are planning has just failed – as so many do – and then generate plausible reasons for its demise. Those with reservations may speak freely at the outset, so that the project can be improved rather than autopsied" (Klein, 2007, p. 18).

10.2.5 *See Complexity Everywhere and Don't Let It Scare You*

Philosopher Søren Kierkegaard put our human futility well: "To secure against insecurity," he wrote, "we set out to become masters of the universe and to hold chaos at bay for one more day" (quoted in Meyers, 2009, p. 178). Sooner or later we realize that neither of these is possible; but that doesn't mean we aren't capable of maintaining a healthy tension between order and chaos, one of the tensions pushing us to the edge while holding us to the center. Comfort with complexity is part of having a humble curiosity: you see turbulence as intriguing rather than frightening.

What makes dealing with chaos so unsettling for many people is that they feel they are being pulled to the margins, a space they can't control, while losing their grip on the center. Some find comfort in an authoritarian leader who vows to fix things for them through, for example, stoking racist anger that "the Other" is to blame for their troubles. Others "hunker down," to use Robert Putnam's (2007) term, shrinking their worlds and social circles so as to "hold chaos at bay for one more day."

Neither of these reactions is healthy, not for individuals or society. Whether the world is truly becoming a more complex and turbulent place, or only feels that way, we seem increasingly unable to embrace complexity without being consumed by it. It doesn't have to be this way. As Lao Tzu wrote in the *Tao Te Ching*:

> Do you have the patience to wait
> till your mud settles and the water is clear?
> Can you remain unmoving
> till the right action arises by itself? (Tzu, 1988, chapter 15)

This to me is the essence of Eastern mindfulness: to make peace with turbulence and change that is ever present; to avoid retreating to absolutist thinking; to allow yourself to experience the tension that awareness of complexity produces, and to turn this tension into constructive disorientation.

The need for comfort with complexity extends beyond the person to the organization. The richest discoveries occur at the boundaries of systems, where they intersect with others, not at their centers (Wenger, 2000). Still, as I've noted earlier, adapting to complexity and turbulence is not most organizations' strong suit. Most often, the tension between the need to *innovate* and the need to *produce* is resolved in favor of the latter, what Mary Uhl-Bien (2018) calls the "order response." Organizational leaders must recognize and engage the tension, not letting it default to the order response. Uhl-Bien's research has shown that pressures for innovation do not typically come from the top brass but from the creativity of an organization's members, agents of change who link up and drive innovation. The role of formal leaders is to spot these innovative nodes, to give them space for trying out new ideas, to manage the inevitable conflict with other parts of the organization, and to link them up with each other and with sponsors having the wherewithal to make real change happen.

10.2.6 Learn How to Learn with Others

As I wrote in Chapter 6, the importance of learning with others may be the most common thread throughout all of the research and theorizing about human learning. The quality of our learning experience improves when others are around and can deteriorate when we are alone. How then might we "cultivate our social fields" (Scharmer, 2018, p. 15) to sow the seeds of empathy, social capital, and authentic engagement, and help them grow? Less metaphorically, how do we create and hold space for learning through dialogue?

I like Peter Rule's (2004) notion of "dialogic space," a concept he developed while doing emancipatory education work in post-apartheid South Africa. He writes,

> By identifying and exploiting cracks of opportunity within the apartheid edifice, the [project] was able to fashion dialogic possibilities. It did this by creating conditions in which participants felt free to communicate openly with one another and, in the process, negotiate new sets of relationships among themselves, with the world and with their futures. These conditions included: a basis of trust (there can be no dialogue without trust); an attitude of openness towards learning from one another; a physical place where participants could meet in relative safety; a project ethos that encouraged participants to express themselves; and a commitment to solving problems through meeting, discussion, reflection and consensus rather than coercion.

This is not to suggest that this dialogue was without conflict, struggle and pain, or that relationships of power were absent from the project, but that these elements, on the whole, were articulated and elaborated within processes of dialogue. (pp. 329–330)

Rule's description of dialogic space captures all of the elements needed for people to learn deeply with others (see Chapter 6 for details). Getting into true dialogic space requires that we challenge a whole set of lazy assumptions:

- that people will leave their biases at the door;
- that a sharing of views in the form of individual monologues will lead naturally to dialogue;
- that participants will feel equally safe, and heard, in the conversation;
- that group learning will occur organically, without first negotiating common understandings and values – and, perhaps, accepting the need to develop some new learning skills.

A learning skill most in need of development today is *listening*. As Julian Treasure (2017), an expert on the effects of sound and speech, has noted colorfully, "our society is crashingly ocular" (loc. 50). We have become adept at picking out visual cues, he avers, and learning which of these to pay attention to (including, as I've noted repeatedly, an assortment of cognitive traps): "People seek out 'proof' on the internet, collecting views that support theirs and ignoring antithetical ones. This is a recipe for polarization" (loc. 77). We are losing our skills at listening, surrounded by such a cacophony that we have a hard time discerning what is worth hearing from all of the "mush." The only antidote, Treasure argues, is skilled conversation marked by active and empathic listening.

Active listening, I would agree, is the necessary first step to learning successfully with others. As I have noted elsewhere in this book, this is a lot harder to do than we might think. In a discussion marked by diverse perspectives, we are usually preoccupied in coming up with a response that supports our own beliefs and refutes others'. We have to learn to listen with intention, focus without judgment on what the other person is saying, check our understanding by reflecting back what we have heard, and summarize the other's message. (In doing so we also have to avoid summarizing the other's point by reducing it to a pejorative overgeneralization, e.g., "Oh, so in other words you think the government should take all our guns away.")

Wendy McGrath and her colleague Peter Eppig, at Antioch University New England, developed a technique they called the "Critical Skills Program." McGrath describes it this way:

> In the Critical Skills Program, we used a collaboration technique that was quite effective when people were dug in [to existing beliefs]. The goal was not a *shared* outcome – but a *higher* outcome, to achieve not common ground but *higher* ground, as it were. Rule 1 – you must work with someone on "the other side." Rule 2 – you can use the pieces (important) of your current viewpoint as resources but they cannot determine the final product. The final "solution" must be something completely different – and better than whatever you came in with. Everyone has to "let go" – but it was effective because people were going someplace new – and in reality – were *not* required to give up their positions, beliefs, ideas. (McGrath, personal communication, January 16, 2019)

Active listening is the first step to building trust, or social capital. Organizational psychologist Frances Frei (2018) suggests that trust will develop when three factors are in play: when the other is perceived as authentic, when his or her arguments are seen to have logical rigor, and when s/he projects empathy. "When all three of these things are working," she said in a recent TED Talk, "we have great trust. But if any one of these three gets shaky, if any one of these three wobbles, trust is threatened." Active listening, as long as it is not experienced as smarmy or disingenuous, contributes to one being perceived as both empathic and authentic. I have discussed the importance of both qualities extensively in this book, and the evidence suggests that if authenticity and empathy are present, then logical arguments are possible, as long as there is a shared interest in reaching agreement.

Some of my work in recent years has been in leadership and change in higher education, most specifically academic departments. My research uncovered six markers of quality in academic departments, one of which was "engagement," where departments asked critical questions of themselves, reflected about their work, and shared individual reflections through dialogue. Consistent with findings in other organizational settings, effective dialogic reflection required "an openness to diverse points of view, seeking to break new ground by sharing meanings, understanding the whole, and uncovering assumptions … When the purpose of the dialogue is to learn from one another, disagreement becomes a source of energy for learning" (Wergin, 2003, pp. 51–52).

Maintaining the "humble curiosity" I referred to earlier includes approaching learning with others with an air of humility about all that we have to learn from them.

10.2.7 Harness the Power of Politics in Learning

The terms "politics" and "political" have had negative connotations for years, no more so than today. Politicians are accused, without irony, of "playing politics," when this is precisely what they were elected to do. In this book I have tried to discuss the politics of learning in a much more positive light.

Recall that in Chapter 7 I wrote that whenever new knowledge threatens to disturb the existing political equilibrium, learning becomes a political act. Even when following all of the principles above, not attending to the politics can doom any attempt at deep learning in a group or organization. We must identify existing power relationships, asking the unasked questions about them, and surfacing assumptions about why things are the way they are. We must speak truth to power, including speaking truth to ourselves about the power *we* may enjoy. We must give voice to the disempowered, including giving them the tools to unleash the power they already have. All of this may sound like a radical, leftist agenda, but it isn't, not really. Constructive disorientation emanates from disturbance, and sometimes it is a disturbance that has to be prompted. Some examples:

- Individuals work most effectively when, as part of mindfulness practice, they routinely invite challenges to their own hegemonic assumptions. As an older White male, I have had to acknowledge and face many examples of my own cluelessness about privilege over the years, and I am afraid I'm not done yet. In retrospect, I wish that I had recognized these myself rather than having had them pointed out to me.
- Communities of practice work most effectively when newcomers at the margins make their ideas known, while those at the center welcome the disturbance to the status quo.
- Organizations work most effectively when, charged with responding to an adaptive challenge – such as, say, reframing a nonprofit's mission to keep it more in line with society's needs – they recognize and welcome contributions from all levels of the organization, including those at the "bottom," while also calibrating how to integrate the products of their work with existing power relationships. They do this knowing all the while that an effective outcome will likely shift the balance of these relationships.

Working the politics requires having a feel for just how hard to push: too gently will get no response, too aggressively will invite a backlash. A useful resource for helping find that sweet spot is Debra Meyerson's (2003) work on "tempered radicals." Tempered radicals, she writes, "operate on a fault line. They are organizational insiders who often succeed in their jobs. They struggle between their desire to act on their 'different' agendas and the need to fit into the dominant culture" (Meyerson, 2004, p. 16). Tempered radicals are not afraid of complexity. They understand that their organizations are constantly evolving, adapting to environmental changes, and so they "push and prod the system through a variety of subtle processes, questioning assumptions, changing boundaries of inclusion, and scoring small wins" (pp. 17–18). Successful ones realize that, given their organizations' default "order response," they need to find kindred spirits and form networks, including sympathetic sponsors who can advise them on how and how hard to push the agenda.

10.2.8 *Invite Disorientation Through Aesthetic Experience*

Just days before writing this I was introduced to Robert Edger, MD, and his wife, Gunn (Gunnbjorg) Lavoll, MD.[2] Both are psychiatrists and Bob is also an artist, a painter. We were discussing a draft of my chapter on constructive disorientation through aesthetic experience, and Bob gave a personal example of how powerful this can be. He and Gunn were part of a group of congregants from a church in Chicago, in South Africa to help commemorate the 100th anniversary of Nelson Mandela's birth. They attended a service held in Desmond Tutu's home parish, where an all-White choir was singing traditional hymns in Zulu and other South African languages. Bob described the disorientation of seeing and hearing a White choir singing in a Black church, and then the experience of witnessing the predominantly Black congregation rising spontaneously, singing, clapping, and dancing, totally responding to the music. What was most exciting were protest songs, specifically "Modimo," which if sung in the apartheid era, could have led to arrest and imprisonment. "The music bonded the races at that moment," Bob said. "It's as if all of the energy these two groups needed to come together could not be expressed in words," I observed. "Music was the necessary catalyst." Bob smiled and nodded.

Earlier in this book I have addressed what is known as "embodied learning." Most of us learn in school that learning is something we do in our heads. Recent advances in cognitive science have established that what we do in our heads is shaped by our experiences, even determined by them. Embodied knowledge is often hidden from our immediate awareness and, as in the example above, hard to put into words. Mindfulness practice can access it; so can aesthetic encounter or expression. As dancer Celeste Snowber (2012) has written, "When we write from our sweat, our words uncover knowing that we did not know" (p. 58). Knowing from our "sweat" applies not just to dance but to many other forms of expression. During my conversation with Bob and Gunn, he noted that, "When I'm painting, I stop thinking." What he meant by this was not that he just makes aimless brushstrokes with random colors; his art is purposeful but driven by how he feels about what he sees unfolding on the canvas.

Aesthetic experience can be an independent path to constructive disorientation and deep learning. Bob and Gunn Edger had an aesthetic experience in the South African church that led to constructive disorientation and deep learning about the bonding power of music. Ethnic and racial tension has been a blight on human history for thousands of years, but the arts can provide a unique, empathic, even joyful setting for expressing painful issues, and expanding our perceptions of the possible.

Art is most powerful as a source of deep learning when it deals with adaptive challenges, such as seemingly intractable racial division. Aesthetic experience gives us license to imagine, at low personal risk, ways of closing the gap between the values we stand for and the realities we face. Aesthetic experience is an invitation – not a directive – to see things differently, and so it unleashes all of the elements of intrinsic motivation: autonomy, efficacy, and relatedness. It is one of the gentlest ways to turn disorientation into *constructive* disorientation.

Imagine how introducing more aesthetic experiences into an organization might create a more welcoming environment for deep learning. For example, think of how aesthetics might transform meeting time into a more generative space, helping people transition from all of the stuff going on in their heads to a mental and emotional place that is more conducive to dealing with, and learning from, problems and issues that lie beneath the formal agenda. Consider using storytelling, having group members share personal experiences related to the topic at hand. Storytelling enlarges the empathic field, especially important when members of a group have diverse life experiences (Yorks & Kasl, 2006). This will only work, of course, when genuine listening is going on and people feel "heard." Or participants could be asked to bring photographs or drawings representing their perceptions of relevant issues and engage others in discussion about what they "see." At a recent conference I attended the organizer[3] had laid out a collection of polished stones, each inscribed with a positive, supportive word, and invited participants to select one and ponder why they had selected it and what the word meant to them. Here are some of the words: serenity, blessings, peace, gratitude, hope, breathe, dream, celebrate. I picked "cherish."

Creative possibilities are endless; just don't be deterred by initial eye-rolling behavior. Take small steps that lie at the edge of participants' comfort zones.

10.2.9 *Engage in Thought Leadership for Deep Learning*

Thought leadership is simply the championing of new ideas so as to transform how we and others think (McCrimmon, 2005). Thought leadership does not depend on one's position in an organization: it is egalitarian and nonhierarchical. The power of thought leadership depends on passion, commitment, and the willingness to stick one's neck out, just far enough to create constructive disorientation in the system.

I began this book by making the case for deep learning and why we need it now more than ever before. We are faced with a confluence of forces: accelerating change, instant and multiple sources of information – many tailored to feed one's biases – and a toxic polarization that both feeds and is fed by a fear of becoming overwhelmed by chaos and "the Other." Drive-by learning is rampant. Reflecting on how we have come to know what we think we know has always been difficult; and now it is more challenging than ever.

We need thought leaders for deep learning. We need people who are willing to be what I have called "leaders in place" (Wergin, 2007), willing to champion the urgency of deep learning. By that I don't mean distributing copies of the deep learning mindset to friends and colleagues. I mean *practicing* deep learning, and helping others do so as well. Not by lecturing or pontificating; not by logic; not by sharing the empirical evidence contained in this book. The path to encouraging deep learning in others is through example, inviting emulation. Lee Shulman, former president of the Carnegie Foundation for the Advancement of Teaching, once told me that the surest way to make change happen in an organization is through what he called "diffusion by envy": demonstrating that what you're doing works (Shulman, personal communication, 2002). A person with a deep learning mindset demonstrates that deep learning works: not by reacting mindlessly to every bit of information that crosses her awareness, and not by hunkering down, trying in Kierkegaard's words to "keep chaos at bay for one more day." A person with a deep learning mindset is mindful of somatic signals and identifies which of these are disorientating. A person with a deep learning mindset uses critical reflection to follow these disorientations, whether quickly, reflecting in action (Schön, 1983), or more slowly and deliberately, in complex situations requiring adaptive learning (Heifetz et al., 2009). A person with a deep learning mindset models for others a center in the midst of turbulence and a ballast in the face of accelerating change.

Notes

1 US readers will recognize this as a true story.
2 I am grateful to my dear friend, mentor and colleague Larry Braskamp for the introduction.
3 Dr. Barbara Lipinski, Antioch University Santa Barbara.

References

Ahl, H. (2006). Motivation in adult education: A problem solver or a euphemism for direction and control? *International Journal of Lifelong Education*, 25(4), 385–405.

Alvesson, M., & Spicer, A. (2014). Critical perspectives on leadership. In D. V. Day (Ed.), *The Oxford handbook on leadership and organizations* (pp. 40–57). New York, NY: Oxford University Press.

Anderson, C., & Keltner, D. (2002). The role of empathy in the formation and maintenance of social bonds. *Behavioral and Brain Sciences*, 25, 21–22.

Argyris, C. (1991). Teaching smart people how to learn. *Harvard Business Review*, 69(3), 99–109.

Argyris, C., & Schön, D. (1978). *Organizational learning: A theory of action perspective*. New York, NY: Addison-Wesley.

Bai, Y., Harms, P., Han, G. H., & Cheng, W. (2015). Good and bad simultaneously? Leaders using dialectical thinking foster positive conflict and employee performance. *International Journal of Conflict Management*, 26(3), 245–267. https://doi.org/10.1108/IJCMA-09-2014-0070

Baltes, P. B., & Staudinger, M. U. (2000). Wisdom: A metaheuristic (pragmatic) to orchestrate mind and virtue towards excellence. *American Psychologist*, 55(1), 122–136.

Bandura, A. (1977). *Social learning theory*. Englewood Cliffs, NJ: Prentice-Hall.

(2002). Reflexive empathy: On predicting more than has ever been observed. *Behavioral and Brain Sciences*, 25(1), 24–25.

Bang, A. H. (2016). The restorative and transformative power of the arts in conflict resolution. *Journal of Transformative Education*, 14(4), 355–376.

Barrett, L. F. (2017). *How emotions are made*. New York, NY: Houghton Mifflin Harcourt.

Basseches, M. (1984). *Dialectical thinking and adult development*. Norwood, NJ: Ablex.

(2005). The development of dialectical thinking as an approach to integration. *Integral Review*, 1, 47–63.

Bassett, C. (2006). Laughing at gilded butterflies: Integrating wisdom, development, and learning. In C. Hoare (Ed.), *Oxford handbook of adult development and learning* (pp. 281–306). Oxford, UK: Oxford University Press.

Batson, C. D., & Ahmad, N. Y. (2009). Using empathy to improve intergroup attitudes and relations. *Social Issues and Policy Review, 3*, 141–177.

Bayne, H. B., & Jangha, A. (2016). Utilizing improvisation to teach empathy skills in counselor education. *Counselor Education and Supervision, 55*(4), 250–262.

BBC News. (2018, December 12). Facebook scandal "hit 87 million users." Retrieved from www.bbc.com/news/technology-43649018.

Blackbum, A., & Hwozdek, C. (2016). Labelled brain. Retrieved from openclipart.org.

Boal, A. (2006). *The aesthetics of the oppressed*. London, UK: Routledge.

Bourdieu, P. (1977). *Outline of a theory of practice*. Cambridge, UK: Cambridge University Press.

Brafman, O., & Brafman, R. (2008). *Sway: The irresistible pull of irrational behavior*. New York, NY: Doubleday.

Brewer, J., Elwafi, H., & Davis, J. (2014). Craving to quit: Psychological models and neurobiological mechanisms of mindfulness training as treatment for addictions. *Translational Issues in Psychological Science, 1*, 70–90. https://doi.org/10.1037/2332-2136.1.S.70

Brock, S. E. (2010). Measuring the importance of precursor steps to transformative learning. *Adult Education Quarterly, 60*(2), 122–142. https://doi.org/10.1177/0741713609333084

Brookfield, S. (2009). Engaging critical reflection in corporate America. In J. Mezirow & E. Taylor (Eds.), *Transformative learning in practice: Insights from community, workplace, and higher education* (pp. 125–135). San Francisco, CA: Jossey-Bass.

Brooks, D. (2016, August 2). How artists change the world. *New York Times*. Retrieved from www.nytimes.com/2016/08/02/opinion/how-artists-change-the-world.html.

Brown, K. W., Ryan, R., & Creswell, J. D. (2007). Mindfulness: Theoretical foundations and evidence for its salutary effects. *Psychological Inquiry, 18*(4), 211–237.

Bruni, F. (2018, December 4). George Bush and the obituary wars. *New York Times*. Retrieved from www.nytimes.com/2018/12/04/opinion/george-hw-bush-obituary.html.

Buller, J. (2015). *Change leadership in higher education*. San Francisco, CA: Jossey-Bass.

Burns, J. M. (1978). *Leadership*. New York, NY: Harper & Row.

Burns, M., Beti, N. B., & Okuto, E. M. (2017). Truth comes in many colors: Theater of the Oppressed for conflict transformation and trauma healing in Kenya. In S. Erenrich & J. F. Wergin (Eds.), *Grassroots leadership and the arts for social change* (pp. 189–205). Bingley, UK: Emerald.

Caffarella, R. S., Armour, R. A., Fuhrmann, B. S., & Wergin, J. F. (1989). Mid-career faculty: Refocusing the perspective. *Review of Higher Education, 12*(4), 403–410.

Chandler, J. L., & Kirsch, R. (2018). Addressing race and culture within a critical leadership approach. In J. Lau Chin, J. Trimble, & J. Garcia (Eds.),

Global and culturally diverse leaders and leadership (pp. 307–321). Bingley, UK: Emerald.

Changeux, J.-P. (2009). *The physiology of truth: Neuroscience and human knowledge* (M. B. DeBoise, Trans.). Cambridge, MA: Belknap/Harvard University Press.

Chater, N., & Loewenstein, G. (2016). The under-appreciated drive for sense-making. *Journal of Economic Behavior & Organization, 126*, 137–154.

Cheng, C. (2009). Dialectical thinking and coping flexibility: A multimethod approach. *Journal of Personality, 77*(2), 471–494.

Cohen, C. (2006). Creative approaches to reconciliation. In M. Fitzduff & C. Stout (Eds.), *The psychology of resolving global conflicts: From war to peace* (Vol. 3, pp. 69–102). Santa Barbara, CA: Praeger.

Coleman, P., & Deutsch, M. (2014). Some guidelines for developing a creative approach to conflict. In P. Coleman, M. Deutsch, & E. Marcus (Eds.), *The handbook of conflict resolution: Theory and practice* (pp. 478–489). San Francisco, CA: Jossey-Bass.

Cranton, P., & Taylor, E. (2012). *The handbook of transformative learning: Theory, research, and practice*. San Francisco, CA: Jossey-Bass.

Csikszentmihalyi, M. (1970). *Flow: The psychology of optimal experience.* New York, NY: Harper Perennial Modern Classics.

(1990). *Flow: The psychology of optimal experience.* New York, NY: Harper & Row.

(1997). Happiness and creativity: Going with the flow. *The Futurist*, September–October, 8–12.

Curry, L., & Wergin, J. F. (1993). *Educating professionals: Responding to new expectations for competence and accountability.* San Francisco: CA: Jossey-Bass.

Daly, B., & Suggs, S. (2010). Teachers' experiences with humane education and animals in the elementary classroom: Implications for empathy development. *Journal of Moral Education, 39*(1), 101–112.

Damasio, A. (1999). *The feeling of what happens: Body and emotion in the making of consciousness.* New York, NY: Pantheon.

(2018). *The strange order of things: Life, feeling, and the making of cultures.* New York, NY: Pantheon.

Davies, L. (2015). Interrupting extremism by creating educative turbulence. *Curriculum Inquiry, 44*(4), 450–468. https://doi.org/10.1111/curi.12061

Davis, D. (2003, September 12). Pro-Nazi filmmaker, Leni Riefenstahl, 101, dies. *Forward.* Retrieved from https://forward.com/news/8105/pro-nazi-filmmaker-leni-riefenstahl-101-dies.

Davis, H. (2002). Too early for a neuropsychology of empathy. *Behavioral and Brain Sciences, 25*, 32–33.

Davis, J., & Thompson, E. (2015). Developing attention and decreasing affective bias. In K. Brown, J. Creswell, & R. Ryan (Eds.), *Handbook of mindfulness: Theory, research, and practice* (pp. 42–61). New York, NY: Guilford Press.

Davis-Manigaulte, J., Yorks, L., & Kasl, E. (2006). Expressive ways of knowing and transformative learning. *New Directions for Adult and Continuing Education, 109*, 27–35.

Day, D. (2014). *The Oxford handbook on leadership and organizations.* Oxford, UK: Oxford University Press.

Dewey, J. [1916] (1985). *Democracy and education* (J. Boydston, P. R. Baysinger, & B. Levine, Eds.). Carbondale: Southern Illinois University Press.

—— (1933). *How we think* (2nd ed.). Boston, MA: D. C. Heath.

—— (1934). *Art as experience.* New York, NY: Minton, Balch & Company.

—— [1938] (1997). *Experience and education.* New York, NY: Free Press.

—— (1981). *The later works of John Dewey, 1925–1953* (Vol. 11: Essays, reviews, Trotsky inquiry, miscellany, and liberalism and social action, J. Boydston, Ed.). Carbondale: Southern Illinois University Press.

Dilworth, L. R., & Willis, V. J. (2003). *Action learning: Images and pathways.* Malabar, FL: Krieger.

Dirkx, J. M. (2008). The meaning and role of emotions in adult learning. *New Directions for Adult and Continuing Education, 2008, 120,* 7–18. https://doi.org/10.1002/ace.311

Dissanayake, E. (2000). *Art and intimacy: How the arts began.* Seattle: University of Washington Press.

Dunning, D. (2011). The Dunning-Kruger effect: On being ignorant of one's own ignorance. In J. M Olson & M. P. Zanna (Eds.), *Advances in experimental social psychology* (Vol. 44, pp. 247–296). Cambridge, MA: Academic Press.

Dweck, C. (2016). *Mindset: The new psychology of success* (updated edition). New York, NY: Random House.

Edelman, D. (2017). Acting up and fighting back: How New York's artistic community responded to AIDS. In S. Erenrich & J. F. Wergin (Eds.), *Grassroots leadership and the arts for social change* (pp. 173–186). Bingley, UK: Emerald.

Elliott, D., Silverman, M., & Bowman, W. (Eds.). (2016). *Artistic citizenship: Artistry, social responsibility, and ethical praxis.* New York, NY: Oxford University Press.

Emerson, R. W. [1841] (2013). *Self-reliance & other essays.* Mineola, NY: Dover Seashore Classics.

Erenrich, S., & Wergin, J. F. (2017). *Grassroots leadership and the arts for social change.* Bingley, UK: Emerald.

Evans, J. S. B. T. (1990). *Bias in human reasoning: Causes and consequences.* Hillsdate, NJ: Lawrence Erlbaum.

Fenwick, T. (2008). Workplace learning: Emerging trends and new perspectives. *New Directions for Adult & Continuing Education, 119,* 17–26.

Ferry, N., & Ross-Gordon, J. (1998). An inquiry into Schön's epistemology of practice: Exploring links between experience and reflective practice. *Adult Education Quarterly, 48*(2), 98–112.

Festinger, L. (1957). *A theory of cognitive dissonance.* Palo Alto, CA: Stanford University Press.

Foucault, M. (1980). *Power/knowledge: Selected interviews and other writings* (C. Gordon, Ed.). New York, NY: Pantheon.

—— (1994). *Ethics: Subjectivity and truth.* New York, NY: The New Press.

(2008). *The government of self and others: Lectures at the College de France, 1982–1983*. New York, NY: Picador.

Fredrickson, R., McMahan, S., & Dunlap, K. (2013). Problem-based learning theory. In B. Irby, G. Brown, R. Lara-Alecio, & S. Jackson (Eds.), *The handbook of educational theories* (pp. 211–217). Charlotte, NC: Information Age Publishing.

Frei, F. (2018, April). Frances Frei: How to build (and rebuild) trust [Video file]. Retrieved from www.ted.com/talks/frances_frei_how_to_build_and_rebuild_trust?language=en.

Freiler, T. (2008). Learning through the body. In S. Merriam (Ed.), *Third update on adult learning theory* (pp. 37–47). San Francisco, CA: Jossey-Bass.

Freire, P. (1970). *Pedagogy of the oppressed*. New York, NY: Seabury.

Friedman, T. (2016). *Thank you for being late: An optimist's guide to thriving in the age of accelerations*. New York, NY: Picador.

Gadamer, H. (1989). *Truth and method* (2nd rev. ed.). New York, NY: Crossroad.

Gadotti, M. (1996). *Pedagogy of praxis: A dialectical philosophy of education*. Albany: State University of New York Press.

Galef, J. (2016, February). Why you think you're right – even if you're wrong [Video file]. Retrieved from www.ted.com/talks/julia_galef_why_you_think_you_re_right_even_if_you_re_wrong.

Gasca, L. (2018). Don't fail fast – fail mindfully. TED Talk, June 2018.

George, R. (2019, March 6). Confirmation bias hurts social science. *Wall Street Journal*, Eastern edition, p. A15.

Gigliotti, A. R., Dwyer, B., & Ruiz-Mesa, K. (2018). Campus unrest in American higher education: Challenges and opportunities for strategic diversity leadership. In L. C. Trimble & E. J. Garcia (Eds.), *Global and culturally diverse leaders and leadership* (pp. 211–232). Bingley, UK: Emerald.

Giordano, A. L., Stare, B. G., & Clarke, P. B. (2015). Overcoming obstacles to empathy: The use of experiential learning in addictions counseling courses. *Journal of Creativity in Mental Health*, *10*(1), 100–113.

Goodfellow, I., Bengio, Y., & Courville, A. (2016). *Deep learning*. Cambridge, MA: MIT Press.

Gorman, S., & Gorman, J. (2017). *Denying to the grave: Why we ignore the facts that will save us*. New York, NY: Oxford University Press.

Gorey, E. (1999). *The unstrung harp: Or Mr. Earbrass writes a novel*. New York, NY: Houghton Mifflin Harcourt.

Greene, M. (1995). *Releasing the imagination: Essays on education, the arts, and social change*. San Francisco, CA: Jossey-Bass.

Grisold, T., & Kaiser, A. (2017). Leaving behind what we are not: Applying a systems thinking perspective to present unlearning as an enabler for finding the best version of the self. *Journal of Organisational Transformation & Social Change*, *14*(1), 39–55. https://doi.org/10.1080/14779633.2017.1291145

Grossman, I. (2018). Dialecticism across the lifespan. In J. Spencer-Rodgers & K. Peng (Eds.), *The psychological and cultural foundations of East Asian cognition:*

Contradiction, change, and holism (pp. 135–180). Oxford, UK: Oxford University Press.
Grow, G. O. (1991). Teaching learners to be self-directed. *Adult Education Quarterly, 41*(3), 125–149.
Ifejika, N. (2006, September 29). What does Ubuntu really mean? *Guardian*. Retrieved from www.theguardian.com/theguardian/2006/sep/29/features11.g2.
Habermas, J. (1984). *The theory of communicative action 1: Reason and the rationalization of society* (T. McCarthy, trans.). Boston, MA: Beacon Press.
Haidt, J. (2012). *The righteous mind: Why good people are divided by politics and religion*. New York, NY: Vintage Books.
Halberstam, D. (1972). *The best and the brightest*. New York, NY: Random House.
Handy, C. (1994). *The age of paradox*. Cambridge, MA: Harvard Business School Press.
Hanhijärvi, T. (2015). *Dialectical thinking: Zeno, Socrates, Kant, Marx*. New York, NY: Algora.
Harris, L., & Fiske, S. (2011). Dehumanized perception: A psychological means to facilitate atrocities, torture, and genocide? *Zeitschrift für Psychologie/Journal of Psychology, 219*(3), 175–181.
Harvard Smithsonian Center for Astrophysics. (1987). *A private universe* [video]. Indianapolis. IN: Annenberg/CPB Project.
Hayes, S., & Yorks, L. (2007). Lessons from the lessons learned: Arts change the world when ... *New Directions for Adult & Continuing Education, 107*, 89–98.
Heifetz, R. (1994). *Leadership without easy answers*. Cambridge, MA: Harvard University Press.
Heifetz, R., Linsky, M., & Grashow, A. (2009). *The practice of adaptive leadership: Tools and tactics for changing your organization and your world*. Boston, MA: Harvard Business Press.
Hoffman, M. (2001). Towards a comprehensive empathy-based theory of prosocial moral development. In A. Bohart & D. Stipek (Eds.), *Constructive and destructive behavior: Implications for family, school, and society* (pp. 61–86). Washington, DC: American Psychological Association.
Horton, M., & Freire, P. (1990). *We make the road by walking: Conversations on education and social change*. Philadelphia, PA: Temple University Press.
Hume, D. [1739–40] (1969). *A treatise of human nature*. London, UK: Penguin.
James, W. (1884). What is an emotion? In R. Richardson (Ed.), *The heart of William James* (pp. 1–19). Cambridge, MA: Harvard University Press.
Jarc, J., & Garwood, T. (2017). Benevolent subversion: Graffiti, street art, and the emergence of the anonymous leader. In S. Erenrich & J. F. Wergin (Eds.), *Grassroots leadership and the arts for social change* (pp. 97–109). Bingley, UK: Emerald.
Jarvis, C. (2012). Fiction, empathy and lifelong learning. *International Journal of Lifelong Education, 31*(6), 743–758.
Jarvis, P. (1999). *The practitioner-researcher: Developing theory from practice*. San Francisco, CA: Jossey-Bass.

Kahneman, D. (2011). *Thinking, fast and slow*. New York, NY: Farrar, Straus & Giroux.

Kahneman, D., & Renshon, J. (2007). Why hawks win. *Foreign Affairs* (January/February), 34–38.

Kallio, E. (2011). Integrative thinking is the key: An evaluation of current research into the development of adult thinking. *Theory & Psychology, 21*(6), 785–801.

Kant, I. (1998). *Critique of pure reason* (P. Guyer & A. W. Wood, Trans.) Cambridge, UK: Cambridge University Press.

Kaplan, A. (1964). *The conduct of inquiry: Methodology for behavioral science*. Scranton, PA: Chandler.

Kasser, V. G., & Ryan, R. M. (1999). The relation of psychological needs for autonomy and relatedness to vitality, well-being, and mortality in a nursing home. *Journal of Applied Social Psychology, 29*, 935–954.

Kavanaugh, J., & Rich, M. (2018). *Truth decay: An initial exploration of the diminishing role of facts and analysis in American public life*. Santa Monica, CA: RAND Corporation.

Kegan, R. (1982). *The evolving self*. Cambridge, MA: Harvard University Press.

(1994). *In over our heads: The mental demands of modern life*. Cambridge, MA: Harvard University Press.

(2000). What "form" transforms? In J. A. Mezirow (Ed.), *Learning as transformation: Critical perspectives on a theory in progress* (pp. 35–70). San Francisco, CA: Jossey-Bass.

Kegan, R., & Lahey, L. (2009). *Immunity to change: How to overcome it and unlock the potential in yourself and your organization*. Cambridge, MA: Harvard Business Press.

Kilpi-Jakonen, E., Vono de Vilhena, E., & Blossfel, H. P. (2015). Adult learning and social inequalities: Processes of equalisation or cumulative disadvantage? *International Review of Education, 61*, 529–546.

Kim, K., & Markman, A. (2013). Individual differences, cultural differences, and dialectic conflict description and resolution. *International Journal of Psychology, 48*(5), 797–808. https://doi.org/10.1080/00207594.2012.711908

King, B. J. (2015, August 27). Pop quiz: How science-literate are we, really? *NPR*. Retrieved from www.npr.org/sections/13.7/2015/08/27/435148051/pop-quiz-how-science-literate-are-we-really.

Klein, G. (2007). Performing a project premortem. *Harvard Business Review, 85*(9), 18–19.

Knowles, M. S. (1984). *The adult learner: A neglected species* (3rd ed.). Houston, TX: Gulf.

Kolb, D. (1984). *Experiential learning: Experience as the source of learning and development*. Englewood Cliffs, NJ: Prentice Hall.

Koven, R. (1977, November 21). A day of symbolism. *Washington Post*. Retrieved from www.washingtonpost.com/archive/politics/1977/11/21/a-day-of-symbolism/050baf56-0509-4a2e-bcad-14d0b4f2e08a/?utm_term=.5abfb178e114.

Kramer, D., & Melchoir, J. (1990). Gender, role conflict, and the development of relativistic and dialectical thinking. *Sex Roles, 23*(9–10), 553–575.

Kreutzer, D. (1995). A facilitation approach to systems thinking breakthrough. In S. Chawla & J. Renesch (Eds.), *Learning organizations: Developing cultures for tomorrow's workplace* (pp. 229–241). Portland, OR: Productivity Press.

Kucukaydin, I., & Cranton, P. (2012). Critically questioning the discourse of transformative learning theory. *Adult Education Quarterly, 63*(1), 43–56.

Labouvie-Vief, G. (1990). Modes of knowledge and the organization of development. In M. Commons, C. Amon, L. Kohlberg, F. Richards, T. Grotzer, & J. Sinott (Eds.), *Adult development, Vol. 2: Models and methods in the study of adolescent and adult thought* (pp. 43–62). New York NY: Praeger.

(2003). Dynamic integration: Affect, cognition, and the self in adulthood. *Current Directions in Psychological Science, 12*(6), 201–206.

(2015). *Integrating emotions and cognition throughout the lifespan*. Cham, Switzerland: Springer International.

Ladkin, D. (2015). *Mastering the ethical dimension of organizations*. Cheltenham, UK: Edward Elgar.

Ladkin, D., & Taylor, S. (2010). Enacting the "true self": Towards a theory of embodied authentic leadership. *Leadership Quarterly, 21,* 64–74.

Lane, D. C. (2018). *Just odds: An illustrated guide to J. E. Littlewood's Law of Miracles*. Walnut, CA: Mt. San Antonio College.

Langer, E. (2016). *The power of mindful learning* (2nd ed.). Boston, MA: Da Capo Press.

Lawrence, P., & Lorsch, J. (1967). Differentiation and integration in complex organizations. *Administrative Science Quarterly, 12*(1), 1–47.

Lawrence, R. (2012). Intuitive knowing and embodied consciousness. *New Directions for Adult and Continuing Education, 134,* 5–13.

Lee, S. (1998). Generativity and the life of Martha Graham. In D. McAdams & E. de St. Aubin, *Generativity and adult development: How and why we care for the next generation* (pp. 429–448). Washington, DC: American Psychological Association.

Lerner, S., & Tetlock, P. E. (2003). Bridging individual, interpersonal, and institutional approaches to judgment and decision making: The impact of accountability on cognitive bias. In S. L. Schneider & J. Shanteau (Eds.), *Emerging perspectives on judgment and decision research* (pp. 431–457). Cambridge, UK: Cambridge University Press.

Lessing, D. (1987). *Prisons we choose to live inside*. New York, NY: Harper Perennial Modern Classics.

Levitin, D. J. (2017). *Weaponized lies: How to think critically in the post-truth era*. New York, NY: Dutton.

Li, Y., Sheldon, K., & Liu, R. (2015). Dialectical thinking moderates the effect of extrinsic motivation on intrinsic motivation. *Learning and Individual Differences, 39,* 89–95. https://doi.org/10.1016/j.lindif.2015.03.019

Lindeman, E. C. (1961). *The meaning of adult education in the United States*. New York, NY: Harvest House.

Lord, C. G., Ross, L., & Lepper, M. (1979). Biased assimilation and attitude polarization: The effects of prior theories on subsequently considered evidence. *Journal of Personality & Social Psychology, 37*(11), 2098–2109.
Lovell, J., & Kluger, J. (2006). *Apollo 13*. Boston, MA: Houghton-Mifflin.
Lucas, H. C. J. (2012). *The search for survival: Lessons from disruptive technologies*. Santa Barbara, CA: Praeger.
Maarhuis, P., & Rud, A. (2017). Dewey, school violence, and aesthetic response: Healing the community through arts after disasters. In L. Hersey & B. Bobick (Eds.), *Handbook of research on the facilitation of community engagement through community art* (pp. 237–266). Hershey, PA: IGI Global.
Mager, R., & Pipe, P. (1983). *Analyzing performance problems: Or, you really oughta wanna*. Atlanta, GA: Center for Effective Performance.
Manuti, A., Impedovo, A. M., & de Palma, D. P. (2017). Managing social and human capital in organizations: Communities of practices as strategic tools for individual and organizational development. *Journal of Workplace Learning, 29*(3), 217–234.
Marshall, J. (2016). *First person action research*. London, UK: Sage.
Marsick, V., & Watkins, K. (2001). Informal and incidental learning. *New Directions for Adult & Continuing Education, 2001, 89*, 25–34.
Martin, J. (2002). *The education of John Dewey: A biography*. New York, NY: Columbia University Press.
Maslow, A. (1998). *Toward a psychology of being* (3rd ed.). New York, NY: Wiley.
McCrimmon, M. (2005). Thought leadership: A radical departure from traditional, positional leadership. *Management Decision, 43*(7), 1064–1070.
McNerney, S. (2011, November 4). A brief guide to embodied cognition: Why you are not your brain [Blog]. *Scientific American*. Retrieved from https://blogs.scientificamerican.com/guest-blog/a-brief-guide-to-embodied-cognition-why-you-are-not-your-brain.
McNiff, J. (2017). *Action research: All you need to know*. Los Angeles, CA: Sage.
McWilliams, J. (2019, April 4). Is more knowledge making us less reasonable? *Pacific Standard*. Retrieved April 4, 2019.
Meissner, P., & Wulf, T. (2015). The development of strategy scenarios based on prospective hindsight: An approach to strategic decision making. *Journal of Strategy and Management, 8*(2), 176–190.
Mercier, H., & Sperber, D. (2017). *The enigma of reason*. Cambridge, MA: Harvard University Press.
Merriam, S. B., Caffarella, R. S., & Baumgartner, L. M. (2007). *Learning in adulthood* (3rd ed.). San Francisco, CA: Jossey-Bass.
Meyers, R. (2009). *Saving Jesus from the Church: How to stop worshiping Christ and start following Jesus*. New York, NY: HarperOne.
Meyerson, D. E. (2003). *Tempered radicals: How everyday leaders inspire change at work*. Boston, MA: Harvard Business School Publishing.
(2004). The tempered radicals: How employees push their companies – little by little – to be more socially responsible. *Stanford Social Innovation Review, 2*(2), 14–22.

Mezirow, J. (1990). *Fostering critical reflection in adulthood: A guide to transformative and emancipatory education.* San Francisco, CA: Jossey-Bass.
 (1998). On critical reflection. *Adult Education Quarterly, 48*(3), 185–198.
 (2000). Learning to think like an adult: Core concepts of transformation theory. In J. A. Mezirow (Ed.), *Learning as transformation: Critical perspectives on a theory in progress* (pp. 3–33). San Francisco, CA: Jossey-Bass.
Mitra, A. (2017). Innovating social change through grassroots leadership practices in the arts. In S. Erenrich & J. F. Wergin (Eds.), *Grassroots leadership and the arts for social change* (pp. 111–126). Bingley, UK: Emerald.
Moody, S. (2019). Interculturality as social capital at work: The case of disagreements in American-Japanese interaction. *Language in Society, 48*(3), 377–402.
Mørk, B. E., Hoholm, T., Ellingsen, G., Edwin, B., & Aanestad, M. (2010). Challenging expertise: On power relations within and across communities of practice in medical innovation. *Management Learning, 41*(5), 575–592. https://doi.org/10.1177/1350507610374552
Motta, M., Callaghan, T., & Sylvester, S. (2018). Knowing less but presuming more: Dunning-Kruger effects and the endorsement of anti-vaccine policy attitudes. *Social Science & Medicine, 211*, 274–281.
Myers, V. (2014, November). How to overcome our biases? Boldly walk toward them. TED Talk. Retrieved from www.ted.com/talks/verna_myers_how_to_overcome_our_biases.
Newman, M. (2014). Transformative learning: Mutinous thoughts revisited. *Adult Education Quarterly, 64*(4), 345–355. https://doi.org/10.1177/0741713614543173
Newport, C. (2016). *Deep work: Rules for focused success in a distracted world.* New York, NY: Grand Central Publishing.
Nisbet, R. (1983). *Prejudices: A philosophical dictionary.* Cambridge, MA: Harvard University Press.
Nolen, S. B., Horn, I., & Ward, C. (2015). Situating cognition. *Educational Psychologist, 50*(3), 234–247.
Nussbaum, M. C. (2001). *Upheavals of thought: The intelligence of emotions.* Cambridge, UK: Cambridge University Press.
Okeke, C. (2018). Crises impacting South African men's participation in early socio-education development of children and possible useful interventions. *South African Journal of Psychology, 48*(4), 476–487.
Palmer, P. (1998). *The courage to teach: Exploring the inner landscape of a teacher's life.* San Francisco, CA: Jossey-Bass.
Pascarella, E., & Terenzini, P. (1991). *How college affects students: Findings and insights from twenty years of research.* San Francisco, CA: Jossey-Bass.
 & Terenzini, P. (2005). *How college affects students. Volume 2: A third decade of research.* San Francisco, CA: Jossey-Bass.
Pederson, R. (2010). Empathy development in medical education: A critical review. *Medical Teacher, 32*(7), 593–600.
Pemberton, J., Mavin, S., & Stalker, B. (2007). Scratching beneath the surface of communities of (mal)practice. *The Learning Organization, 14*(1), 62–73. https://doi.org/10.1108/09696470710718357

Pennycook, G., & Rand, D. (2019). Who falls for fake news? The roles of bullshit receptivity, overclaiming, familiarity, and analytic thinking. *Journal of Personality* [e-journal version]. doi: https://doi-org.antioch.idm.oclc.org/10.1111/jopy.12476

Piaget, J. (1954). *The construction of reality in the child*. New York, NY: Basic Books.

Polanyi, M. (1966). *The tacit dimension*. Chicago, IL: University of Chicago Press.

Preskill, S., & Brookfield, S. (2009). *Learning as a way of leading: Lessons from the struggle for social justice*. San Francisco, CA: Jossey-Bass.

Preston, S., & de Waal, F. B. (2002). Empathy: Its ultimate and proximate bases. *Behavioral & Brain Sciences, 25*, 1–72.

Putnam, R. (2000). *Bowling alone: Collapse and revival of American community*. New York, NY: Simon & Schuster.

— (2007). E pluribus unum: Diversity and community in the twenty-first century. *Scandinavian Political Studies, 30*(2), 137–174.

Riegel, K. (1973). Dialectic operations: The final period of cognitive development. *Human Development, 16*, 346–370.

— (1976). The dialectics of human development. *American Psychologist, 31*(10), 689–700.

Rittel, H., & Webber, M. (2017). Dilemmas in a general theory of planning. In J. Stein (Ed.), *Classic readings in urban planning* (pp. 52–63). New York, NY: Routledge.

Roberts, L. (2015). *Reflected best self engagement at work: Positive identity, alignment, and the pursuit of vitality and value creation*. Oxford, UK: Oxford University Press.

Rodgers, C. (2002). Defining reflection: Another look at John Dewey and reflective thinking. *Teachers College Record, 104*(4), 842–866.

Roessger, K. (2014). The effects of reflective activities on skill adaptation in a work-related instrumental learning setting. *Adult Education Quarterly, 64*(4), 323–344.

Roseman, C., Ritchie, M., & Laux, J. (2009). A restorative justice approach to empathy development in sex offenders: An exploratory study. *Journal of Addictions & Offender Counseling, 29*(2), 96–109.

Rosenberg, M. (1979). *Conceiving the self*. New York, NY: Basic Books.

Rowe, N., Baker, N., & Khatab, A. (2017). The shape of water ... Palestine, Badke and let's make noise for Gaza: Three journeys of intercultural choreographic practice in Palestine. In S. Erenrich & J. F. Wergin (Eds.), *Grassroots leadership and the arts for social change* (pp. 281–298). Bingley, UK: Emerald.

Rule, P. (2004). Dialogic spaces: Adult education projects and social engagement. *International Journal of Lifelong Education, 23*(4), 319–334. https://doi.org/10.1080/0260370420000233476

Ryan, R., & Deci, E. (2017). *Self-determination theory: Basic psychological needs in motivation, development, and wellness*. New York, NY: Guilford.

Ryan, S. (1995). Learning communities: An alternative to the "expert" mode. In S. Chawla & J. Renesch (Eds.), *Learning organizations: Developing cultures for tomorrow's workplace* (pp. 279–291). Portland, OR: Productivity Press.

Scharmer, O. C. (2018). *The essentials of Theory U: Core principles and applications.* Oakland, CA: Berrett-Koehler.

Schön, D. (1983). *The reflective practitioner.* New York, NY: Basic Books.

Scott, K. S. (2017). An integrative framework for problem-based learning and action learning: Promoting evidence-based design and evaluation in leadership development. *Human Resource Development Review, 16*(1), 3–34.

Seligman, M. (1991). *Learned optimism.* New York, NY: Knopf.

Senge, P. (2006). *The fifth discipline: The art and practice of the learning organization* (rev. ed.). New York, NY: Doubleday.

Shatz, C. J. (1992). The developing brain. *Scientific American, 267*(3), 60–67.

Sherif, M., & Hovland, C. I. (1961). *Social judgment: Assimilation and contrast effects in communication and attitude change.* New Haven, CT: Yale University Press.

Shermer, M. (2011). *The believing brain.* New York, NY: Henry Holt & Company.

Shore, Z. (2008). *Blunder: Why smart people make bad decisions.* New York, NY: Bloomsbury.

Shtulman, A. (2017). *Scienceblind: Why our intuitive theories about the world are so often wrong.* New York, NY: Basic Books.

Sinclair, A. (2007). *Leadership for the disillusioned: Moving beyond myths and heroes to leading that liberates.* Crows Nest, Australia: Allen & Unwin.

——— (2016). *Leading mindfully: How to focus on what matters, influence for good, and enjoy leadership more.* Crows Nest, Australia: Allen & Unwin.

Sloman, S., & Fernbach, P. (2017). *The knowledge illusion: Why we never think alone.* New York, NY: Riverhead Books.

Snowber, C. (2012). Dance as a way of knowing. *New Directions for Adult and Continuing Education, 134,* 53–60. https://doi.org/10.1002/ace.20017

Sogunro, O. (1998). Impact of evaluation anxiety on adult learning. *Journal of Research & Development in Education, 31*(2), 109–120.

Spencer-Rodgers, J., Anderson, E., Ma-Kellams, C., Wang, C., & Peng, K. (2018). What is dialectical thinking? Conceptualization and measurement. In J. Spencer-Rodgers & K. Peng (Eds.), *The psychological and cultural foundations of East Asian cognition: Contradiction, change, and holism* (pp. 1–34). Oxford, UK: Oxford University Press.

Stanovich, K. E., West, R. F., & Toplak, M. E. (2013). Myside bias, rational thinking, and intelligence. *Current Directions in Psychological Science, 22*(4), 259–264.

Stark, J. (2014). The potential of Deweyan-inspired action research. *Education and Culture, 30*(2), 87–101.

Staw, B. M. (1983). Motivation research versus the art of faculty management. *Review of Higher Education, 6,* 301–321.

Stewart, T. A. (1997). *Intellectual capital: The new wealth of organizations.* New York, NY: Doubleday.

Stitzlein, S. (2014). Habits of democracy: A Deweyan approach to citizenship in America today. *Education and Culture, 30*(2), 61–86.

Swart, T., Chisholm, K., & Brown, P. (2015). *Neuroscience for leadership: Harnessing the brain gain advantage*. New York, NY: Palgrave McMillan.

Swick, K. (2005). Preventing violence through empathy development in families. *Early Childhood Education Journal, 33*(1), 53–59.

Tart, C. T. (2001). *Waking up: Overcoming the obstacles to human potential*. Lincoln, NE: IUniverse.com.

Taylor, E. W. (1994). Intercultural competency: A transformative learning process. *Adult Education Quarterly, 44*(3), 154–174.

Terenzini, P. T. (2014). Remarks: Proceedings from Penn State Conference on Engaged Scholarship, University Park, Pennsylvania.

Thompson, K., & Gullone, E. (2003). Promotion of empathy and prosocial behavior in children through humane education. *Australian Psychologist, 38*(3), 175–182.

Torbert, W. (2004). *Action inquiry: The secret of timely and transforming leadership*. San Francisco, CA: Berret-Koehler.

Treasure, J. (2017). *How to be heard: Secrets for powerful speaking and listening* [Kindle edition]. Coral Gables, FL: Mango Publishing Group.

Tuchman, B. W. (1984). *The march of folly: From Troy to Vietnam*. New York, NY: Knopf.

Tzu, L. (1988). *Tao Te Ching: A new English version, with forward and notes* (S. Mitchell, Trans.). New York, NY: HarperPerennial.

Uhl-Bien, M. (2018, May 31). Plenary address: Developing and mobilizing next generation leaders. Presentation to Next Generation Leadership, International Leadership Association Regional Conference, Pretoria, South Africa.

Uhl-Bien, M., Marion, R., & McKelvey, B. (2007). Complexity leadership theory: Shifting leadership from the industrial age to the knowledge era. *Leadership Quarterly, 18*, 298–318.

Uzefovsky, F., & Knafo-Noam, A. (2017). Empathy development through the life span. In J. Sommerville & J. Decety (Eds.), *Social cognition: Development through the life span* (pp. 71–97). New York, NY: Routledge.

Vaill, P. (1996). *Learning as a way of being: Strategies for survival in a world of permanent white water*. San Francisco, CA: Jossey-Bass.

Vanderah, T., & Gould, D. (2016). *Nolte's the human brain: An introduction to it functional anatomy* (7th ed.). Philadelphia, PA: Elsevier.

Vince, R. (2004). Action learning and organizational learning: Power, politics, and emotion in organizations. *Action Learning: Research and Practice, 1*(1), 63–78.

—— (2012). The contradictions of impact: Action learning and power in organizations. *Action Learning: Research and Practice, 9*(2), 209–218.

Vince, R., Abbey, G., & Langenhan, M. (2018). Finding critical action learning through paradox: The role of action learning in the suppression and stimulation of critical reflection. *Management Learning, 49*(1), 86–106.

Vosoughi, S., Roy, D., & Aral, S. (2018). The spread of true and false news online. *Science, 359* (6380), 1146–1151. Retrieved from www.sciencemag.org/about/science-licenses-journal-article-reuse.

Vurdelja, I. (2011). *How leaders think: Measuring cognitive complexity in leading organizational change* (Doctoral dissertation). Antioch University, Yellow Springs, OH.

Vygotsky, L. S. (1978). *Mind in society: The development of higher psychological processes*. Cambridge, MA: Harvard University Press.

Wang, W., Yang, N., Li, X., Xiao, H., Gao, M., Yan, H., & Li, S. (2019). A pathway analysis of exploring how HIV-related stigma affects social capital among people living with HIV/AIDS in China. *Psychology, Health, & Medicine*, pub. online March 21, 2019.

Warwick, R., McCray, J., & Board, D. (2017). Bourdieu's *habitus* and field: Implications on the practice and theory of action learning. *Action Learning: Research and Practice, 14*(2), 104–119.

Warzel, C. (2018). He predicted the 2016 fake news crisis. Now he's worried about an information apocalypse. *Buzzfeed News*. Retrieved from www.buzzfeednews.com/article/charliewarzel/the-terrifying-future-of-fake-news.

Wason, P. C. (1960). On the failure to eliminate hypotheses in a conceptual task. *Quarterly Journal of Experimental Psychology, 12*(1), 129–140.

Weick, K., & Putnam, T. (2006). Organizing for mindfulness: Eastern wisdom and Western knowledge. *Journal of Management Inquiry, 15*(3), 274 287.

Weick, K., & Sutcliffe, K. (2006). Mindfulness and the quality of organizational attention. *Organization Science, 17*(4), 514–524.

Welner, K. (2013). Consequential validity and the transformation of tests from measurement tools to policy tools. *Teachers College Record, 115*(9). Retrieved from https://nepc.colorado.edu/publication/TCR-Consequential-Validity.

Wenger, E. (1998). *Communities of practice: Learning, meaning, and identity*. New York, NY: Cambridge University Press.

——— (2000). Communities of practice and social learning systems. *Organization, 7*(2), 225–246.

Wergin, J. F. (2001). Beyond carrots and sticks: What really motivates faculty. *Liberal Education, 87*(Winter), 50–53.

——— (2003). *Departments that work: Building and sustaining cultures of excellence in academic programs*. San Francisco, CA: Jossey-Bass.

——— (Ed.). (2007). *Leadership in place: How academic professionals can find their leadership voice*. San Francisco, CA: Jossey-Bass.

Wergin, J. F., & Alexandre, L. (2016). Differentiation and integration: Managing the paradox in doctoral education. In P. Blessinger & D. Stockley (Eds.), *Emerging directions in doctoral Education* (pp. 225–242). London, UK: Emerald Group.

Wergin, J. F., Mazmanian, P., Miller, W., Papp, K., & Williams, W. (1988). CME and change in practice: An alternative perspective. *Journal of Continuing Education in the Health Professions, 8*, 147–159.

Will, G. F. (2018, September 12). Trigger warning: An embarrassing fragility on college campuses. *Washington Post*.

Willer, R. (2016, September). *How to have better political conversations* [Video File]. Retrieved from www.ted.com/talks/robb_willer_how_to_have_better_political_conversations?language=en.

Wilson, J. C. (2011). Service-learning and the development of empathy in US college students. *Education & Training*, *53*(2–3), 207–217.

Wilson, S. (1988). The "real self" controversy: Toward an integration of humanistic and interactionist theory. *Journal of Humanistic Psychology*, *28*, 39–65.

Wlodkowski, R. (2008). *Enhancing adult motivation to learn: A comprehensive guide to teaching all adults* (3rd ed.). San Francisco, CA: Jossey-Bass.

Wright, M., Skaggs, W., & Nielsen, F. A. (2016). The cerebellum. *WikiJournal of Medicine*, *3*(1). Retrieved from https://en.wikiversity.org/wiki/WikiJournal_of_Medicine/The_Cerebellum.

Yeo, R., & Marquardt, M. (2010). Problems as building blocks for organizational learning: A roadmap for experiential inquiry. *Group & Organization Management*, *35*(3), 243–275.

Yorks, L. (2005). Adult Learning and the generation of new knowledge and meaning: Creating liberating spaces for fostering adult learning through practitioner-based collaborative action inquiry. *Teachers College Record*, *107*(6), 1217–1244. https://doi.org/10.1111/j.1467-9620.2005.00511.x

Yorks, L., & Kasl, E. (2002). Toward a theory and practice for whole-person learning: Reconceptualizing experience and the role of affect. *Adult Education Quarterly*, *52*(3), 176–192.

(2006). I know more than I can say: A taxonomy for using expressive ways of knowing to foster transformative learning. *Journal of Transformative Education*, *4*(1), 43–64.

Index

accountability, 69, 89, 96, 104, 132
ACT UP, 132
action research, 27, 166, 167
adaptive, 57
Alexandre, L., 142
analytic thinking, *see* critical thinking
Apollo 13, 154
Argyris, C., viii, ix, 6, 49, 75, 81
Aristotle, 19, 27, 52, 70, 86, 89, 112, 145
   episteme, 27, 52, 70
   phronesis, 27, 28, 52, 70, 73
   techne, 27, 52, 70, 86
art
   defined, 123
   as cultural vaccination, 130
   music as a tool for deep learning, 127
   as path to community healing, 124
   as pathway to deep learning, 137–138
   performance as pathway to deep learning, 132–135
   photography as tool for deep learning, 130
   and politics, 135–137
   street art as tool for deep learning, 129
autonomy, 34, 40, 41, 43, 46, 60, 63, 65, 80, 104, 137, 144, 150, 174

Bacon, Francis, 9, 167
Baldwin, James, 127
Bandura, A., 64, 92
Banksy, 129, 130, 131, 132, 135, 139n6
   "Girl With a Balloon," 129
Barrett, L., theory of constructed emotion, 31
Basseches, M., 147, 149, 152
bias, 2, 29, 60, 74, 137, 144, 163
   affective, 54
   belief persistence, 15, 16, 18, 110
   causal assumptions, 13, 15
   confirmation/myside, 9, 10, 11, 12, 15, 18, 32, 45, 53, 110, 146, 163
   confronting, 162–164

diagnosis bias, 110, 111
Dunning-Kruger effect, 12, 14
enabling vs. disabling, 163
exposure anxiety, 111
intuitive beliefs, 14, 15, 53, 54, 87
intuitive theories, 84
loss aversion, 61, 110, 111, 167
patternicity, 13, 15
reductive thinking, 13, 14, 15, 55, 111
Boal, A., 87, 122, 134
   Theatre of the Oppressed, 134, 135
Bourdieu, P., 50, 79, 120
Brafman, O., 17, 110, 121
Brafman, R., 17, 110, 121
brain, anatomy of, 20–22
Brookfield, S., 75, 78
Brooks, D., 129
Bruni, F., 150
Burns, J., 97

Cartesian thinking, 25
challenge, 35, 36, 50, 52, 58, 59, 60, 63, 66, 67, 71, 140, 141
   adaptive, 60, 70, 77, 88, 98, 143, 172
Challenger disaster, 162
cognition, ix, 6, 8, 16, 19, 22, 25, 27, 31, 49, 75, 129
   embodied, 27
cognitive dissonance, 7, 12, 15, 31, 36, 45, 51, 53, 54, 60, 66
cognitive science, 18
communities of practice, 100–102, 105, 143
community, 29, 34, 65, 74, 95, 101, 118, 124, 125, 130, 131, 134, 136, 137, 138, 144
competence, 35, 36, 40, 41, 46, 48, 58, 59, 63, 64, 66, 71, 82, 101, 105, 140, 141, 143
consciousness
   defined, 84
constructive developmentalism, 43–45

Index

constructive disorientation, x, 70, 74, 75, 84, 96, 108
  barriers to, 146
  defined, 57, 66
  enabling in others, 65, 71
  necessary conditions for, 66, 84, 101, 137, 141, 159, 162
  through art, 126–129
  what makes disorientation constructive, 60–65
critical theory, 79, 103
Csikszentmihalyi, M.
  effort imperative, 59, 142
  flow theory, 58, 59, 66, 67, 69, 70, 71, 140, 141, 142
    addictive potential of, 59

Damasio, A., 32, 33, 84
dance, as a tool for deep learning, 125, 129, 131, 132, 174
Davies, L., 57, 62, 80
  educative turbulence, 80
deep learning mindset, 84, 87, 106, 138, 151, 156, 160, 175
deep work, 68, 71, 73
dehumanized perception, 92
Dewey, J., x, 25, 26, 42, 43, 48, 50, 57, 58, 64, 67, 73, 74, 75, 88, 96, 101, 108, 113, 116–119, 124, 139, 140, 154, 156n3, 158, 166
  Art as Experience, 123–124
  bourgeois democracy, 118
  criteria of experience, 42
  intelligent action, 48, 74
  learning and democracy, 109
  mis-education, 48, 96
  mis-educative, 26, 154
  and open-mindedness, 118
  routine action, 48
dialectic, 43, 74, 118, 143, 144, 145, 149
  definition, 145
dialectical thinking, 145–150, 156
  and aesthetic experience, 148
  defined, 146
  developing, 150–154
  elements of, 152
  systems thinking as necessary for, 154
  vs. absolutist and relativistic thinking, 146
  vs. other forms of thought, 147
dialectics, 52
dialogue, *see* discourse
diffusion by envy, 175
Dirkx, J., 125

discourse, x, 3, 88, 106, 108, 114, 115, 120, 121, 121n4, 128, 138, 143, 144, 145, 159
  active listening, 170, 171
  dialogic space, 169
  maieutic discussion, 118
disequilibrium, *see* constructive disorientation
disorienting dilemma, 28, 29, 30, 32, 35, 38, 48, 53, 70, 84, 139, 146, 151, 158, 160, 162, 165
Dissanayake, E., 125
diversity, group, 14, 62, 90, 95, 96, 97, 99, 102, 103, 104, 111, 118, 122, 129, 144, 154
double-loop learning, 49
Dreyfus Affair, 10
Dweck, C., 166

Edelman, D., 132, 133
Edison, Thomas, 10
educative turbulence, 62
efficacy, viii, 34, 37n8, 40, 57, 60, 64, 65, 66, 71, 78, 80, 104, 137, 165, 174
Emerson, Ralph Waldo, 89
emotion, 1, 7, 19, 25, 33, 35, 49, 78, 86, 124, 148
  role of, 16, 18, 25, 29, 31–32
  role of in deep learning, 122, 128
empathic field, 129, 138, 139, 144, 174
empathy, 90–94, 98, 106, 122, 126, 129, 136, 169, 171
equilibrium, in learning, 110, 121, 123, 135, 136
Erenrich, S., 129
essential tensions, forms of
  the center and the edge, 142–144
  intuition and deliberation, 141
  the self and the other, 144
experience, 15, 27, 41, 47, 74, 114, 164
  aesthetic, ix, 125, 128, 129, 136, 138, 158, 173, 174
exposure anxiety, 17, 110, 111

Facebook, 4, 12, 111
fake news, 1
Foucault, M., 112, 114, 115, 117, 119, 120, 121n4
Franklin, Benjamin, 19
Freire, P., 26, 29, 48, 49, 87, 90, 108, 112, 113, 114, 115, 117, 119, 134
  banking model, 26, 48
  conscientization, 112, 134, 138
  praxis, 29, 49, 113
Friedman, Thomas, 3, 4

Gadamer, H., 163
Gadotti, M., 155
Galileo, 19, 25
goal displacement, 69
Graham, Martha, 125
Greene, M., 125
growth mindset, 166

Index

Habermas, J.,
  distantiation, 76
habitus, 50, 52, 120
Haidt, J., 7, 16, 94, 95, 97, 112
Handy, Charles, 4
Hegel, G., 145
hegemonic assumptions, 78, 79, 102, 103, 104, 172
Heifetz, R., 57, 76, 98, 107n4, 108, 140, 155, 176
  productive zone of disequilibrium, 58, 65, 66, 140
Highlander Research and Education Center, 113, 119
Horton, M., 112, 113, 114, 115, 117, 119
Hovland, C., 127, 139n4
Hume, David, 6

Ibsen, Henrik, 38
identity
  defined, 33
immunity to change, 17, 61, 84, 153, 167
  competing commitments, 17
incidental learning, *see* intuitive learning, learning:intuitive
Infocalypse, 3, 4
International Center for the Advancement of Scientific Literacy, 23
intuition, 15, 28, 73, 141, 164
intuitive learning, 85–87

James, W., 25
Jarvis, C., 93
Jarvis, P., 27, 49
JR, 130, 131, 132, 135

Kahneman, D., 8, 9, 14, 24, 28, 68, 71, 73, 74, 110, 111, 141, 164
Kant, Immanuel, 4, 145, 156n4
Kasl, E., 128, 129, 144, 174
Kegan, R., 5, 17, 18, 43, 44, 45, 46, 47, 48, 50, 61, 70, 144, 149, 153, 154, 160, 164, 167
  self-authoring, 45, 50, 53
  socialized mind, 45, 47, 53
Kierkegaard, S., 168, 175
knowing
  embodied, 86
Kolb, D., 26, 67

Labouvie-Vief, G., 148, 150
Ladkin, D., 39, 46, 80, 92, 161
Lahey, L., 17, 18, 61, 70, 153, 154, 164, 167
Langer, E., 53
leadership
  embodied, 92
  transformative, 97

learning
  action, 67, 71, 89, 98–100, 103, 105, 108
  critical, 104
  adaptive, 36n1, 57, 58, 60, 61, 63, 67, 68, 70, 77, 79, 80, 88, 104, 137, 139n2, 154, 176
  adult, ix, 28, 30, 58, 66, 114, 119, 126
  collaborative, 98
  cooperative, 167
  deep
    barriers to, 31, 47, 48, 68, 74, 89, 98, 111, 155
    definition of, vii, viii, 158
    necessary conditions for, ix, x, 32, 35, 38, 49, 52, 60, 62, 64, 68, 70, 73, 84, 86, 90, 95, 119, 121, 129, 141, 159
    as a political act, 109
    as political consciousness, 112–116
    why so hard, 6–18
    why so important, 1–6
  double-loop, 75, 77
  drive-by, 1, 19, 32, 68, 70, 175
  embodied, 27, 131, 138, 159, 173
  experiential, 25–31, 89, 113, 166
    experiential learning cycle, 26
  incidental, 81
  instrumental, 84
  intuitive, 84, 87, 97, 138, 159
  mindful, 76, 79, 84, 85, 87, 138, 141, 142, 151, 156
  mytho-poetic, 125
  observational, 92
  organizational, 50, 104, 108, 115
  participatory, 97–100
  physiology of, 22
  problem-based, 67, 83, 89
  self-directed, 48, 50, 67
  single-loop, 75, 76
  transformative, viii, ix, x, 28, 29, 30, 44, 55, 70, 76, 86, 87, 88, 105, 108, 125, 126, 128
  workplace, 81
learning organization, 50, 81
learning paradox, 153–154
Lee, Spike, 127
Lessing, D., 160
Lindeman, E., 75
Littlewood's Law of Miracles, 13
loss aversion, 17

Marshall, J., 166
Marx, K., 145
Maslow, A., 39, 40
  Maslow's hierarchy, 39, 40
  self-actualization, 40
meaning schemes, *see* mental models
mental models, ix, 14, 23, 28, 31, 35, 36, 75, 81, 84, 153, 159, 161

Mercier, H., 10, 11, 15, 16, 77, 94, 95, 96, 97, 107n3
Meyerson, D., 173
Mezirow, J., 28, 29, 44, 45, 48, 70, 73, 75, 76, 77, 78, 96
 assimilative learning, 78
 objective reframing, 77
 subjective reframing, 77
mindfulness, 46, 53, 54, 76, 79, 84, 141, 153, 155, 156, 158, 160–162, 166, 168, 174
 defined, 53
minimal power differentials, 102–105
Mitra, A., 130, 131
Moore's Law, 3
motivation, 33, 40, 41, 58, 63, 78, 105, 159
 autonomous, 63, 65, 66, 67, 69, 70, 104
 characteristics of, 33
 defined, 33
 intrinsic, 60, 62–65, 67, 70, 71, 79, 104, 137, 174
 and learning in adults, 32–35
 organizational, 64
Myers, V., 162, 164

Newman, M., 99
Newport, C., 68
Nisbet, R., 143
Nussbaum, M., 31

order response, 61, 169, 173
organizational mindlessness, 80, 161

Palmer, P., 34
Parks, R., 119
parrèsia, 120, 121
Pauling, L., 10
Piaget, J., 43, 147
Picasso, P., 128
Polanyi, M., 85
polarized attitudes, 18
political capital
 defined, 111
politics, 4, 74, 103, 105, 106, 108, 114, 115, 120, 121, 121n4, 138, 143
 defined, x, 109
 harnessing power of, 172–173
Popper, K., 73
positive psychology, 40
post-truth, 1
practice-based research, 27
procedural justice, 120, 121, 135
project premortem, 168
prospective hindsight, 167
Putnam, R., 95, 96, 168

RAND Corporation, 2
rationalist delusion, 7, 112
rationality, 6, 29, 145, *see* reasoning
reasoning, 8, 9, 11, 13, 15, 16, 77, 78, 89, 95, 112
recognition, 34, 65, 105
reductive thinking, 111
reflection, 4, 26, 29, 31, 32, 49, 50, 53, 73, 74, 86, 98, 100, 103, 114, 119, 124, 131, 142, 153
 criteria for, 74
 critical, ix, x, 4, 29, 88, 108, 113, 114, 115, 119, 121, 126, 128, 129, 141, 146, 153, 156, 159, 176
 characteristics of, 75
 and development of expertise, 81–84
 and mindful learning, 78
 defined, 73
 on practice, 81
relatedness, 40, 41, 46, 60, 64, 80, 88, 95, 104, 137, 150
Riefenstahl, L., 136
Riegel, K., 148, 149
Rogers, Carl, 91
Roosevelt, Eleanor, 88
Rowe, N., 131
Rule, P., 169
rumor cascades, 3

Scharmer, O., 157n11, 160, 166
Schön, D., 49, 60, 75, 81, 83, 176
 reflection in action, 49
 technical rationality, 60, 77
self, the, 38, 46, 52, 63, 84, 88, 89, 91, 144, 149, 150, 164, 165
 essentialist views of, 39–42
 interactionist views of, 42–45
 reflected best self, 41
self-actualization, 40, 88
self-determination theory, 40, 43, 46, 63, 65, 67, 88, 95, 150
self-development theory, 40
Senge, P., 38, 50, 51, 65, 75, 108, 140, 155
 creative tension, 51, 57, 65, 66, 140
 personal mastery, 50, 51
shallow learning, *see* drive-by learning
shallow work, 68
Sherif, M., 127, 139n4
Shermer, M., 6, 9
Shore, Z., 17, 110, 111
Shtulman, A., 15
Shulman, L., 175
Sinclair, A., 161, 163
social, 94–97
social capital, 80, 90, 98, 101, 102, 104, 106, 111, 118, 121, 132, 144, 159, 169, 171

social learning field, 138
social learning systems, 101, 102, 103, 143
Socrates, x, 4, 38, 145
Sperber, D., 10, 11, 15, 16, 77, 94, 95, 96, 97, 107n3
Staples, M., 122, 127
Staw, B., 64
strategic planning, 51, 69, 71
synapses, *see* brain
systems sensing, 155

tacit knowledge, 83, 85, 148
Tao Te Ching, 145, 168
Tart, C., 46, 157n12, 161
tempered radicals, 173
Tetlock, P., 96, 97
thought leadership, 175–176
Torbert, W.
   action inquiry, 46
   action logics, 47
      conventional, 47, 51
      postconventional, 47, 50, 51, 53, 147
   liberating structures, 98
Treasure, J., 170
truth decay, 1
Tuchman, B., 18n4, 110
Twain, Mark, 19, 68

Twitter, 1, 3, 14, 68, 111
Tzu, L., 140, 145, 146, 168

Ubuntu, 150
Uhl-Bien, M., 61, 119, 169

Vaill, P., 5, 38, 47, 48, 49, 50, 81, 83, 98, 105, 161
   institutional learning, 5, 6, 48, 81
   permanent white water, 5, 6, 47, 48, 50
   reflective beginner, 49, 51, 83, 98, 161
   reflexive learning, 50
Vince, R., 103, 104
Vurdejla, I., 152
Vygotsky, L.
   scaffolding, 58, 105
   zone of proximal development, 58, 66, 67, 140

Weick, K., 161, 162
Wenger, E., 100, 101, 102, 143, 169
Wergin, J., 34, 63, 83, 86, 129, 142, 171, 175
Will, George, 121n2
Willer, R., 91, 94
wisdom, 28, 52, 143, 145, 148
Wlodkowski, R., 33, 34, 35, 93, 94

Yorks, L., 97, 98, 99, 100, 107n6, 128, 129, 144, 174